CIVIL SOCIETY AND THE
AID INDUSTRY

The Institute for Development Research
44 Farnsworth Street
Boston, MA 02210-1211

ABOUT THE NORTH-SOUTH INSTITUTE

For more than 20 years, The North-South Institute (NSI) has built a reputation for sound research and analysis of Canadian foreign policy, offered an independent voice on the urgent importance of world development issues, and brought those issues before the Canadian public and decision makers. Established in 1976, it is the only independent, non-governmental research institute in Canada focused on international development.

The Institute's research supports global efforts to strengthen international development cooperation, improve governance, enhance gender and social equity in globalizing markets, and prevent ethnic and other conflict. The results of this research are shared – through publications, seminars, and conferences – with policy makers, educators, business, and media, as well as with interested groups and individuals, to help generate greater understanding and informed discussion of the problems and opportunities facing Canada and countries in the developing world.

A charitable, not-for-profit corporation, The North-South Institute is non-partisan and cooperates with a wide range of Canadian, overseas, and international organizations. NSI also collaborates closely with the International Development Research Centre and the International Institute for Sustainable Development in promoting knowledge-based development programs and policies.

CIVIL SOCIETY AND THE AID INDUSTRY
THE POLITICS AND PROMISE

Alison Van Rooy

The North-South Institute

Earthscan Publications Ltd, London

First published in the UK in 1998 by
Earthscan Publications Limited

Copyright © Alison Van Rooy, 1998

A catalogue record for this book is available from the British Library

ISBN: 1 85383 553 6 paperback
        1 85383 554 4 hardback

Typesetting and page design by PCS Mapping & DTP, Newcastle upon Tyne
Printed and bound by Biddles Ltd, Guildford and Kings Lynn
Cover design by John Burke Design

Cover photo © Her Majesty in Right of Canada / CIDA / ACDI / Roger Lemayne.
Her Majesty in Right of Canada is not responsible for any unauthorized use of
images acquired from CIDA's IDPL

For a full list of publications please contact:

Earthscan Publications Limited
120 Pentonville Road
London N1 9JN
Tel: (0171) 278 0433
Fax: (0171) 278 1142
E-mail: earthinfo@earthscan.co.uk
http://www.earthscan.co.uk

Earthscan is an editorially independent subsidiary of Kogan Page Limited and
publishes in association with WWF-UK and the International Institute for
Environment and Development.

This book is printed on elemental chlorine free paper from sustainably managed
forests.

TABLE OF CONTENTS

ACKNOWLEDGEMENTS

This book owes its existence to many interested, and interesting, watchers of international affairs. Greatest thanks go to the research and advisory team members, Katalin Ertsey, Alan Fowler, Nicolás Lynch, Wachira Maina, Kamal Malhotra, Ferenc Miszlivetz, Pepi Patrón, Mark Robinson, Paikiasothy Saravanamuttu and Ian Smillie for their imagination and humour. Thanks, in generous measure, also go to members of The North–South Institute staff and to research assistants Donna Chiarelli and Kari Glynes Elliot. For comments on drafts and for helpful direction, we are grateful to others too numerous to name. Finally, for his encouragement and more than his fair share of housework, I thank my husband, Neil Hart.

The assistance by the following organizations was critical for the success of the research programme. Their continuing support of research in development is another sign of the richness of internationalism:

- The International Development Research Centre, Ottawa, Canada;
- The Canadian International Development Agency, Ottawa, Canada;
- The Swedish International Development Cooperation Agency, Stockholm, Sweden;
- The International Centre for Human Rights and Democratic Development, Montreal, Canada; and
- The K M Hunter Charitable Foundation, Peterborough, Canada.

Alison Van Rooy,
Ottawa
March 1998

ABOUT THE RESEARCH TEAM

The Editor

Alison Van Rooy, Senior Researcher, The North-South Institute. Van Rooy's recent work on civil society, official development assistance (ODA), and the role of non-governmental organizations (NGOs) includes numerous articles, policy papers, speeches and presentations in addition to *A Partial Promise? Canadian Support to Social Development in the South* (NSI, 1995) and *The Altruistic Lobbyists: The Influence of Non-Governmental Organizations on Development Policy in Canada and Britain* (DPhil, 1994). Her Rhodes scholarship was supplemented by a research fellowship at the Canadian Department of Foreign Affairs and International Trade where she wrote on improved practices for consultation with civil society organizations. She was a Canada World Youth participant to Sri Lanka, and has been involved as a development educator for young people.

The Authors

Katalin Ertsey, NGO activist and researcher, Budapest. Ertsey has been involved in civil society organizing in Hungary and in other parts of Europe, working with groups focused on gypsy rights, youth, culture and NGO training and advocacy. A journalist by training, she has been part of noted research teams on civil society at The Center for European Studies, the Hungarian statistics department, the Rockefeller Brothers Fund and Johns Hopkins University.

Wachira Maina, Institute of Economic Affairs, Nairobi. A lawyer and political scientist, Maina earned his degrees at Nairobi, Columbia and the University of Leeds. He has written about NGO capacity, human rights and constitutional reform and is currently working on research on the effectiveness of donor support to Kenyan civil society organizations.

Ferenc Miszlivetz, Center for European Studies, Budapest. As a leading writer on changing Hungarian civil society, Miszlivetz is also Director of the Monus Illes Academy for Democratic Society and a frequent visiting lecturer in Europe. He is a contributing editor to several journals and is a Leverhulme Fellow at the Institute of Development Studies at Sussex, an Associated Fellow at the Transnational Institute in Amsterdam and a MacArthur Fellow in International Peace and Security. Dr Miszlivetz also served as an advisor on the team.

Pepi Patrón, FORO Nacional/Internacional. A political philosopher trained in Belgium, Patrón has been central in FORO's Agenda Perú project, a country-wide debate on the Peruvian state of governance. Also involved with Transparencia, an NGO concerned with government accountability, and with youth mobilization efforts, Patrón is publishing this year her original research on civil society and social space in Peru. Dr Nicolás Lynch has been a special advisor on the Peruvian case study.

Mark Robinson, Institute of Development Studies, University of Sussex, Brighton. Dr Robinson is a rural/political sociologist with special interests in democratization, governance and aid conditionality; politics of public policy management and institutional reform; private sector provision of public services; and official and NGO approaches to poverty alleviation. Educated at Cambridge and Sussex, he has published widely on the role of NGOs and civil society within development thinking and practice.

Paikiasothy Saravanamuttu, Centre for Policy Alternatives (CPA), Colombo. His academic career at the LSE and as a lecturer at the University of Southampton focused on international relations, conflict resolution, protection of minorities, federalism and South Asian security. Saravanamuttu is also a Visiting Lecturer at the University of Colombo, a member of the Sri Lankan Ministry of Foreign Affairs' Study Group and a political columnist.

The Advisors

Alan Fowler, Development writer and consultant, Addis Ababa. With 20 years of experience working primarily in the NGO sector in Kenya, Fowler is a prolific writer on non-governmental issues, including their role in supporting civil society. His doctorate, from the Institute of Development Studies in Sussex, focused on the role of NGOs in Africa's democratization; his latest book, *Striking a Balance* (Fowler, 1997b), examines NGO management and organization.

Kamal Malhotra, Co-Director and Co-Founder of *Focus on the Global South*, Bangkok. Now engaged with Focus' programme of progressive development policy research and practice, Malhotra has also been a director with Australia's Community Aid Abroad and with the International Institute of Rural Reconstruction in the Philippines. An Indian national, Malhotra has also served with UNDP and UNIDO, and is also currently part-time Regional Advisor to Save the Children UK on Macroeconomic Policy and Children in Southeast and East Asia.

Ian Smillie, Development writer and consultant, Ottawa. As one of Canada's most prominent independent voices on NGOs and development, Smillie has long worked in Africa and Asia as a consultant on development issues. He was co-founder of InterPares and Executive Director of CUSO. His most recent book is *The Alms Bazaar*, published by IT Publications in Britain and the International Development Research Centre.

ACRONYMS

Parentheses indicate translation or explanation.

ADEX   (Exporters' association)
AIC   African Inland Church
AIPCA   African Independent Church of Africa
APRA   (Popular Revolutionary American Alliance)
ASBANC   (Peruvian Association of Banks)
BRAC   Bangladesh Rural Advancement Committee
CADE   (IPAE's Annual Executives' Conference)
CASIN   Centre for Applied Studies in International Negotiation
CCSS   Central Council of Social Services
CEDEP   Centro Brasileño de Documentación y Estudios de la Cuenca del Plata
CEE   Central and Eastern Europe
CGD   Centre for Governance and Development
CIDA   Canadian International Development Agency
CIPART   Citizen's Participation Project
CITE   (Intersectoral Committee of State Workers)
COEECI   (Coordinating Body of the International Foreign Cooperation Institutions)
CONFIEP   (National Confederation of Private Entrepreneurs' Institutions)
COPEME   (Association of NGOs supporting small and micro-entrepreneurs)
CSDP   Civil Society Development Program
CRM   Civil Rights Movement
CSO   civil society organization
CWY   Canada World Youth
DAC   Development Assistance Committee
DANIDA   Danish International Development Assistance
DFID   Department For International Development
DG   democracy and governance
EFC   European Foundation Centre
EU   European Union
FES   Friedrich Ebert Stiftung
FIDA   (International Federation of Women Lawyers)
FMM   Free Media Movement

FONCODES (National Fund for Compensation and Social Development)
GDP   Gross Domestic Product
GMF   German Marshall Fund
GNP   Gross National Product
ICES   International Centre for Ethnic Studies
ICFTU   International Confederation of Free Trade Unions
ICHRDD   International Centre for Human Rights and Democratic
           Development
ICNL   International Center for Not-for-Profit Law
IDB   Inter-American Development Bank
IDESI   (Institute for the Development of the Informal Sector)
IDP   Instituto Diálogo y Propuesta
IDRC   International Development Research Centre
IEP   Instituto de Estudios Peruanos
IFI   International Financial Institutions
IMF   International Monetary Fund
INFORM   Information Monitor of Human Rights
INP   (National Planning Institute)
INTRAC   International Non-governmental Organisation Training and
           Research Centre
IPAE   (Peruvian Institute of Business Administration)
IPAL   Instituto para América Latina
IRI   International Republican Institute
JVP   Janata Vimukthi Peramuna (People's Liberation Front)
KAP   (Dutch Embassy Small Project programme)
KCC   Kenya Cooperative Creameries
KFA   Kenya Farmers Association
KHRC   Kenya Human Rights Commission
LIEN   Link Inter-European NGOs
LSK   Law Society of Kenya
LST   Law and Society Trust
LTTE   Liberation Tigers of Tamil Eelam
MDDR   Movement for the Defence of Democratic Rights
MIRJE   Movement for Inter-Racial Justice and Equality
MONLAR   Movement for National Land and Agricultural Reforms
MRTA   Movimiento Revolucionario Túpac Amaru
MSZOSZ   (Hungarian trade union)
NCCK   National Council of Churches of Kenya
NFF   National Forum Foundation
NGO   non-governmental organization
NIOK   (Nonprofit Information and Training Center)
NIS   National Intelligence Service
NLG   Dutch guilders
NORAD   Norwegian Agency for Development Cooperation
NPI   New Partnerships Initiative
OAS   Organization of American States

ODA	official development assistance
OECD	Organization for Economic Co-operation and Development
OFASA	Obra Filantrópica de Asistencia Social Adventista
PAFFREL	Peoples Action for Free and Fair Elections
PCEA	Pentecostal Church of East Africa
PHARE	Poland and Hungary Aid for Reconstructing the Economy
PRONAA	National Program for Food Assistance
quangos	quasi-NGOs
RBF	Rockefeller Brothers Fund
RECAP	Research and Civic Awareness Program
SANASA	(Federation of Thrift and Credit Societies)
SDA	Seventh Day Adventists
SECTI	(Executive Department for International Technical Cooperation)
SEED	Support to Eastern European Democracies
SIDA	Swedish International Development Cooperation Agency
SLFP	Sri Lankan Freedom Party
SOEs	State-owned enterprises
SSA	Social Scientists Association
TACIS	(EU's economic assistance program to the former Soviet republics)
TAF	The Asia Foundation
TESZ	(Legal successor of the People's Patriotic Front)
UNDP	United Nations Development Programme
USAID	United States Agency for International Development
USIS	United States Information Service
UTHR	University Teachers' Human Rights

LIST OF FIGURES, TABLES AND BOXES

FIGURES

TABLES

BOXES

I | INTRODUCTION: ALL ROADS LEAD TO ROME

Alison Van Rooy

WHY BOTHER ABOUT CIVIL SOCIETY?

Why bother about civil society? The answer is that talk about civil society is shaping the very way in which we 'do' international relations. That conversation pulls together global ideas, values, institutions and money in a fascinating, and sometimes disturbing, fashion. This book chronicles one part of the story and highlights some of the promises and dangers that the language of civil society brings with it. In many ways, civil society is the Rome of today's internationalism; wherever we may begin, we will arrive at this debate sooner or later.

Certainly, Southern, East European and Northern writing about the role of civil society has grown in volume and depth. Various definitions describe civil society as the whole of humanity left over once government and for-profit firms are excised, covering all those organizations that fill in the spaces between the family and the State and the market. From this sphere are to come the agents of change that will cure a range of social and economic ills left by failures of government and the marketplace: autocracy, poverty, disenfranchisment, oppression, social malaise. Cornucopian expectations for social change have been heaped on this idea and, indeed, for some Northern donors in particular (both official and non-governmental), the 'discovery' of civil society has promised a solution to the enduring problems of development and democratic change (the topics of chapters 1 and 2). Many donors have devoted official development assistance (ODA) dollars to a range of civil society projects throughout the world, and the number and variety of those projects increases daily. Civil society is the topic of the day.

Yet serious questions remain about the whole enterprise. How is the language concerning civil society being used? Where did it come from? What are donors actually doing when they report on strengthening civil society? What *could* they reasonably do? What are the issues and implications, both for good and for ill, of this growing sector of the international aid business? This study tries to ask, and begin to answer, some of the most vexing of these questions.

This book, therefore, adopts a part of the civil society conversation and looks at it in detail, but the answers are relevant to civil society watchers from many other perspectives. The language wielded in development organizations in Northern countries is taken apart to ask: Why talk about civil society at all? Why now? What will civil society do for the problems of development and for the problems of development practitioners? The donor practices that flow from these analyses are then examined in four countries in particular: Hungary, Kenya, Peru and Sri Lanka. Analysts from each country look at the programs of donor organizations and compare that picture to the dynamics of civil society organizing underway at home. How are donors shaping the evolution of civil society in each country? The picture produced by layering those two images tells us a great deal about how the globalization of ideas is working.

The choice of countries is deliberate. We wanted to show examples from countries with active civil societies, active international donor involvement in trying to shape those civil societies and disparate political and social histories so we could examine some of the universals attributed to civil society. It also matters, in the big picture, that some countries are markedly less dependent on international aid than others. Looking only at official aid (leaving aside contributions from non-official sources), it becomes clear that foreign aid to Kenya is most susceptible to the pull of donors (see Table 1.1). Against the background of falling private capital flows, aid carves out a substantial 8 per cent of the formal economy. Hungary, at the other end of the scale, generates less than 1 per cent of its gross national product (GNP) from aid, dwarfed by the nearly 19 per cent earned in private capital flows. These differences in leverage matter as we explore the power dynamics that run through the aid industry.

The book is organized to help us explore those power dynamics and how civil society organizations have come into the picture. It begins with the historical debate on civil society and attempts to explain its resurgence in popular discourse (Chapter 1). Chapter 2 describes why that debate has become so exciting to development practitioners in particular, and why (and how and how much) it has climbed into policy documentation and programming imperatives. Chapters 3 to 6 are case studies of those development interventions as well as histories of civil society mobilization in Hungary (because our awareness of the debate in the North is tightly linked with changes in the late 1980s in Eastern Europe), Kenya (because of the keen recent interest in the international community to alter the political shape of that country), Sri Lanka (because Northerners have seemingly run out of ideas for ending the long embittered civil war) and

Table 1.1: Aid and the Economy

	Gross National Product (GNP)		Overseas Development Assistance (ODA)		Private Flows	
	GNP in 1995 current dollars	GNP per capita in 1995 current dollars	Total net ODA 1995	ODA as a percentage of GNP	Net private capital flows 1995	Net private capital flows 1995 as a percentage of GNP
	1	2	3	4	5	6
Kenya	8778	280	732	8.34	(42)	(0.5)
Sri Lanka	12,776	700	556	4.35	140	1.1
Peru	57,043	2300	427	0.75	3532	6.2
Hungary	42,024	4120	210	0.50	7841	18.7

Sources:
Column 1:   OECD, 1997: Table 44; and for Hungary, imputed from World Bank, 1997: Table 1
Column 2:   OECD, 1997: Table 44; and for Hungary, World Bank, 1997: Table 1
Column 3:   OECD, 1997: Table 33; and for Hungary, imputed from World Bank, 1997: Table 1
Column 4:   Imputed from columns 1 and 3 for Kenya, Sri Lanka, Peru; source for Hungary is in 1994 dollars and is from World Bank, 1997: Table 3
Column 5:   World Bank, 1997: Table 3
Column 6:   Imputed from columns 1 and 5
All figures in US$ millions

Peru (because over a decade of terrorist violence and an authoritarian regime have changed how Peruvians have, and can, organize in civil society). Those stories are gathered into a discussion in the final chapter on how, in both conceptual and practical terms, agents of outside intervention can (if they should) be shaping their activities.

Through these stories, we have sought to answer questions about civil society and foreign aid. Our conclusions, summarized in the final chapter, suggest that there are powerful lessons to be learned. The aid community, inhabited by good, bad and sometimes irrelevant policies and programmes, may be taking an important step forward.

ORIGINS

If that is where our study ends, perhaps it would be useful to make a note about where it began. It is maybe not surprising, if indeed all roads lead to Rome, that this study arose from a different idea altogether. A number of years ago, The North-South Institute published a successful book on the debates and dilemmas of the Canadian development non-governmental organization (NGO) community, called *Bridges of Hope?* Our initial wish was simply to update the book to include new data and a discussion of some of the recent issues in the community. A reference group, representing various important constituencies in the Canadian development world, met a few times in 1994 and 1995 to pull together the key threads of the study.* It immediately became clear that Canadians were debating what their colleagues throughout the international development community were talking about: What is civil society? Is it a new name or a new idea? How can we strengthen it? How will that change our work?

The original study proposal, much smaller in scope than the current work, was put aside in favour of more interesting but more difficult questions about the role of foreign agents in strengthening or, for that matter, harming civil society organizations in other parts of the world. That initial reference group helped shape the study, leading to a two-year project to explore the role of Northern governmental, multilateral, and non-governmental agencies and foundations in supporting Southern and Eastern European civil societies.

With those questions in mind, the study design became larger, more international, more encompassing and more expensive. With a generous initial grant from the Canadian International Development Agency (CIDA), Ottawa, the Institute was able to pull together a research team from four countries and an advisory team to balance the group's interdisciplinary profile (see About the Research Team, pviii). With a team in place, and a first meeting held in Ottawa in June 1996, the study was put into motion with the support of the International Centre for Human Rights and Democratic Development, Montreal, the K M Hunter Charitable Foundation, Peterborough, Ontario, and a large contribution from the International Development Research Centre (IDRC), Ottawa. A second meeting was held in England in May 1997, and the final manuscript was completed over the autumn. As the study neared its end, another substantial grant was extended by the Swedish International Development Cooperation Agency (SIDA), Stockholm.

To meet the pragmatic goals of the study in a complex field, the research involved a number of activities, summarized below. An initial widely-distributed discussion paper was prepared to frame the debate (and, eventually, to shape much of Chapter 1); workshops with the research team were held at the beginning and middle of the writing process to shape the study and generate its conclusions; empirical case studies of donor policy and practice in each of the countries were undertaken, including workshops, surveys, extensive interviews and project data

---

* The members of that team were: Tim Brodhead, McConnell Family Foundation, Montreal (one of the authors of *Bridges of Hope?*); Zack Gross, Marquis Project, Brandon; Shelina Kassam, then of the British Columbia Council for International Cooperation, Vancouver; Gabrielle Lachance, then Executive Director of the Canadian Catholic Organization for Development and Peace, Montreal; Yianna Lambrou, then of the International Development Research Centre, Ottawa; Lily Mah-sen, CUSO, Ottawa; Katherine Pearson, then of the Canadian Council for International Cooperation, Ottawa; Gauri Sreenivasan, then of CUSO, Ottawa; and Doug Williams, Canadian International Development Agency, Ottawa.

analysis, as well as primary and secondary literature surveys; and a host of discussion papers, articles, meetings and correspondence was generated to contribute to the policy debate. This book is, therefore, only one, although one of the most visible, manifestations of the research.

Through this set of activities, we generated the pages and arguments that follow. We hope that these roads may lead you to to some of the same conclusions.

1 CIVIL SOCIETY AS IDEA: AN ANALYTICAL HATSTAND?

Alison Van Rooy

From what reaches of political philosophy have we resurrected the notion of 'civil society'? Why? Why now? This chapter runs through some of the history of civil society as an idea and focuses on six of its current incarnations:

1) value;
2) collective noun;
3) space;
4) historical moment;
5) anti-hegemony; and
6) anti-state.

In this way, it tries to address a main frustration – that many of the most interesting ideas earned in a long history have been lost by simplifying civil society down to an 'analytical hat stand', suitable for almost any political agenda (White, 1993: 64). In trying to understand what civil society is and why we might want one, a simplified set of arguments has been imported into Northern aid policy – the subject of Chapter 2.

This chapter, therefore, begins by reclaiming some of the most interesting ideas within the history of civil society. Ideas that were born in a particular time and place in Western philosophy have been resurrected today to answer very modern problems. The focus on civil society has grown in the 1990s because of concerns with globalization, political change in the post-Cold War era and a sense of dismay about the quality of society, particularly in industrialized countries. Although the language has seeped deeply into Northern thinking about development in other countries, the debate tells us more perhaps about development, and underdevelopment, in the 'developed' parts of the world.

WHAT IS CIVIL SOCIETY?

Civil society has wandered its way through the academic world on a tortuous path. Ideas have been attached and detached, origins have been ascribed and divorced, social meanings have been generated and debunked. What we have today is not one object of inquiry, but several. This section describes the six most familiar viewpoints normally generated on the topic of civil society and examines them with an eye to the questions posed in the next chapter: how do ideas about civil society improve the prospects for development and democracy?

History of the Idea: Nothing New but Very Much Changed

The term 'civil society' has a long history in political philosophy, and its definition had been altered with Roman, Lockean, Hegelian, Marxist and Gramscian interpretations long before it was resurrected in the 1990s. Indeed, the disentanglement of those debates has become an intellectual industry of its own in recent years (Keane, 1988; Cohen and Arato, 1992; Kumar, 1993; Chandhoke, 1995; Hall, 1995), but a brief resume will be useful here. To understand why the term has been brought back to life, we need to know some of its genealogy.

As we see in the following paragraphs, there are two phases in the family history of civil society as theory. The first, dating from the Romans, grappled with why and how humankind should be governed, who should govern and under what conditions. From the Scottish Enlightenment in the eighteenth century, however, we see a line drawn starkly between the governed and the governors: all of a sudden, there is a State that needs to be defended against, and a civil society that harbours the citizenry and trains them to keep the State at bay.

The Latin notion of *civilis societas*, which entered European thinking around 1400 from the writings of Cicero, designated those living in a civilized political community, creating a state to serve the community's interests. Civil society was, therefore, different from private, or domestic, society. It was the company of men (literally) who fulfilled their public and social roles. The norms of how to live together in such a society further endowed *civilis societas* with moral value and authority (Thomas, 1997). The important note to underline in the Roman tradition is the idea of the State as instrument of civil society, not as its antithesis.

The Roman tradition stretched over 2000 years. Up until the eighteenth century, it made sense that civil society and political society were interchangeable ideas, vested with moral virtue: 'the joining together of people

---

BOX 1.1:   BIG NAMES IN CIVIL SOCIETY THEORY

The Classics

Adam Ferguson	*An Essay on the History of Civil Society*, 1767
Antonio Gramsci	*The Prison Notebooks*, six volumes beginning in 1948
G W F Hegel	*Philosophy of Right*, 1821
John Locke	*A Letter Concerning Toleration*, 1689
	An Essay Concerning Human Understanding, 1690
Thomas Paine	*The Rights of Man*, 1791–2
Alexis de Tocqueville	*Democracy in America*, 1835–40

Today's Literature

Andrew Arato and Jean Cohen	*The Political Theory of Civil Society*, 1992
Ernest Gellner	*Conditions of Liberty: Civil Society and Its Rivals*, 1994
John A Hall	*Civil Society: Theory, History, Comparison*, 1995
John W Harbeson, Donald Rothchild, Naomi Chazan	*Civil Society and the State in Africa*, 1994
John Keane	*Democracy and Civil Society*, 1988
	Civil Society and The State, 1988
Adam Seligman	*Civil Society*, 1992
Edward Shils	*The Virtue of Civil Society*, 1991

---

in a society (in the modern sense) is by its nature a political act and establishes a political community (and with it a common good), (Castiglione, 1994: 86), an idea that remained true from Aquinas to Locke. For Kant, Hume, Rousseau, Hobbes and others up to the Scottish Enlightenment, 'state', 'civil society' and 'political society' were used synonymously (Keane, 1988: 35–71; Castiglione, 1994: 86; Ghils, 1995: 138). For such thinkers, the meaningful division was not between the State and society, but between society and the state of nature.

Keane dates the actual philosophical turnover to the century between 1750 and 1850, when he describes the important changes in ideas typified by the writings of Adam Ferguson, Thomas Paine, G W F Hegel and Alexis de Tocqueville. From Ferguson, we have the idea that one must guard against authoritarianism by developing independent 'societies' within civil society; from Paine, the more radical idea that the State itself (not just bad states) impeded civil society's hopes for social equality and liberty; from Hegel, the countervailing idea that a civil society that was too free might be conflict-producing, hence needing State control; and from de Tocqueville, the contradictory idea that even a democratically chosen government might suffocate civil society if sufficient vigilance by independent citizen associations was not maintained. All, however, drew a line between the State and civil society that had not existed before. These are the anchors of today's thinking on civil society.

The first harbinger of change predated the Enlightenment. Locke, writing in the seventeenth century, certainly maintained the idea that the State and civil society were consanguineous. Because Locke and other proponents of natural law saw each individual to be naturally free, civil society was a compromise, a contract in which each gave up some liberty to ensure the liberty of others. When individuals gave up the law of nature and subsumed their will under the public will, then civil society was possible, as long as all obeyed the laws under which they voluntarily placed themselves. Government was, therefore, to be seen as a trust by the people; society was seen to exist before government. The State maintained its role as instrument for public good – again, it was not seen as the antithesis of the public good. Yet in Locke's careful theoretical negotiations lie the beginnings of doubt – the State was not necessarily good, but existed in a carefully scrutinized relationship of trust.

The pre-modern tradition continued with Adam Ferguson, one of the Scottish Enlightenment thinkers. Ferguson, struggling to counterbalance the unrestricted individualism he and other moral philosophers perceived at the early stages of capitalist development, argued that civil society was an improvement (not a compromise) on the state of nature, which was primitive and rude. Civil society was less political than social. With Ferguson, 'civil' took on its connotation of polite and refined behaviour.

With Adam Smith, another element was added to the State–society mix: the economy. For the first time, the philosophers of eighteenth-century Britain began to talk about a distinct dimension of social life: 'The 'economy' now defines a dimension of social life in which we function as a society potentially quite outside the ambit of politics' (Taylor, 1990: 107). The idea that one could talk about anything within the public sphere that was not politics was a novel idea. It suggested, as Calhoun explains, that self-organization was possible.

> *Whether or not free markets are necessary for political freedom, the crucial early contribution of markets to the idea of civil society was as a demonstration of the possibility of self-organization. Market led thinkers like Adam Ferguson and Adam Smith to the idea that the activity of ordinary people could regulate itself without the intervention of government.* (Calhoun, 1993: 271)

By the time the nineteenth century rolled around, the switch had been completely made. French adventurer Alexis de Tocqueville wrote a wildly influential account of his travels in the new republic of the United States. *Democracy in America*, written between 1835 and 1840, described an America of community spirit, volunteerism, and incessant association forming (de Tocqueville, 1988). It was this single characteristic that de Tocqueville felt was society's ultimate, and best, defence against tyranny by the State. French and American republican sentiments aside, his work illustrated a sentiment throughout Northern Europe that social, economic and political life outside of the official apparatus of the State was both possible and necessary.

There were some, of course, who worried about the implications of a society unrestrained by the State. Hegel, writing in 1821, argued that it was necessary for the state to harmonize competing interests in society. For him, the State was the protector, suggesting that civil society could not remain civil unless it is ordered politically, subjected to 'the higher surveillance of the State' (Hegel, 1976: 397, translated by Keane, 1988: 52). The problem was that freedom gained in economic enterprise allowed individuals to be liberated from feudal relations, family yokes, serfdom and servitude, yet in tearing the individual away from those ties, the marketplace created an atomized individual, rootless and unmoored. Civil society – associations, clubs, networks, institutions – provided a second home. The danger was that civil society carried with it no guarantee of moral behaviour or service to the common good, guarantees only possible through the more ethical laws of the State. For Hegel, and later for Marx, civil society became synonymous with self-interested and egotistical society (Lipschultz, 1992: 398; Castiglione, 1994: 89; Rosenblum, 1994: 548; Palmer, 1997).

By the end of middle of the nineteenth century, however, the late Enlightenment thinkers were entirely overcome by the power of the industrial revolution. The debate on civil society fell out of favour; it had had 'a brief but remarkable career in Europe until the second half of the nineteenth century, when it fell (or was pushed) into obscurity and disappeared almost without trace' (Keane, 1988: 1).

Gramsci, the most familiar of modern interpreters, resurrected the conversation almost 100 years later while imprisoned during World War II. In trying to understand why Italian workers were not forming the revolution Marx had predicted, he sought answers in the notion of hegemony – a control so pervasive that it becomes imperceptible. He then described civil society in a much different sense from his forebears: not as a part of society, but as a sphere in which battles for and against capitalism are fought. That sphere is occupied by a struggle for material, ideological and cultural control over all of society, including the State. The State is not, as in the Hegelian view, the expression of universal will, but rather the potential instrument of domination by the forces of capital (Bobbio, 1988; Thomas, 1997). His ideas gained tremendous currency this century, particularly in Latin America, and have been used to fuel opposition to authoritarian regimes and their ideological incarnations. For most English-speaking audiences, however, Gramsci was relegated to courses on political philosophy.

As change in Eastern Europe bubbled throughout the 1980s, however, civil society took on yet another lease of life. The floating university of Poland's pre-Solidarity days, the Czechoslovakian 'velvet' underground, and Hungary's circles of freedom came to Western attention, described by Eastern Europeans as the resurgence of civil society. Eastern Europeans, of course, had read Gramsci, and described their protest to outsiders using his language. Bronislaw Geremek, for example, a Polish historian and Solidarity leader, writes,

> *Moral resistance, though seemingly hopeless against systems*
> *that are based on political and military force, functions like*
> *a grain of sand in the cogwheels of a vast but vulnerable*
> *machine. The idea of a civil society, even one that avoids*
> *overtly political activities in favor of education, the*
> *exchange of information and opinion, or the protection of*
> *the basic interests of particular groups, has enormous anti-*
> *totalitarian potential.* (Quoted in Bahmueller, 1997)

Geremek's thoughts resonate strongly with Gramsci's prison notebooks, except this time the enemy is a totalitarian socialism, not a totalitarian capitalism. These words found fertile ground with Westerners, taken by surprise that their cold war had apparently been 'won' from within.

By the late twentieth century, civil society had thus been constructed in contrast to the State, the law, nature, morality, capitalism and socialism. Today, these debates, elaborated by the authors in coming sections, have been thrown together in a bit of a conceptual grab-bag, and have come out with surprising moral connotations.

There are various real reasons for the resurgence of interest in civil society, as the following pages will argue. The modern Western context for the debate is concern about societal well-being at home, the decline of the welfare state, triumph over the end of the communist experiment in East and Central Europe and (bit by bit) in China – all these feed into the conversations about civil society.* As we continue the search for theoretical explanations and practical solutions to these problems, we reach for civil society in a utopian manner, using 'civil society' as code for values and institutions we think may present an answer – our analytical hatstand. Eric Hobsbawm, among others, critically describes these yearnings as 'strange calls for an otherwise unidentified "civil society" or "community" which are the voice of lost and drifting generations. They are heard in an age when such words, having lost their traditional meanings, have become vapid phrases' (in Roche, 1995).

Is civil society a vapid phrase? The accusation is probably well earned. This chapter suggests, however, that the guilt is not in too little meaning but, rather, too much. The modern mix-and-matching from the centuries-old debate on civil society has produced at least six viewpoints, or facets on the debate, used frequently in the academic and non-academic litera-ture on development today. The following discussion of those facets almost necessarily sets up straw men, however, for few would argue that the

---

* The literature on civil society in China, and whether the social and economic transitions we are witnessing actually indicate the emergence of a civil society, is vast. For a review of some of that literature, and cases made for and against, see the Wakeman and Chamberlain articles in the special 1993 issue of *Modern China*.

debate on civil society focuses on one facet alone or can be reduced to one stark statement. The analysis is none the less important, for the diagnosis and prescriptions that follow from one theoretical emphasis have real implications in practice. This section thus describes civil society alternately as values and norms, as a collective noun, as a space for action, as a historical moment, as an anti-hegemonic movement, and as an antidote to the State. Like tangled balls of wool, these viewpoints need to be unravelled so that their colours are more visible.

Civil Society as Values and Norms

For some, like Adam Ferguson 200 years earlier, the 'civil' in civil society is the operative word. Today, the link between civil society and civility is most often associated with the writing of Edward Shils, 'the virtue of civil society is the readiness to moderate particular, individual or parochial interests and to give precedence to the common good' (Shils, 1991: 16). Civil society thus describes the kind of well-behaved society that we want to live in, the goal for our political and social efforts. This ideal society is trustful, tolerant, co-operative – ambitions held to be universal and to be universally good. Invocation of civil society, therefore, becomes a statement of a moral goal, not a description of a thing. Civil society is synonymous with good society.

The current motors for this train of thinking are not difficult to uncover. North Americans in particular seem convinced that their societies are travelling away from a civil society rather than toward it. Elshtain, in her 1993 Massey Lectures, catalogues the problems of modern America:

> *The growth of cynicism and the atrophy of civil society; too much privatizing, acquisitive individualism that translates 'wants' into 'rights'; an increase in disrespect, even contempt for, the rule-governed practices that make democracy work, from the franchise to due process; a politics of displacement that disdains any distinction between public and private and aims to open up all aspects of life to the harsh glare of publicity; a neglect of practical politics in favour of rageful proclamations of one's unassailable and unassimilable identity as a member of a group; impatience with democratic citizenship and growing enthusiasm for identities based on race, gender, or sexual preference over that of the citizen; a waning of our ability to transmit democratic dispositions and dreams to succeeding generations through education. This is not a pretty picture.* (Elshtain, 1993: 120)

These fears of the decline of the family and of social cohesion have been incessant themes in American popular media, and in academic circles, through communitarian thought (Aaron et al., 1994) and the work of the democratic right (Yankelovich, 1994). Whether these fears reflect reality –

Putnam (1995) presents interesting counter examples of social cohesion – is almost beside the point. Our fears have become the basis for action.

The most compelling new ingredient in the debate on decline is the notion of 'social capital', an idea associated with Robert Putnam's book on *Making Democracy Work* in Italy. He and his team set out to explain why Northern Italy was so prosperous and Southern Italy so bedraggled. Their answer was that people had learned to live together, to trust one another, and to build up relationships through non-market activities that also strengthened market transactions. This social glue, called 'social capital', is described as the strength of family responsibilities, community volunteerism, selflessness, public or civic spirit – the same moral element that underlies the civil society debate.*

The challenge posed by the advocates of social capital is *how* to build up the social capital needed to reach a civil society. The solution most commonly offered is a return to the vision described de Tocqueville: an America of community spirit, volunteerism and association. Elshtain writes:

> *The 'loss of civil society' lies in the background to our current discontents, helping to account for why democracy itself is going through an ordeal of self-understanding as we near the end of the century. It is through the associational enthusiasms of civil society that the democratic ethos and spirit of citizens have been made manifest.* (Elshtain, 1993: 6)

In practical ways, of course, Northern governments have long supported the culture of association at home: many regularly fund organizations, promote discussions and subsidise volunteerism. The difference today is that we are now lending analytical weight and academic names to this moral vision: 'promoting volunteerism' sounds less like a serious policy goal than the weightier aim of 'building social capital'.

This domestic debate, with its refurbished vocabulary, has quickly been applied to changes outside of the Western circle as well. As the walls in Eastern Europe came tumbling down, questions rose about the purported end of alternative models of government, the expansion of democracy worldwide, the near universal acceptance of liberal market economics and the impact of this globalization on governance, culture, markets and daily life. How did all of that change come about? For many, the key trigger, if not the key cause, was the desire for civil society by Eastern Europeans themselves.

There are innumerable examples of this post-collapse enthusiasm for civil society. One triumphant source is an electronic journal funded by the United States Information Agency but run by CIVITAS, an organization of

---

* A related issue is the use to which the idea of social capital, like civil society, is being put. There is a normative debate over the use of the term to describe social cohesion as a good thing unto itself, and as a prerequisite for economic development – another tool in the arsenal of neoliberals. For a description of World Bank thinking on this topic, see Grootaert (1996) on the link between social capital and development.

civic educators that met initially in Prague in 1995 'to discuss the importance of a civic culture to the successful consolidation of democratic governance in countries in transition from dictatorship' (from their website at <http://civnet.org/>). In the first issue of the magazine, *Journal for a Civil Society*, Bahmueller alternately calls civil society a location of voluntary and independent thought and action, an antidote to modern alienation, a means for conflict resolution, a method to disperse power, a supplement or substitute for government, a school in the art of democratic citizenship, a preserver of certain values against the corrosive effects of modern culture, a source of creativity, a means for the individual to escape capture by the perspective of any one group and as the source of civil behaviour. Although the author throws in a warning, 'Not every aspect of civil societies as we find them is good or desirable' (Bahmueller, 1997), the caution rings hollow against the avalanche of its possibilities.

In the face of the disintegration of old political forms in the former Soviet Union and China especially, the appeal of the idea of civil society lies in the possibility of a different, moral socio-political vision that could match the emancipatory vision of socialism, yet embrace Western democratic notions. As Kumar writes,

> *The terms of civil society, its attractive combination of democratic pluralism with a continuing role for State regulation and guidance, make it appear hopeful to societies seeking to recover from the excesses of State socialism; at the same time it seems to offer help in the refashioning of radical politics in those societies where socialism has lost whatever appeal it once possessed.* (Kumar, 1993: 375)

It is this appeal that is the most dangerous for clear thinking, however. If we understand civil society as an ethical goal, then we have left unanswered, or even unasked, questions about how and why we are unhappy with our current society, about the systems and relationships that keep it in place and about the ways in which power – and whose power – generates our less-than-ideal situation.

An even greater danger, as we will see in the following, is the assumption that civic virtue is somehow self-evident and universal. Hall, among others, argues that it is important to separate a quest for civil society from a search for civic virtue, pointing to the presence of slavery, militarism and nationalism as one-time 'civic virtues' (Hall, 1995: 10). Indeed, civil society may generate what Slovenian commentator Tomaz describes as 'totalitarianism from below' (Tomaz, 1990: 309) – the notion that whatever appears in the civic realm must necessarily be in the public interest. The case of China is perhaps particularly illustrative. Chamberlain, concerned about the slapdash application of the term 'civil society' to explain the changes in China, warns that,

> *The term has come to signify nothing less than the 'reign of virtue'. Whatever political arrangement – whatever configuration of state and society – encourages its development is deemed good and worthy of support, and whatever arrangement stands in its way is to be condemned and altered.*
> (Chamberlain, 1993: 200)

Last, and perhaps most critically for our discussion of the aid industry, Westerners and others may import their own culturally specific normative goals into other contexts. As one critic warns, because civil society is a

> *... fundamentally normative concept, to operationalize it empirically would be either (1) to make the mistake of optimistically misreading into events and structures characteristics that are not there, or (2) to impose our own ideas of what should be occurring in the Third World instead of acknowledging and encouraging events to unfold according to the logic of a given country's own historical development.*
> (Bickford, 1995: 207)

The implication for policy analysts, therefore, is first to recognize the normative motors that drive the debate. These are important, but they are distinct from our observations of civil society itself. In short, although we need to know *why* we are interested in civil society, we also have to know *what* we are seeing.

Civil Society as a Collective Noun

Civil society is most often defined as if it were a collective noun, the sum of all the organizations we feel are responsible for bringing civility closer to home. In practice, civil society has been made synonymous with the voluntary sector (or the Third Sector), and particularly with advocacy groups, non-governmental organizations (NGOs), social movement agents, human rights organizations and others actors explicitly involved in 'change work'. Most often, these groups are circumscribed by a definition that excludes those belonging to the marketplace and the State (although there is, as we shall see, real debate over the exclusion of the private sector and lower orders of government), and by according them a positive moral mandate. Most definitions further specify that civil society organizations do not include those groups interested in acquiring political power, hence the usual exclusion of political parties (Diamond, 1991: 6–7).

These civil society organizations (CSOs) are seen as fomenters of democratic ideas, the genuine voices of the economically (and otherwise) oppressed, the underdogs scratching away at the underpinnings of autocracies in China, the Soviet Union, Eastern Europe, Asia, Africa and Latin America. Worldwide, these organizations and movements are seen to be stirring the soup of discontent and revolt. As one NGO collective writes,

> *Brought out of decades of collaboration and work with popular communities, unprotected sectors of society, marginalized, excluded and poor people of our Americas, the NGOs and groups participating in this Initiative believe Civil Society (CS) to be a real alternative to the environmental destruction, to the inhumane inequality of the economic system and to the uncertainty of this Century's end.* (Hemispheric Partnerships, 1997)

The response from the academic community to this burgeoning has included a number of efforts. The first, not surprisingly, has been to count: just how many non-profit organizations are there? Based in the empirical tradition of American political science, the work of Salamon and Anheier is the most prominent in this field, having grown from domestic research into organizations in Western countries (1994). From their studies of Brazil, Egypt, Ghana, India and Thailand, they offer an empirical effort at describing the shape of a nonprofit sector in each country, even where those words are not used (Anheier and Salamon, 1998; see Box 1.2). They show variations in the shape and structure of the sectors, historical and cultural patterns (including links to colonialism, religion, authoritarianism, the presence of a middle class and the nature of development ideology), the pattern of their considerable growth in recent years, and the ways they finance themselves. One shared element is that development NGOs – those intermediary organizations that serve as funnels from the outside world – are a substantial minority.

From a policy perspective, however, there are a number of difficulties with the empirical focus on counting civil society. One is that the term is equated, in practice at least, with *particular* sectors or kinds of organizations – those that we like – even if the definition is meant to encompass a larger population. In development circles, civil society is further reduced to 'NGO'.

Another problem is the assumption that the mere presence of organizations necessarily leads to a civil society working in the public interest. Does the proliferation of groups necessarily indicate the improvement of society? Ernest Gellner, the most prominent voice in the civil society debate today, says no. He points out that we shouldn't include all associations as members of civil society:

> *there are the segmentary communities, cousin-ridden and ritual-ridden, free perhaps of central tyranny, but not free in a sense that would satisfy us; there is centralization which grinds into the dust all subsidiary social institutions or sub-communities, whether ritually stifling or not; and there is the third alternative which is the one we seek.* (Gellner, 1995: 35)

His view is that it matters deeply what kinds of organizations inhabit civil society. Calhoun complains in a similar vein that 'the burgeoning literature

BOX 1.2: NON-PROFITS IN THE DEVELOPING WORLD

Brazil
- Non-profits work country-wide, of which 45,000 are in Sao Paulo alone and 16,000 in Rio
- Most are small, with budgets of less than US$30,000
- Total employment is easily one million, or about 2 per cent of total employment
- Most are funded by fees and charges rather than by funds from abroad

Egypt
- Non-profits exist nationwide
- Of these (noting overlap), 17,500 are membership-based, 9,500 are charitable and 3,200 work in development
- Most are urban, but 30 per cent work in rural areas
- Included are 22 professional groups whose members number 3 million

Thailand
- Of the some 11,000 registered non-profits country-wide, 2,200 are based in Bangkok
- Most have less than US$4,000 in assets
- Many more are non-registered
- An important segment of the sector is made up of traditional cremation societies

India
- At least 2 million associations are at work country-wide
- Ghandian non-profits alone employ 600,000
- NGOs receive some US$460 million in foreign funds

Ghana
- 800 formal non-profits are registered
- International groups are particularly prominent

Source: Salamon and Anheier (1998)

on 1989 in China identifies civil society too often with non-State business institutions and media proliferation *per se* (often failing to clarify relations among economic, political, social, and cultural dimensions of analysis)', (Calhoun, 1993: 271). Rosenblum adds to this critique by warning 'that enthusiasm for associational life eclipses the political and legal institutions necessary to sustain it', (Rosenblum, 1994: 555). Echoing Gramsci, civil society is a sphere of ideology, power and political and legal institutions – not only of organizations.

A corollary argument is that not all civil society organizations are bad either. On the domestic scene, Barber complains of the way that public interest groups have been marginalised as 'special interests' in America. Americans have lost the idea, he suggests, of a common interest – all interests are seen to be particular, each to be weighed as if none represented the common good. He points to the dismissal of environmental groups:

> *Although pursuing a genuinely public agenda of clean air for*
> *all, including the polluters, they have been cast as the*
> *polluters' twin – another special-interest group whose inter-*
> *ests are to be arbitrated alongside those of toxic-waste*
> *dumpers; over time, they have begun to behave that way,*
> *hiring lobbyists in Washington to push their own particularis-*
> *tic agendas. Under such conditions, the 'public good' could*
> *not and did not survive as a reasonable ideal.* (Barber, 1996:
> 272)

If civil society organizations are neither inherently morally good nor bad, a
further criticism is that the moral presumption of worth has made us blind
to ambiguous and conflicting motives within civil society. Robinson and
White warn that,

> *Actual civil societies are complex associational universes*
> *involving a vast array of specific organizational forms and*
> *a wide diversity of institutional motivations. They contain*
> *repression as well as democracy, conflict as well as coopera-*
> *tion, vice as well as virtue; they can be motivated by*
> *sectional greed as much as social interest. Thus any attempt*
> *to compress the ideas of civil society into a homogeneous*
> *and virtuous stereotype is doomed to fail. It is also intellec-*
> *tually harmful not only because it misrepresents the reality*
> *of civil societies, but also because it distorts development*
> *discourse more broadly by encouraging similarly simplified*
> *but overwhelmingly negative conceptions of other societal*
> *agencies, whether State or market.* (Robinson and White,
> 1997: 3)

The virtuous stereotype also means that most observers are not sure what
to do with neutral organizations (like bridge clubs) and those that have
uncivil outcomes (such as neo-Nazi associations). Indeed, if one broadens
the notion of civil society to include all associations, as White notes, one
may simply be describing society, thus rendering the 'civil' redundant
(White, 1993: 66). We may also be missing social processes that are critical
to development if we focus on social agitators alone.* We may well miss
the football clubs in which politics are discussed; girl guides, which shape
leadership; racist attacks, which spawn civil liberty movements. Most donor
definitions give only passing reference to these 'diverse and sometimes

---

* The literature on social movements has much to add to correct this myopia. Writing on
global civil society, Macdonald and Healy point out that the 'understanding of global civil
society overlooks the often deeply-entrenched nature of social divisions. As well, their
ontological individualism conceptualizes groups within civil society as voluntary associations
of free, rational individuals. As a consequence, this perspective is incapable of appreciating
the collective dimensions of forces for social change and the dynamic construction of group
identity among these actors' (Healy and Macdonald, 1997: 12).

contradictory social interests' without thinking how those conflicts fundamentally affect development.

A final problem, also related, is a large-scale unwillingness in the literature to look at the dynamics among and within organizations. This was certainly the point of Gramsci's contributions: understanding the ideological and other forces within civil society, as well as those operating between civil society organizations and the State, was the key to emancipation. As we see in the following chapters, there are a host of forces at play, including both private and public incentives for movement into the civil sphere. Without this kind of internal differentiation, the idea of civil society loses explanatory value – either as theory or as a tool for policy decisions. NGOs themselves are certainly willing to be critical: a volume crafted by NGO workers Sogge, Saxby and Biekhart asks very pointed questions about their own corner of civil society. Titled *Compassion and Calculation?* (1996), the book discusses the motivations and dynamics within the international NGO community, arguing that power relationships there – particularly between local groups and foreign aid agencies – is a critical determinant of success.

Civil Society as a Space for Action

Civil society has also been used as a metaphor for the space organizations occupy – usually described as the enabling environment in which they prosper (or wilt), rather than the more battle-riven terrain of Gramsci's writings. The United Nations Development Programme's (UNDP) definition is typical:

> *Civil society is, together with State and market, one of the three 'spheres' that interface in the making of democratic societies. Civil society is the sphere in which social movements become organized. The organizations of civil society, which represent many diverse and sometimes contradictory social interests are shaped to fit their social base, constituency, thematic orientations (e.g. environment, gender, human rights) and types of activity. They include church-related groups, trade unions, cooperatives, service organizations, community groups and youth organizations, as well as academic institutions and others.* (UNDP, 1993: 1)

The notion of space is most often used by sociologists and other watchers of social movements in an effort to explain why and how groups form in the first place. Bryant, for example, writes about civil society as 'a space or arena between household and State, other than the market, which affords possibilities of concerted action and social self-organization' (Bryant, 1993: 399). This notion, of course, holds radical promise for activists. In Sethi's vision of 'the new politics', for example, Southern civil societies, whether foreign or domestic development groups, charities for relief, action groups devoted to consciousness-raising and mobilization of the oppressed, protest groups, political groups, pre-party political formations or support groups are the 'locus of action' by actors bent on change (Sethi, 1993). Civil society becomes a space for (possible) revolution.

The target of that action differs according to political persuasion, however. For some, like prominent American writer Larry Diamond, civil society is the sphere that battles the State and keeps it in check. Civil society is, therefore:

> *the realm of organized social life that is voluntary, self-gener-*
> *ating (largely), self-supporting, autonomous from the State,*
> *and bound by a legal order or set of shared rules. It is*
> *distinct from society in general in that it involves citizens*
> *acting collectively in a public sphere to express their inter-*
> *ests, passions, and ideas, exchange information, achieve*
> *mutual goals, make demands on the State and hold State*
> *officials accountable.* (Diamond, 1994: 5)

For still others, the notion of spheres simply provides a way to categorize organizations. Throughout the policy literature, we see diagrams such as Figure 1.1 used to describe civil society, drawn with clear boundaries around the State, the market and 'civil society', a residual category of non-State, non-market actors.

There are a couple of problems with this kind of description. One is that the circles are frequently drawn in even, egalitarian sizes, neatly overlapping. The intent is schematic, but the effect is to depict a vision of balance and segregation that may not exist in reality. As this book under-lines, the population of organizations (in numbers or in their relevance to political or economic forces) is rarely so well balanced. Another problem is

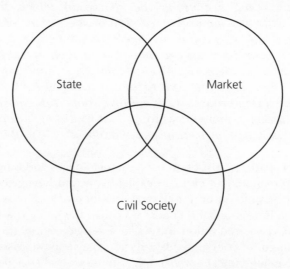

Figure 1.1: Modelling Civil Society

that this description divides the world by organizational type, hiding other aspects of an organization's role or function in society. Even if one allows overlapping identities (unions, for example as part market, part civil society), the effect is, none the less, of sorting by organizational identity rather than by purpose, goal, vision, method, function or some other more interesting distinction. Uphoff, writing on the work of NGOs, has been one of the critics of a too-tidy segmentation of organizations, preferring instead to locate organizations along a spectrum of involvement in each sector, rather than assigning them to any one in particular (Uphoff, 1993).

Taylor argues that it may be a stretch to even talk about civil society as distinct from the State – in the West at any rate. Certainly, it is hard to draw clear dividing lines in countries like Germany, Sweden and the Netherlands. Taylor asserts indeed that the anti-corporatist mood of our times has been responsible for bringing the civil society debate to the fore: the very debate on civil society is an outgrowth of anti-corporatist sentiment (Taylor, 1990: 98).

Perhaps it is this sentiment that has allowed us to think of the State as pointedly distinct from civil society. What has happened in much of the policy writing on civil society is a misappropriation of the idea of terrain into a simpler sphere, and final simplification into a neat circle drawn around organizational types.

Civil Society as a Historical Moment

Others describe civil society as a historical moment, either a real or idealized description of society when a set of prerequisites was in place. Adam Seligman, in *The Idea of Civil Society*, argues that civil society might have existed in the historical past, but has since become a fragile construction; the conditions that sustained it have radically changed in today's world. His prerequisites are the primacy of the individual, rights-bearing and autonomous, and a shared public space in which agreed rules and norms – morality – are sustained and followed (harking back to Cicero). Those norms must be universal for civil society to have meaning – nationalism, excessive individualism or ethnicity kills it. This civil society, built upon Anglo-European thought and the Scottish Enlightenment, cannot be created from without; it is the outcome of history.

Similarly, Gellner, in *Civil Society and its Rivals*, argues that the historical and social prerequisites for a civil society, notably the creation of atomized liberal individuals, are rare outside of Western states. Castiglione picks up the same argument, combating as well the notion of civil society as a simple sphere. 'Civil society is not simply an abstract space of free relationships between individuals and groups, not directly controlled by a centralized power, but the specific product of historical and cultural conditions, which result from both social and political practices and traditions' (Castiglione, 1994: 82–3). In short, they argue that it matters *deeply* how and what kind of organizations are formed. Any organization will not do.

Blaney and Pasha, searching for civil society in India and Africa, also argue that the starting point for civil society is 'the stabilization of a system of rights, constituting human beings as individuals, both as citizens in relation to the State and as legal persons in the economy and the sphere of free association', (Blaney and Pasha, 1993: 4). They suggest, however, that this mix of prerequisites cannot simply be assumed to exist in other countries. Their argument is that civil society exists because of a capitalist system – one that depends on the division of labour, on inequality, on the perceived division between the political and the economic.

This cultural specificity is also argued by Hutchful, who suggests that changing our notion of civil society to fit the African case may well have substantial repercussions for the theory itself (Hutchful, 1995–6). As a historical moment, the notion is associated with fundamental transformations in Western society and economy that do not necessarily apply to the African condition (capitalist modernization, urbanization, the communications revolution and growth of literacy, the dissolution of traditional bonds and the decline of religious consciousness). By way of contrast, African 'associational life' (Bratton, 1986) is most often made up of ascriptive groupings (organizations one is born into) rather than voluntary ones, and ones that may be entwined with the State and ravaged by outside forces (ethnicity, sectarianism, etc). Callaghy, in *Civil Society and the State in Africa*, argues that:

> *Much associational life has very little to do with the creation of norms, especially civil ones ... In fact, group interaction ... may easily lead to the development of norms that do not further the development of the public sphere, much less a civil, open, tolerant, and participatory one based on established rights, as commonly presumed.* (Callaghy, 1994: 235)

Throughout the literature on what foreign donors can do to support civil society, this precondition approach is rife. Other factors most often cited include the rights needed to participate in organized groups, a democratic political system of some sort (the main entry point for most donors), a culture of association that allows the organization of groups for moral ends (the most interesting debates in this aspect talk about African associational life; see Bratton, 1986; Hutchful, 1995–6); and perhaps a middle class with disposable income and time to support organizations.* All these elements – government structure, culture, class – are nationally specific, mutable elements and, in many countries, now undergoing rapid change.

The interesting thing about a historical view of civil society, after all, is that it raises questions about how civil society emerges and why it might disappear, a topic that Oxhorn develops, for example, in trying to understand why civil society in Latin America has gotten weaker with the advent

---

* On the role of the bourgeoisie in the establishment of civil society, see Moore (1966), Hall (1995: 18–20) and Szelenyi (1988).

of democracy (Oxhorn, 1995). The policy outcome for some international donor agencies has subsequently been a quest for the foundations, the pre-requisites of civil society. Donors have thus trained their analytical sights on the ingredients that are most mutable. Can one create a system of rights? What about a culture of association? As we shall see in the next chapter, the potential for successful intervention on such an enormous field becomes small – or, at best, very long term.

Civil Society as Anti-Hegemony

One of the most radical viewpoints on the civil society debate argues that civil society is not conducive to modern liberalism (in politics or economics) but is instead its antithesis. Arguments like Gellner's are put on their head by writers who interpret civil society as a reaction to (and not the intended result of) the atomization of liberal culture. For the purposes of our study, this vision of civil society has a couple of important implications.

First, a number of authors point out that many civil society organizations are disengaged from formal political processes and work in part underground. As Melucci argues, these movements build solidarity outside and underneath conventional institutions of civil society and the State, in small groups submerged in everyday life (Melucci, 1988). Arato and Cohen describe these new movements as having a unique social base, a particular social and political nature and a set of demands that are an alternative type of democratic action (Arato and Cohen, 1992; see Seligman, 1992: 11–17). In arguing about values and norms (gender and power, environment, gay and lesbian identities), movements may or may not ever join in political action or seek political power. If one defines civil society primarily in terms of its relationship with the State, therefore, one may well miss this aspect of civil organizing.*

A second element is the importance of anti-Westernism. In some parts of the South, particularly among Indian academics, a school of thought on New Social Movements has been particularly anti-Western in its inspiration, claiming a higher moral ground and re-appropriating the language of civil society for its own purposes. Kothari reasons that social mobilization arises from 'a reaction to the perpetuation of a homogeneous consumer culture and desires kindled by a homogenizing popular media' (Kothari, 1996: 14) and that the capacity of Third World people to play an active role 'is discounted by the centralization of economic and political power primarily because of the critical loss (and lack) of control over productive resources' (Kothari,1996: 15). The challenge is therefore to build a 'democratic State that can act as a buffer against predatory capital (domestic and transnational) and as a non-partisan arbiter in domestic conflicts' (Kothari, 1996: 16).

---

* Jean Bethke Elshtain warns, however, that this populist fervour is inimical to civil society. Identity politics, the notion of rights without responsibilities, the anti-government sentiment expressed in direct versus representational democracy – all these work against collective action (Elshtain, 1993).

This anti-hegemonic debate focuses on the link between a certain kind of atomized individual and the nature of production, from which (in familiar Marxist terms) the State evolves. This argument is certainly acknowledged in various traditions: Bickford writes that 'the historical relationship between the development of capitalism and the origins of civil society is important and it is hardly coincidental that civil society sees a resurgence in the age of neo-liberalism' (Bickford, 1995: 212). Gellner, in his turn, argues that the civic spirit that animates democracy also provides the spirit that fulfills contracts and obligations without endless enforcement, hence contributing to economic growth (Gellner, 1991: 501) – one of Putnam's points about Italy (Putnam, 1995).

For donors, the implication of this link between oppression and the development of certain types of civil society is the realization that their intervention may be utterly unwanted – a symptom of the perceived cultural and economic dominance of Western ideas.

Civil Society as an Antidote to the State

Another overlapping viewpoint describes civil society by its activities in opposition to a centralized or autocratic State. As White writes, the use of civil society 'implies a certain power relationship between State and society such that there are limitations on the State's capacity to pervade and control society, and a certain power on the part of members of a society to insulate themselves from, and exert influence upon, the State' (White, 1993: 65). Promoting civil society has come to mean limiting the State.

This central defining opposition runs counter to the body of theory on civil society; in no previous literature does civil society exist in *opposition* to the State – they are always a conceptual pair. Chamberlain writes that the modern use of civil society seems to be underwritten by the premise that 'the existence and viability of civil society varies directly with the distance (or absence) of State power. But this seriously distorts the meaning of the term. Historically conceived, civil society is as much a creature of the State as it is of society' (Chamberlain, 1993: 204). Yet in today's policy talk, explored in more depth in the following chapter, civil society and the state are pinned at opposite ends of the good guy–bad guy spectrum. 'We have arrived at a crucial historical moment where the State appears to be of little consequence to societal projects' (Chandhoke, 1995: 33). We are apparently interested in civil society in large part because it is placed as the antithesis to the State, even as the State gives it room to function.

Part of the reason is a Western, perhaps primarily American, loss of faith in both the abstraction and the physical manifestation of the State. Chandhoke's thesis is just that:

> *If the decade of the 1970s witnessed political theory's obsessive preoccupation with the state, the decades of the 1980s and 1990s, are distinguished by an almost identical obses-*

> *sion with civil society, but this had led political theory into a*
> *theoretical impasse for, if the preoccupation with the state*
> *had marginalized civil society, the preoccupation with civil*
> *society has succeeded in marginalizing the state.*
> (Chandhoke, 1995: 14)

This anti-statism is particularly strong in American policy schools, though it is hardly contained there. Jessica Matthews, head of the National Endowment for Democracy, makes a symptomatic argument when she suggests that 'The end of the cold war has brought no mere adjustment among states but a novel redistribution of power among states, markets and civil society.' Much of that shift in power she attributes to the electronic communications revolution because it 'disrupts hierarchies, spreading power among more people and groups', such that today, 'NGOs are able to push around even the largest governments' (Matthews, 1997: 50, 52). For Matthews, not only *should* states wield less power, but also they actually *are* less powerful in the face of the civil society onslaught.

Even the less evangelistic proponents of civic action would agree in part. Arguing against the long-time dismissal of NGOs as important agents in world politics, Wapner suggests that political scientists missed the point: 'Being forced to acknowledge the centrality of the State, they failed to ask what constitutes relevant political behaviour, what power is, and which dimensions of collective life are most significant for bringing about changes in human practices'. As he elaborates, 'The failure of governments to respond, however, does not necessarily mean that the efforts of activists have been in vain. Rather, they influence understandings of good conduct throughout societies at large. They help set the boundaries of what is considered acceptable behavior' (Wapner, 1995: 319, 326). In short, civil society organizations (CSOs) matter even if the State is stronger.

Another issue is the inclusion of the market within civil society. If the debate is really about the State, then civil society has somehow come to mean everything else. Keane relates this train of thought to those on the political right in Western Europe who granted the term civil society with 'a kind of natural innocence and deployed (it) as poorly defined synonym for the market and other forms of 'private' life which are supposed to be good because of their opposition to State power' (Keane, 1988: 13). The problem, of course, is that society is then seen to be divided into two simple parts, washing away all that is complex and contradictory and inter-connected. Sales makes a similar complaint, arguing that civil society is often confused with the private sphere, which includes 'such heteroge-neous elements as families, social movements, political parties, underground enterprises or large multinationals – in short, everything not directly managed by the State' (Sales, 1991: 296). If we cannot generalize about civil society organizations, it certainly makes little sense to talk about multinationals in the same breath.

Another issue focuses on the internationalization of civil society. Civil society is seen by some as a response to global changes in statehood itself, not merely its domestic manifestation; Lipshultz argues that we are seeing a rise in global civil society *because* of a leaking away of sovereignty (Lipshultz, 1992). The right to sovereignty, although formally still recognized, he argues has undergone steady attrition in practice. Environmental degradation; the universalization of human rights (and the notion that foreign actors can act upon the transgression of rights in other countries); civil wars; drug trafficking; and other transborder and intraborder activities are no longer seen to belong to the governments that control the territory upon which they take place.

The implication here is at least twofold. One is that civil society organizations themselves are taking on transborder roles, stirring up inter-nation discourse – an element that has had important consequences in the countries studied in this volume. The other is that the shifting of sovereignty has implications in turn for the legitimacy of states. In some cases, the international community has accepted that civil society organizations are more representative of the populace and more true in their rendition of the world than are their governments. In the world of international activism and organizations, there is a widely accepted notion that true democracy may involve the circumvention of governments altogether. This sentiment also explains in part why foreign agencies have often given themselves permission to intervene in other countries under certain conditions. Amalric argues that,

> *Advocacy groups can claim to speak in the name of civil society only if it can be argued that civil society is misrepresented by existing political institutions. The legitimacy of civil society groups is therefore dependent upon the existence of a deficit in democracy, a gap between actual democratic practices and some democratic ideal.* (Amalric, 1996: 7)

Just who decides on the deficit of democracy thus becomes an additional debate. It also becomes an issue when the enabling environment provided by the State also disappears. John Hall argues that,

> *The notion that groups, albeit of the right type, should balance the State is subtly wrong. This manner of conceptualizing state–society relations leaves much to be desired because it tends to see the state exclusively as a threat. In Eastern Europe in recent years, this led many reformers to seek virtually to abolish the state, in the belief that civil society would work best in its absence. The current situation of Russia, bereft of the rule of law, demonstrates the weakness of this view. The state is needed by civil society for protection and so as to ensure basic social conditions, such as, in recent years, the protection of women inside the household.* (Hall, 1995: 15–16)

This element of the debate means that this study should address the under-lying rationale of donors' civil society programming. Is the idea of the State itself implicitly under question? If so, how is its future being shaped? If not, is the motivation centred on the activities of a *particular* government or regime? The distinction between State and government is important, of course. Donors bent on getting rid of a particular regime will interact differently with groups in civil society than will donors trying to reshape the State itself (in particular, in response to lending conditionality). In the one case, outsiders may promote opposition groups or information campaigns; in the other, they may interact with service organizations that might absorb State responsibilities. Those differences in turn raise differ-ent kinds of questions about civil society autonomy in function, if not in type, from the State – are groups simply sub-contractors of State services? Are service organizations tied to State strings, therefore, outside of civil society? To get to the answers, we must accept that the lines between State and society are irrevocably blurred and interdependent. The task then is to look at those blurred relationships and ask how they are affecting the development of a country's peoples.

KEEPING ANALYSIS SEPARATE FROM HOPE

In designing a study to investigate what others are calling civil society, we must also explain what we mean by civil society. The difficulty in building a definition from these viewpoints, along with all the theoretical, norma-tive and other baggage they drag behind them, is considerable. There are at least four major categories of difficulty, identified by Alan Fowler, one of the book's advisors and a frequent commentator on NGO issues (Fowler, 1997a: 2–3), and expanded in the following.

The Objections

Western and Northern Bias

Theories in use today largely draw upon limited Western experiences. Critics, like French academic Le Roy, argue that Western ideas based on puritan traditions of civil society are transferred *in toto* on to Southern societies, hence mobilizing only a small fraction of Westernized elites into action.* His argument is premised on the notion of civil society as a histor-ical moment – a moment that does not necessarily exist in other countries and cultures, but that is, none the less, fruitlessly cookie-cuttered on to non-Western political forms.

---

* Personal letter, translated by the author, 1996. Original: 'Nous transposons dans les sociétés du sud, spécialement en Afrique pour ce qui me concerne, des représentations qui ne sont propres qu'à nos traditions occidentales, spécialement la tradition puritaine pour ce qui concerne la notion de société civile. Ainsi ne mobilise t'on qu'une fraction des élites occidentalisées, apte à se situer positivement face aux enjeux d'un État revisité selon des critères non seulement anglo-saxons mais nord-américains'.

Others, however, find usefulness in a universalist approach. *Civil Society and the State in Africa*, an important book by Harbeson and others, argues overall that civil society theory is helpful as a 'formula for analysing State–society relations in Africa because it embodies a core of universal beliefs and practices about the legitimation, and limits to, State power' (Harbeson et al., 1994: 52). That formula serves as a checklist for looking at all societies, and thus identifying which ingredients of civil society are present. Taylor agrees, 'Western democracy wasn't written in our genes. At the same time, the chauvinistic idea that representative institutions cannot take root outside of their home culture is refuted by the existence of such societies as India and Japan' (Taylor, 1990: 101).

In general, however, a North–South line is overwhelmingly drawn through the academic literature and theory. A workshop organized by the International Non-Governmental Organization Training and Research Centre in Oxford in 1995 identified just this split in a debate on the definition of civil society:

> *(The Southern participants) questioned whether the whole concept was not donor driven, whether northern interpretation of the concept was not imperialism in a new guise and whether many in the north had not forgotten the long history of struggles for rights by civic groups all over the world...*
> *One could argue that the 'split' in the group reflected the distinction between the liberal interpretation of civil society with its emphasis on pluralism, diversity, co-existence and consensus and those that adhere to a tradition associated with Marx and Gramsci, which sees civil society as inherently conflictual as well as being recursively related to the state.* (Roche, 1995: 3)

Any definition must recognize that political split and examine its implications. As the visions of civil society shift, changes in policy and practice may follow.

Theoretical Myopia

Choosing viewpoints on civil society, therefore, entails political choice – theories on civil society are outgrowths of other perspectives: Marxist, liberal and social democratic, among others. Although most visions of civil society are not necessarily incompatible with each other, they do have different implications in their emphases. We must be conscious of the implications of the choice and identify those subterranean politics as they arise. Wood, a Marxist, offers a warning that is useful to those of all political persuasions: civil society, 'this conceptual portmanteau, which indiscriminately lumps together everything from households and voluntary associations to the economic system of capitalism, confuses and disguises as much as it reveals' (Wood, 1990: 65). This book thus explores whether the idea has more value as a slogan than as a theoretical concept.

Normative Bias

Theories tend to be used in moral and normative ways, confusing what is with what should be. The point of political theory, of course, is to explain the world in a way that will lead us toward desired ends. The problem is that those normative lenses may not allow us to see all relevant events, actors and processes because we are not looking for them. If we insist that non-State organizations (civil society as collective noun) should be necessary for democracy, for example, we may well not see those organizations that are inimical to democracy's presence. As Chandhoke writes, 'whereas civil society has become a crucial concept in the construction of radical projects in the contemporary world, an inadequate, one-sided or a romanticized understanding of the concept can lead to flawed political practices' (Chandhoke, 1995: 77).

Organizational Bias

Political theories of civil society get mixed up with theories about organizations, hence forgetting the enabling environments in which those organizations are born. In our rush to understand complex processes, we have a natural tendency to reach for the concrete. Civil society has too often become equated with organizations, and those organizations then become the centre of our inquiry: what do they look like, how do they work, how do they form and why? In our fascination with trees, we do not see forests.

Defining Civil Society

Given those warnings, how are we to forge a definition? Why we need to find a definition should be clear: investigating civil society is important if we think that the idea might have merit for social projects in this, and the next, century. The issue is not simply that 'ideas about civil society are being used today for a variety of ends'. The real issue is that those ideas do matter, for they shape our analyses of the problems we see in our own societies and in those of others, and those analyses sometimes are followed up by programmes, projects and cash. Moreover, we argue that there are important meanings in the idea and in our attempts to make sense of it, and in those meanings lie inspiration for social change. Yet if we allow civil society to be theoretically impoverished, to mean all things to all people, to exist as a residual category once all other slices of human life are drawn away, then it deserves abandonment (Fierlbeck, 1996).

Any definition must, therefore, address major objections before being useful and must explicitly describe the combination of viewpoints used. Those clarifications will not mean that this, or any, definition is final but, rather, that it is useful for a particular purpose. The purpose of this book is both to examine what civil society has meant in the aid industry (and so

to interrogate the versions under use by donors) and to propose alternatives based on a less ethnocentric, more theoretically curious, more
normatively transparent and more comprehensive definition.

A working definition for this study, therefore, takes into account this
mix of elements and objections. We define civil society as both an observable reality (civil society as a collective of conflicting, interdependent,
inter-influential organizations) and a good thing (that having a civil society,
warts and all, is better than not).

Civil society is an observable reality

The reality of civil society is the population of groups formed for collective
purposes *primarily* outside of the State and marketplace. We acknowledge
that not all of civil society's purposes are for the collective good and not
all improve the quality of public life. We also acknowledge that voluntary
(versus ascriptive) membership is not the sole qualification for inclusion,
but that the nature of membership may be an important element in the
organization's role and function within civil society. For the purposes of
this study, therefore, our definition is narrowed further to look at organizations involved in performing particular functions. We are concerned with
the function of groups and not their overall population; hence, we
examine only those organizations active in the shaping of democratic and
developmental goals in their country. Other studies for other purposes
may well look at other organizations.

Civil society is a good idea

The normative statement is that civil society is a good thing; many of the
groups that interest us form to compensate for the failures of the State, the
market or other parts of society to fulfill their aspirations. The idea assumes
that a third sector is necessary to guarantee a just society, and that the
formation of civil society itself – a population of groups and the enabling
environment necessary for their survival – is, therefore, a good thing. For
the purposes of this study, we include not only a description of particular
groups and their functions, but also an examination of efforts to expand
the enabling environment for all organizations (including the culturally
specific preconditions for their existence).

Wielding this rather clunky definition, the following chapters build a
set of arguments about why and what donors are doing and with whom
(the observable reality), and judgements of how they might better serve
the goals of development and democracy (the normative assessment). This
is a weighty task. Hall acknowledges that 'civil society is complicated, most
notably in being at one and the same time a social value and a set of social
institutions' (Hall, 1995: 2). By trying to distinguish between what we are
seeing and whether what we see is helping or hindering, the chapters make
recommendations for action. As such, we have tried to keep analysis
separate from hope.

2 OUT OF THE IVORY TOWER: CIVIL SOCIETY AND THE AID SYSTEM

Alison Van Rooy and Mark Robinson

> *In the Third World itself, governmental officials, social movement activists, international donors and other actors adopt the dominant paradigm of the moment and take it out of the ivory tower and into play – using its framework to generate certain questions and answers, to direct (governmental, international and philanthropic) funds, and to advance certain programmatic priorities over others. In the 1990s, civil society is fast becoming one of these dominant paradigms. (Bickford, 1995: 203–4)*

Ideas about civil society *do* matter: ideas carry implications for action, for good and for ill. Oxfam's Roper-Renshaw, for example, cautions against the appeal of an unexamined rush towards 'civil society', warning that 'because development is so complex, an organizing concept like civil society is very appealing... However, oversimplifications lead to distortions, poor analyses and poor outcomes' (Roper-Renshaw, 1994: 48–49). In the same vein, World Vision's Alan Whaites writes, 'the ways in which development NGOs perceive civil society, and consequently plan projects to facilitate and enhance the work of civil associations, can have a significant long-term effect on the evolution (or lack of it) of civil society in the countries in which they work' (Whaites, 1996: 240). Indeed, those interventions may be counterproductive to the project of social transformation.

This chapter, therefore, goes further by delving into the relationship between ideas and action to examine how talk about civil society has descended from the ivory tower and been absorbed into the international aid system in practice. To illustrate that absorption, the text includes segments from interviews with donor representatives, as well as excerpts from policy documentation, reports and statistics.* The chapter uses these sources of information to examine how language about civil society is used in the industry, what kinds of activities are attached to that language and what successes and dangers have been identified along the way. The pages that follow try to show *how* those ideas have mattered: who gets money, who doesn't; who is invited to the table, who isn't; whose interests are served by programme A rather than programme B. The language about civil society is, therefore, language about, and language that shapes, power relationships.

The way to avoid unexamined rushes towards civil society is to look carefully at the goals of donor programming, whether by Northern governments in their bilateral budgets, by the large multilateral bodies like the UNDP and the World Bank, by foundations such as Ford and Mott, or by individual Northern NGOs such as Oxfam and Caritas. The first part of this chapter, written by Alison Van Rooy, therefore, looks at three sets of answers to the question, 'What is civil society *supposed* to do?' from the vantage point of foreign contributors to civil society. The first two sets of answers, improving development and promoting democracy, will be familiar: but a third set, 'the other agenda', offers some surprises.

The second part of the chapter, written by Mark Robinson, looks at the history of programming in recent years and tries to explain how dollars (and marks and pounds) are being spent in the aid industry to support civil society. The last section takes these policy and practice questions and suggests how they inform the cases to follow. In the tangled realities of the aid, culture, history, politics and economic change that emerge in the stories of Kenya, Hungary, Peru and Sri Lanka, signposts to the larger questions might help. The third section, by Alison Van Rooy, is thus meant to arm the reader with map and compass for the stories that follow.

WHAT IS CIVIL SOCIETY SUPPOSED TO DO?

Alison Van Rooy

The greater part of this chapter looks at the discussions of civil society in donor policy talk. It takes apart those conversations, highlighting objec-

* Information from interviews with representatives from a number of donor agencies, largely US-based foundations, is included in this chapter. It is understood that these individuals speak from their own experience and do not necessarily represent the views of their organizations. I would like to offer my thanks to: Nancy Muirhead, Rockefeller Brothers, NY; Krystyna U. Wolniakowski, German Marshall Fund, Washington; John Anelli, International Republican Institute, Washington; Lisa Maclean and Kate Kelsch, National Democratic Institute, Washington; Sonam Yangchen, UNDP, New York; Gary Hansen, Civil Society Unit, USAID, Washington; Jon Blyth, Mott Foundation, Flint, MI; Bill Shambra, Lynde and Harry Bradley Foundation, Milwaukee; John Hurley, MacArthur Foundation, Chicago; Mary Shipsey Gunn, The David and Lucile Packard Foundation, Los Altos, CA; Steve Pierce, The Inter-American Development Foundation, Rosslyn, VA; Doug Williams, Ivan Roberts and Maury Miloff, CIDA, Hull; and Paul Light, Pew Charitable Trusts, Philadelphia.

tions from various sources and describing the breadth of the theoretical landscape. For almost every justification, of course, there is a counter-argument from elsewhere in the literature. At the end , we do not leave the debate scattered (like Humpty Dumpty, as one reviewer complained, in too many pieces to be fixed). As we will see, donors have shown different behaviours in response to (or despite) the debate on civil society and many of their activities have made important strides in the promotion of development and democracy. What we will suggest, however, and what the conclusion will underline, is that those strides are pretty small in comparison with the range of tasks at hand. Working at the margins, donors can, at best, fashion small miracles. Let us begin, however, with a review of what civil society is *supposed* to do.

Improving Development

Throughout the 1980s, donors noted with growing enthusiasm the work of first Northern and then Southern community organizations (see Box 2.1). Non-governmental organizations (NGOs), an umbrella phrase for grassroots, intermediary and international groups, were described as important players in a country's overall development* – more effective, less costly and more innovative than official donors or even home governments and more able to reach the poorest citizens.**

In the past decade, however, talk about the worthiness of NGOs as a resource for foreign and domestic government interventions has broadened. Now, the focus is on civil society organizations (CSOs), whose numbers include the familiar corpus of NGOs working in the North 'on behalf of' those in the South and grassroots and intermediary organizations working in the South as well.***

NGOs or CSOs?

CIDA: 'As new, non-NGOs arrive on CIDA's horizon, the term 'civil society' has allowed the agency to encompass the new actors. In Latin America, certainly, we have realized that we have neglected social issues in pursuit of economic ones. In looking

---

* We use the term 'development' to refer to positive changes in the material, social, political and physical status of a country's peoples. At the same time, however, we are aware that development is a concept that has also referred to a history of foreign intervention and carries the burdens of failures, misconceptions and dependency between North and South.
** Noteworthy milestones in the literature, both in support and in criticism of this view, include: Drabek (1987), Cernea (1988), OECD (1988), Fowler (1990), Korten (1990), Riddell and Robinson (1995), Sogge (1996).
*** A recent trend has been to fund Southern organizations directly, skipping the Northern partner altogether, on the grounds that Southern NGOs/CSOs are less expensive mechanisms for distributing official development assistance (Bebbington and Riddell, 1995: 880). This strategy is controversial for Northern NGOs, of course, who see their role to be more active than that of intermediary alone.

Box 2.1 Spending on NGOs

Easily US$1 billion in aid money is now spent via NGOs (figure 2.1),* and in some countries, the proportion spent via NGOs reaches 11 per cent (figure 2.2). The figures are *in addition* to the nearly US$6 billion that Northern NGOs raise from other sources (OECD, 1998). Even multilateral agencies have joined the enthusiasm. The World Bank, for instance, now reports growing levels of NGO involvement – 40–50 per cent of projects in 1994–96 had some kind of NGO involvement (World Bank, 1996: 7).**

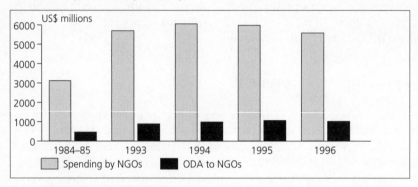

Source: Table 21 (OECD, 1998)

Figure 2.1: *Development Assistance Committee (DAC) official development assistance (ODA) to NGOs and NGO spending current US$ millions*

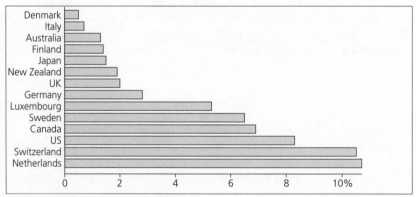

Source: Table 26: OECD, 1998

Figure 2.2: *Percentage of DAC Member ODA spent through NGOs, 1994–95*

---

* The quality of the figures for spending on NGOs is very poor, however. For a comprehensive note on the problems with DAC data, see Smillie and Helmich (1993: 40–41).
** In some cases, however, 'involvement' has meant incidental consultation or subcontracting. As World Bank watcher Nelson writes,' "Participation" refers to mobilizing communities or associations to carry out some project objective and only rarely priority setting or planning'(Nelson, 1997: 21).

for ways to channel support through non-governmental sources to support democracy in Peru, we began to talk about civil society'.

UNDP: *'We were receiving feedback, especially from our Middle East posts, that the term "NGO" was seen to mean "anti-government", whereas "civil society" was seen to be more neutral'.*

Inter-American Foundation: *'Many use "civil society" synonymously with "NGOs", but I don't think that equation is useful because once you focus on the functions of organizations, you realize that you need strategic alliances (among many kinds of organizations)'.*

The distinction between NGO and CSO is important because the policy and power implications are different. Rightly or wrongly, NGOs are often described in service–delivery roles, whereas CSOs are depicted as political agents.[*] In his survey of donor policy on civil society, Robinson writes:

The developmental emphasis on institution-building and participatory development focuses attention on NGOs and local membership organizations, whereas a concern with democratization highlights the more political role played by civic organizations, such as trade unions, professional bodies and groups representing women, students and youth. The former emphasizes the role of civil society in service provision and programme implementation, whereas the latter addresses the contribution of civic organizations to the process of democratization and in holding governments to account for their policies and actions. (Robinson, 1996: 3)

POLITICAL AGENTS

USAID: *'Civil society "is defined as nonstate organizations that can (or have the potential to) champion democratic/governance reforms." (Hansen, 1996: 3)'*

IRI: *'Our unofficial definition is of civil society as citizens organizing for political or economic change'.*

---

[*] This pattern seems to be true in other countries as well. In Uganda, Ghana and Tanzania, Dicklitch and Hutchful both find that very few NGOs do anything but provide services that indirectly support a quasi-authoritarian government (Dicklitch, 1997, Hutchful and Schmitz, 1992).

The reality is far more complex, of course; both types of organizations frequently play multiple roles simultaneously, often in a contradictory fashion as we shall see in the following chapters. For purposes of analysis, however, the two major strands – the promotion of development and the promotion of democracy – are treated as separate policy issues in our review of donor thinking. In answer to the question, 'What is civil society supposed to do for *development?*' at least three answers are usually offered: CSOs can help generate economic growth, improve equity and function as replacements for waning State services.

The Putnam Principle: Civil Society and Social Capital Build Economies

With the crumbling of the Berlin Wall, there has been a visible retrench-ment in the West of the values underlying the free market system. Those values include individualism and open markets in association with minimal government, curbed by democratic checks and balances.* Yet in exporting models for liberalized economies, donors and others are aware that neces-sary *social* prerequisites for a functioning market are rarely in place. How do you create 'economic individuals' in practice? Who trains citizens in the values necessary to entrepreneurialism? How do you get people interested in opening markets and curbing governments in the first place? One answer has been to encourage associational life.

THE PUTNAM LINK

Mott: *'We are finding that this economic health is a much more important variable for realizing civil society than we had thought. For example, in countries like Russia or the Ukraine, where the standard of living has fallen dramatically with democ-racy, the whole building of civil society is like building a house of cards: while we may talk about advances toward civil society, we must acknowledge that little will happen unless there are increased economic opportunities and economic security.'*

This train of thought is associated with Robert Putnam's work on social capital that demonstrated a link between civil society and, as a by-product, improved economic performance (see Chapter 1). This link has in turn been made in donor writing. The Organization for Economic Co-operation

---

* Gellner attributes this retrenchment in large part to the role of economic prosperity, rather than territorial aggrandizement, as the chief means of acquiring national greatness (Gellner, 1991: 496), a familiar argument. As the criteria for greatness changed, centrally planned economies were dismissed as viable means of organizing production, and the fixation turned to the mechanisms – rather than the principle – of installing a free market system.

and Development (OECD), for instance, notes in its document on *Participatory Development and Good Governance* that 'it has become increasingly apparent that there is a vital connection between open, democratic and accountable systems of governance, and respect for human rights, and the ability to achieve sustained economic and social development' (OECD, 1993: 3). Even though improved economic performance is not a *necessary* outcome of greater civil organizing, donor support to civil society is frequently justified as a direct measure of support to the creation of a vibrant free market.

Indeed, much of US talk about civil society in the former Soviet Union approaches the debate from this angle.* Gary Hansen, one of the main writers within the United States Agency for International Development (USAID) on this topic, argues 'that the transition from statist to market-based economies can be more effectively consolidated with the growth of advocacy groups that champion such reforms' (Hansen, 1996: 2). For the agency's New Partnerships Initiative (NPI), the economic and political marketplaces are deeply intertwined:

> *Civil society thrives in a dynamic and competitive economy and in an open, democratic political environment. At the local level, economic requirements translate into an expanding small business sector that stimulates employment, entrepreneurship and a spirit of independence and self-help. Democratic local governance provides a political environment that is responsive to local needs, stimulates participation, and can be held accountable to citizens. NPI focuses on three sets of local institutions – nongovernmental organizations, competitive small businesses, and democratic local governments – that together can significantly enhance the effectiveness of private and public development efforts and can help reduce the distortions and inequities in closed economies and political systems.* (USAID, 1995: i)

This rationale has also generated a thick body of literature on the link between civil society and the free market in China, as foreign investors watch the liberalization of the economy with interest. Here the debate focuses on the degree to which support to entrepreneurial organizations, in combination with privatizing reforms to government structures, will open up the economy to external intervention. White makes just this argument: 'there is a close relationship between the spread of market relations and the differentiation of ownership brought about by the Chinese economic reforms on the one hand and the rise of new forms of

---

* The American opinion is particularly important because USAID spends easily more than any other donor in this area and has generated the most full and coherent policy material. In so setting the scene for their DAC colleagues, the Americans have set the civil society agenda.

social organization and the adaptation of existing social organizations on the other' (White, 1993: 67). Howell's work has been similarly focused on the relationship between the rise of the free market and the evolution of Chinese civil society. Indeed, her definition of civil society organizations *includes* business within the familiar corpus of civil society organizations because the overwhelming dominance of the State eclipses distinctions in other spheres (Howell, 1994).

These kinds of reasons are mirrored broadly elsewhere in the community. The German political foundation Friedrich Ebert Stiftung, for instance, is of the opinion that:

> *Decentralized and pluralistic decision-making is a precondition for democratic structures, even in the economy. In this regard, intermediary institutions, settled between the State and the individual, play an important role: organizations of small-scale craftsmen and smallholders, chambers of commerce and industry, associations for environmental protection as well as self-help groups, promoting the improvement of the socio-economic condition of women. The creation, strengthening, and further development of such institutions of the so-called 'civil society' is an essential prerequisite for an efficient and socially sustainable functioning of a market economy.* (FES, 1995: 22 in Robinson, 1996: 8)

The policy implication of this reasoning is that support to civil society organizations can speed up economic growth. The inclination in practice, however, is to narrow the definition of civil society to concentrate on organizations whose functions are geared around the marketplace rather than other sectors. Support to 'civil society' then becomes narrowed in project proposals to support to pro-entrepreneurial organizations, moving away from the broader associational argument made by Putnam. A further inclination is to push to the sidelines discussion of the State's role in shaping the economy. The State's responsibilities then fade from the civil society debate, even while a return to the State has become more prominent in mainstream development analyses.* The complex links between State guidance, civil society activity, economic performance and other factors (as in the case of the East Asian miracle and current crisis) fall prey to oversimplification.

THE PRIVATE CIVIL SECTOR?

Bradley: *'We have always been interested in securing free markets and promoting traditional values, and civil society is another way of describing that.'*

---

* The 1997 World Development Report, for example, is focused on the role of the State.

Inter-American Foundation: *'We don't use the term "civil society" too much because we are working closely with business sectors, and many business organizations consider themselves part of civil society. Therefore, I prefer to use the terms governmental, for-profit, and not-for-profit – the latter two are civil society.'*

Civil Society Generates Equity

Civil societies are also assumed to foster the activism that brings about *equitable* development: development for the poorest first. Although there are certainly counter cases (the Philippines and India, with strong civil societies, are notably inequitable), the argument is that a healthy civil society is a prerequisite for effective and equitable State policy. But one needs to ask what donors, and others, mean by 'equity' and how they intend to reach it. There are, as always, different answers.

Reaching the poorest
One key reason for adopting a civil society approach is to reach the poorest through organizations that either represent them, or can reach them more reliably than can governments.

THE GRASSROOTS ADVANTAGE

Bradley: *'There are grassroots organizations solving the most serious problems of society, often without notice, below the radar screen, largely based on faith. Our job is to find more of these organizations.'*

This is the most familiar rationale for support to NGOs (see Riddell and Robinson, 1996a and 1996b), not only for delivering services more equitably and effectively, but also for leveling the political playing field. German aid, for instance 'places priority on building up channels of political representation among the most marginalised groups in society' and Norwegian aid pointedly refers to the bolstering of the capacity of socio-economic groups that lack voice (Reinermann, 1995: 8 and OECD 1993: 46, respectively, both in Robinson, 1996: 7).

Turning the tables
The goal of reaching the poorest, however, is only one part of the development picture. In more radical quarters, this approach should be replaced by an equity strategy that addresses the larger problem of the failure of the State and marketplace to provide equitable development – the anti-hegemonic approach. Indeed, many of the New Social Movements have nothing to do with delivering assistance to the poorest. Some, like

the anti-Miss Universe immolators in India protesting against Western cultural imperialism, the climate change activists in Canada and the pro-Islamic forces in the Persian and Saudi peninsula, are advocating a world different from the current consensus. In these visions, civil society rejects – and does not build – the foundations for the marketplace thriving in the Northern world (see Wignaraja, 1993).

GREEDOMANIA

Mott: *'In the US, greedomania, where a minute percentage of the population holds the most wealth, and where the standard of living of the labour force is declining in real terms, there is a major threat to the future stability of US society. The idea that the economic system must provide some sort of measure of income distribution is very important.'*

Promoting human rights

Another aspect of the equity debate draws on the growing acceptance of the idea of rights. The entire discussion around civil society is inextricably wound up in the claim-making capacity of rights, a language that has changed the whole tenor of debate, particularly by the standard-setting Northern Europeans. The Dutch, for example, explain that 'a human rights approach to development ... should enable even the most marginalized and powerless of people and groups to make a legal claim against the State' (Netherlands, 1996: 78). In an example from Kenya, USAID commentators have noted a similar power in rights language,

> *The rights discourse might well go on at all levels of society including the media, think tanks, community-based organizations and even in frequently maligned and seemingly ubiquitous seminars that are, in fact, quite useful for a civil society coming out of a long repressive phase when agendas need (to) be set and central issues – frequently revolving around 'rights', broadly defined – are inevitably discussed.*
> (Holmquist et al., 1995: 90)

In rights language, we see a meeting of both liberal and radical interpretations of equity. On the one hand, claim-making is directed at the State to guarantee a limited set of political and civil rights; on the other, claim-making for much wider economic and social rights is directed at a larger set of actors (companies, domestic elites, government departments charged with economic and social policy, international lending organizations and so on). Policy designed to support civil society for equity reasons, therefore, returns to the normative question: What *should* be the role of the State and other players? Who has the right to stake claims from whom?

It becomes clear that equity does not mean the same thing to all stake-holders – it may mean a leveling of the political playing field (all should have voice and equal opportunity), or a leveling of the entire field (all should have a share in the economic, political and social pie as well).

Civil Society Replaces State Aid

Pressures to decrease the size of governments in the South (primarily through loan conditionality) has highlighted yet another role for civil society organizations. The dismantling of the State has led to the expectation that domestic groups will partly take over, through sub-contracting or by default, the provision of key services. As in the solution prescribed for the ailing welfare State in the North, we see the following prophecy in the South: 'As government budgets, staff and foreign aid resources have shrunk or, in many cases, failed to materialize, NGOs have sprung up to fill the gap in supply of services, materials, technology, training, credit and communication with rural villagers and urban slum dwellers' (Schearer, 1995: 7). For donors, this phenomenon generates at least two policy issues.

Undermining (what's left of) the State

One issue is the danger of inadvertently weakening key enabling structures and thereby undermining broader policy goals. Has support to civil society organizations undercut key functions left with the State? In the extreme case of Mozambique, for example, that argument is justifiable:

> *Relief agencies – and NGOs in particular, some of which have programmes larger than those of the largest bilateral donor – have become the chief provider of public welfare and important sources of employment. They also further weaken government structures by siphoning off the remaining trained and competent local professionals, from deputy ministers to drivers, who are attracted by the higher and regular salaries paid by the outsiders.* (Donini, 1995: 436)

Support to CSOs, however, need not undermine the State. In some cases, CSO activity might strengthen the State or otherwise promote broader development goals. Smillie, one of the advisors for this volume, has argued that in Zimbabwe, for example, where NGOs provide 40 per cent of the health services and are paid to do so, the government has been strengthened through its effective management of improved services. In another example, however, he argues that the work of the Bangladesh Rural Advancement Committee (BRAC) has *rightly* siphoned off competent personnel from the official and corrupt primary school system, thus better serving the cause of development through literacy training in its 33,000 schools, albeit through the weakening of the State system (personal communication, 1997).

COMBINED SOLUTIONS

MacArthur: *'It became clear that issues with which we are concerned – environment, population, etc – involve actors these days that go beyond the government. There are many kinds of day-to-day mechanisms that people don't think about where civil society organizations play a role in developing solutions, monitoring and implementation'.*

Governments do not always welcome this push toward CSOs, of course. In the case of Mexico, for example, the Inter-American Development Bank (IDB) has shown particular interest in civil society strengthening, organizing a number of meetings in the mid-1990s to explore the topic. The approach elaborated by IDB focuses on civil society as an alternative or complement to a shedding State: 'The re-definition of the role of the State includes strengthening the capacity of citizens to assume responsibilities – some of which are economic – that the State has been shedding and to monitor and supervise the act of governing' (Hernández, 1996: 6). However, Hernández emphasizes that there is 'a gap between what is discussed in Washington and what happens in the IDB here (in Mexico). Civil society and the IDB do not have a mechanism for regular discussion and collaboration on the design and implementation of IDB projects in Mexico' (Hernández, 1996: 6). Currently, only 1 per cent of total IDB financing for Mexico flows through civil society organizations, and government resistance will likely keep that figure low.

Dumping social services

Another issue for donors and others is the dynamics of delegation. Eastern Europeans in particular have complained of the dumping of services on to the voluntary sector – the expectation that voluntary agencies will take over the work without a corresponding transfer of funding and the development of a mutual relationship with the State. As a student of the Hungarian case notes, 'the lingering "need" of the State to exercise control while abandoning services creates a rather interesting and unique environment – one that is largely unexplored in theory'.* A similar argument is made by Hutchful and Schmitz about Africa, 'In the wake of structural adjustment and privatization measures, governments may see the voluntary sector's role as a way to relieve themselves of public welfare responsibilities' (Hutchful and Schmitz, 1992: 9). The issue for donors is whether their interventions contribute to the strengthening of CSOs or, inadvertently, their weakening.

There have been numerous studies on the role of CSOs in providing social services, either instead of or in addition to the services provided by the State:

---

* Zoltan Toth (Personal communication, 1997).

At a time when many developing countries are undergoing fiscal stress caused by an excessive imbalance between revenues and expenditures, shifting the burden of responsibility from the State to the voluntary sector for the financing and provision of public goods and welfare services presents an attractive means of reducing official outlays. Second, there is a perception that developing country States do not have the capacity to finance and deliver services of a cost and quality that are adequate to the needs of consumers and that State provisioning is characterized by high levels of inefficiency and sub-standard services. (Robinson and White, 1997: 2)

What Robinson and White discover in their review of the secondary literature on non state provisioning of state services, however, is that voluntary provision of social services is full of holes: incomplete coverage, amateurism, high turnover, duplication, unsustainability, differing approaches, core area concentration and problems with equitable distribution according to gender, ethnicity and class (Robinson and White, 1997). Tvedt, in his review of the Norwegian government's policies towards NGOs, makes a similar point. The message must be that the State has an irreplaceable role:

Organisations can function as a cordon sanitaire (…); they are both a disguise (of the real problem) and a buffer (between people and government), but they cannot solve the initial problem. They help to segregate a social problem from the government's responsibility and install what has been called a 'a tyranny of structurelessness' (…) An illusion is created: a lot of activity is going on even if hardly anything of importance is being done for the population at large. In this way, NGOs may in a broader perspective be seen, not as representatives of 'civil society' against the State, but as a means by which the status quo is maintained. (Tvedt, 1995: 48)

Building Democracy

Civil society is more irrevocably linked to democracy, however, than to vague notions of development. As chapter 1 argued, it was in Eastern Europe that the equation between civil society and democracy was most forcefully made to outsiders. As Seligman writes:

For what characterizes the demand for a 'return' to civil society for those living 'East of the Elbe' is most essentially a call for the institutionalization of those principles of citizenship upon which modern liberal democratic polities in the

> *West are based. In this sense, for many in East Central*
> *Europe, civil society is but a different term used to charac-*
> *terize those institutional features which are taken to define*
> *democratic regimes, based on the principles of citizenship.*
> (Seligman, 1992: 5)

Indeed, Seligman suggests that civil society was used to talk about democracy because the word democracy itself had been appropriated by the Communists as a political slogan (Seligman, 1992: 6). If 'democracy' could not be used, 'civil society' filled in the vacuum. For many theorists, the link is more than strategic; it indicates cause and effect. Larry Diamond of the American *Journal of Democracy*, for example, identifies at least six ways in which civil society can promote democracy:[*]

1   Civil society is a reservoir of political, economic, cultural and moral resources to check the power of the State.
2   The diversity of civil society will ensure that the State is not held captive by a few groups.
3   The growth of associational life will supplement the work of political parties in stimulating political participation, à la Tocqueville's 'large free schools'.
4   Civil society will eventually stabilize the State because citizens will have a deeper stake in social order. Furthermore, although civil society may multiply the demands of the State, it may also multiply the capacity of groups to improve their own welfare.
5   Civil society is a locus for recruiting new political leadership.
6   Civil society resists authoritarianism (Diamond, 1991: 7–11).

There is strong evidence to link healthy civil societies with the existence of democracies. Too little caution, however, is usually exercised in jumping from this list of potential roles to the actual *formation* of democracy – the causative links between civil society and democracy are not necessarily straightforward (Simone and Pieterse, 1993: 41–69). Roniger questions this link when he writes, 'Late twentieth-century societies, governments, and parties have embraced the rhetoric of civil society and have claimed they stand for genuine, popular democracy. Yet, both in historical and contemporary terms, this identification is more conceptual than factual' (Roniger, 1994: 209). Civil society may be weak where democracy flourishes (Japan), or strong where democracy is also strong (India) or even detrimental to democracy itself (Russia). He goes on to argue that,

> *Historically, both the idea and the reality of civil society*
> *have preceded the development of democracy. While there*
> *are points of convergence around pluralism and the disper-*

---

[*] See also Diamond (1995) and White (1995).

> *sion of interests and social forces, the pluralistic character of civil society neither ensures democracy nor implies a strengthening of the open domain of public life.* (Roniger, 1994: 210)

The bundle of potential links between civil society and democracy, therefore, reflects an optimistic world view that, although welcome, does not necessarily help us to analyse the process of democratization in the countries of our case studies.* Even if we accept that civil society is a necessary condition for democracy, we must be careful of the assumption that it is sufficient (Bernhard, 1993). Civil society *can* eventually stabilize the State, as Diamond suggests, but it can do the opposite (like in the former Yugoslavia where civil society associations turned to factionalism), can circumvent the State altogether (as in Italy where society is affluent enough to build parallel structures to avoid the corrupt State systems)** or can be tightly intertwined with the State (Vietnam).***

This call to specificity is important. Hutchful and Schmitz, for example, examine the literature on democracy and Africa, arguing that:

> *As criticism of governments has mounted, many have turned to the concept of civil society in an attempt to identify possible sources of political renewal and democratic potential in Africa. The term has been used somewhat indiscriminately, often more as a shorthand for disillusionment with the State of state-centred analysis than as a rigorous tool for understanding African realities. Certainly there has been little systematic attempt to understand the specific features of civil society in Africa and the implications that this might have for democratization for the design of political institutions. There is also a tendency in much of the new writing to empty civil society of political and ideological content, portraying it as virtually homogenous and inspired by the same political project – the installation of democracy.* (Hutchful and Schmitz, 1992: 8)

This section, therefore, takes a look at what democracy promotion via civil society has meant in practice. A short list derived from donor literature includes civil society as an antidote to the State, civil society as democratic institution builders and civil society as creators of a democratic culture.

---

* Indeed, in some analyses, this connection between civil society and democracy has been called naive, arguing to the contrary that in Latin America 'the "resurrection" of civil society during democratic transitions invariably gives way to the "eclipsing" of civil society as relatively small groups of elites come to control democratic politics in an increasingly undemocratic fashion' (Oxhorn, nd: 2, see also Oxhorn, 1995).
** In *The Idea of Civil Society* (1992), Seligman gives parallel examples from Jerusalem, Budapest and Los Angeles.
*** For a view on Vietnam, see Gray (1997).

An Antidote to the State

One of the reasons for the interest in civil society is its supposed place as an antidote to the State. Democracy is seen to be impossible without the support of the countervailing powers of civil society.

TAKING BACK CONTROL

Bradley: *'Our intention is to return to a state of affairs in the US and abroad where citizens have a greater degree of control over their lives. We hand life over to the experts, not only in govern-ments but also in other areas. All of this has diminished the life of the citizen and his or her ability to make choices; like choos-ing schooling, as was possible in times past. This ability has been eroded considerably, so we have tried to restore a state of affairs in which citizens could take more control.'*

The Dutch aid program, for instance, is premised on just that notion: 'for a pluralist and civic society, the development of intermediaries between the citizen and State is of great importance. Dutch NGOs operating in developing countries have actively supported the strengthening of counter-vailing powers within society' (Netherlands, 1993: 2 in Robinson, 1996: 7). The USAID New Partnerships Initiative program (which promises to raise funding via NGOs and CSOs to 40 per cent of the US aid budget) has this similar statement: 'NPI embodies recent advances in development theory – advances that recognize the critical economic and political role of civil values and of the rich variety of voluntary associations that constitute civil society. NPI will focus significant resources on strengthening civil society and helping to restructure the relationships between States and civil societies' (USAID, 1995: i).

Those restructuring and countervailing powers, no less, can also replace much of the State's functions. A recent piece in the *Economist* reflects on Latin America, 'In partnership with government, the region's multiplying self-help community groups can improve anything from primary health care to housing to environmental protection' (*Economist*, 1996b: 15). Anything? Such faith in the organizations of civil society and such prejudice against the State (as opposed to particular regimes), is remarkable.

Not all donors have adopted this same creed, however. The University of Leeds research study on donor thinking study found that,

> *The most substantial differences found are between, on the one hand, the World Bank and ODA (Overseas Development Administration) and on the other, SIDA (Swedish International Development Agency), underpinned by different conceptions of the role of the State in development. The former two agencies appear concerned to improve the performance of*

the State only in its minimal role of providing the 'enabling environment' for a radical free market economy. In contrast, SIDA's starting point is a broader perception of the State's role, particularly in the context of Africa, as the most important actor in dealing with the current crisis. (Crawford, 1996: xi)

Some within the Washington circle have accepted the idea that the State must be strengthened, however, not abandoned. Tagged the 'Santiago Consensus' and heralded by John Williamson, formerly of the Institute for International Economics, this revised consensus talks of strengthening central State institutions, heightening supervision of deregulated and privatized agencies, bolstering judicial systems and targeting social spending, using local government and NGOs when logical, to those most vulnerable (*Economist*, 1996a: 19).

In this revised version, civil society takes its place beside the State and is supported by an enabling environment provided in part by the State. The countervailing powers of civil society may thus paradoxically need a healthy State system to work.

Democratic Institution Builders

Most people are used to talking about democracy as a noun: a set of institutions that guide how we are governed, especially the existence of free, fair and periodic elections in a multi-party system supported by the rule of law (Stout, 1996: 25). In the majority of interpretations, such elements are an agreed minimum: the Leeds study found unanimity among donors on the importance of free and fair elections within a multi-party system, even though there was little congruence on the broader definition of democracy (Crawford, 1996: x).

DEEPENING DEMOCRACY

NDI: *'In the deepening of democracy in (East and Central Europe), we noticed that many people weren't involved and that apathy was hampering democracy. In our goal to support democratic development in societies undergoing political transitions, we identify a number of essential institutions that need strengthening: the political parties, the parliament, the local government bodies, the relationship between civilians and the military and elections. Equally important, there is the mass of citizens that need to participate in the "new" democratic decision-making. ... While early involvement was with "critical" elections that saw us leave after the vote, we are now facing different challenges. Civil society appeared as an idea as we began to ask how we could deepen the democratic process. The outcome is that our grants are now longer-term and larger, and since our grants are longer-term, our approach is more developmental.'*

> Rockefeller Brothers: *'We are interested in the consolidation of democracy, and so have approached civil society from the vantage point of pluralism. We want to strengthen citizen involvement, help to institute checks on government, promote advocacy and build partnerships among the three sectors of government, non-profits and business.'*

At the same time, it is clear that the formal institutionalization of democracy (elections or multi-partyism) does not equal democracy in its fullest sense. In his assessment of US democracy promotion in the 1980s, for example, Carothers writes:

> *The Reagan administration's 'elected government equals democracy' formula ignored the crucial question of how much actual authority any particular elected government had, whether, for example, an elected government's authority was largely curtailed by traditional power groups in the country, such as the military or an economic elite, or whether certain attributes of the elected government itself, such as its own gross ineptitude or corruption, effectively negated its claim to being a functioning representative government.* (Carothers, 1991: 245)

Certainly, pressure to reform government *can* come from civil society organizations, thus generating donor assertions that civil society needs to be strengthened to consolidate effective and democratic institutions of government (Crawford, 1996: x). It is for this reason, for example, that USAID has chosen deliberately to limit its support to CSOs to *civic advocacy* groups; those that focus on democratic reform (Hansen, 1996). Many argue, however, that the existence of a broad civil society, including but not limited to civic organizations, is what is need for long-term democratic change. This is certainly the case according to Gyimah-Boadi, a director of the Institute of Economic Affairs in Accra who makes a strong link between civil societies in Africa and the process of democratic opening. Key in the mix he describes is the presence of middle-class professional bodies, the churches and development NGOs, although he argues all are weakened by constraints that the aid community could help alleviate: poor funding, weak organizational capacity, weak accountability (Gyimah-Boadi, 1997).

It is a mistake, however, to assume that civil society organizations necessarily focus on democratic opening. Chandhoke writes:

> *Civil society can in one sense be identified with democratization and liberalization, but it is a far more comprehensive and deeper concept than democracy. Democracy can*

become, as it has often become, identified with the practices of the State. And these 'democratic' practices have often been reduced to rituals and staged political events, such as elections, parliamentary representation and plebiscites which are meant to reaffirm the legitimacy of the State. Democracy has become, somewhat unfortunately, an empty shell which serves a useful purpose for the State, but which gives us little indication of state–society or inter-societal relations. (Chandhoke, 1995: 25)

Indeed, democratization may not even come at the wish of the populace, but from outside forces. One example is the 1991 opening of the Kenyan State to multi-partyism. Although many observers credited a mixture of domestic demands and donor elbow-pinning, a closer reading shows that President Daniel arap Moi was trading institutional political reform for avoidance of stringent economic reform. In the end, his reading was astute: the opening of multi-partyism fragmented the opposition and probably delayed his loss of power. Did civil society organizations force changes in democratic institutions in Kenya? The answer becomes more complex when a less-than-straight causal arrow is drawn.

Another problem is the assumption that civil society organizations are necessarily interested in democratic politics. Rosenblum makes this criticism, complaining that this assumption depreciates 'other uses of civil society – private relations and personal satisfactions, economic ambitions, cultural identity, ideology, and individual expressivism. The danger is the colonization of social life by political culture' (Rosenblum, 1994: 555). Sales has a similar critique: 'Without wanting to participate directly in the political process, ecological groups criticize the way enterprises manage resources, while the feminist movement questions the organization of the couple, the family, domestic life, and the workplace as well as identities, values and language' (Sales, 1991: 307–8). Here, the message is that civil society matters deeply outside of the sphere of those organizations engaged in a visible battle with the State.

The Culture of Democracy

For some, the whole point of democracy is its value as a way of life, not only as a way of government. Hadenius and Uggla understand the value of participating in CSOs as practice in playing at democracy, as a training ground for harmonious living. Their analysis echoes some of the ideas arising out of Putnam's work: that the social capital emerging from collaboration with CSOs spreads into all other areas of life (Putnam, 1995). This sentiment is echoed throughout the work of many aid agencies, including the aptly named Foundation for a Civil Society:

We believe that Civil Society is the environment in which

democracy flourishes. It is where myriad seeds sown by many take root to form community values based on individual responsibility – an uneven, often frustrating and enormously rewarding process. As we in the United States know only too well, democracy is messy... initially, many Western foundations, governments, international organizations and individuals, whose goals and methods seemed reasonably clear in the euphoria of the lifting of communism, were involved in efforts in Central Europe. As a result, free expression, entrepreneurship, market economics, fair elections and macro-economic reforms took root breathtakingly quickly. (Luers, 1996: 2/3)

DEMOCRATIC CULTURE

Mott: 'Civil society is often defined by its preconditions, by its characteristics, its processes and its outcomes; for our purposes, civil societies are free societies where governments, private sectors and independent sectors are balanced, where civility is respected by Rule of Law, democratic governance and human rights, where citizens participate in communities and in mediating organizations comprising a vibrant sector, where racial and ethnic diversity is respected and where economic systems and policies support and reward individual initiative and provide security to those with specials needs. (In Eastern Europe, civil society is defined as the voluntary sector; but we do not: we believe in a balance of the three sectors.) In a healthy civil society, people act civilly toward one another, care about families, communities and fellow citizens and take democratic freedoms seriously by taking actions to nourish these freedoms'.

Those habits are not conflict free, of course: democracy, conflict and conflictual debate are not antithetical concepts and democracy does not necessarily (or even often) imply harmony. It is possible, however, to learn civility. It is thus that civil society,

... is also an arena where individuals come to recognize themselves as social beings. Members of this sphere learn civility, i.e., the importance of treating others with respect and tolerance, because individual self-realization is bound up with and dependent upon the self-realization of other individuals. Civil society possesses a pedagogic character since it educates the individual in the values of collective action. (Chandhoke, 1995: 34)

However important in conceptual terms, this train of reasoning produces vague and unmeasurable goals in the practical world of foreign assistance (Robinson, 1996: chapter 4), a problem common enough in the development field. How can one design programmes to teach harmonious living? Many believe one can strengthen civil society by encouraging joining as a social activity. Echoing de Tocqueville's thoughts of civil society as an open school for democracy, for example, Roniger writes,

> *Civil society can be nurtured through involvement in parti-*
> *cipatory activities and grassroots organizations, through the*
> *establishment of centers of sociability like coffeehouses,*
> *clubs, and voluntary associations; though increased public*
> *interaction – in the framework of open lectures, recreational*
> *locales, and museums; by means of communication –*
> *written and electronic that empower and substantiate the*
> *citizen's sense of autonomy from the logic of regulation by*
> *the State.* (Roniger, 1994: 208–9)

For aid workers, however, these are difficult to justify unless they can be shown to lead to desired results. Although 'participation' has become central in the development lexicon, the usual reason is that participation leads to more effective projects. Funding participation for its own sake runs counter to the input–output models on which development assistance is frequently designed. Moreover, there is no guarantee that CSOs necessarily undertake such democratic training roles. In Dicklitch's study of Uganda, she points out that:

> *The simple proliferation of a number of voluntary associa-*
> *tions will not guarantee a transition to democracy or a more*
> *democratic civil society. Unless those organizations possess*
> *internal capacity, practice internal democracy, are commit-*
> *ted to autonomy (from the State) and are committed to the*
> *preservation of democratic rights and principles – whether*
> *directly or indirectly – they will not necessarily help create*
> *an environment which would be nurturing to the develop-*
> *ment of democracy.* (Dicklitch, 1997: 8)

Dicklitch's study is more than anecdotal. Her findings that many Ugandan NGOs were 'briefcase' agencies, run by urban elites as a lucrative alternative to an impoverished civil service, is echoed in other circles (Hutchful and Schmitz, 1992: 29; chapters 5 and 6 in this volume).

The issue here is not that organizations cannot promote democratic values, but that there is no necessary connection between the formation of associations and the democratization of society. An important next step, then, is to 'problematize' civil society and remove some of its utopian characteristics while maintaining its emancipatory potential. The next section suggests ideas for further deconstruction.

Other tasks for civil society

The focus on democracy and developmental goals, despite the critical tone adopted so far in this chapter, is important. Asking for clarification, pushing at definitions, examining activities in real life – all these are meant to improve, not discard, the good programs of the donor community. There are a number of other motivations, however, for using the term civil society in donor-speak that deserve harsher treatment. Highlighted here are three visible motivations, some hinted at earlier: an excuse for supporting friends now that the cold war is over, a way to disguise free-marketeering, and a natural, if not defensible, desire to be doing the same thing as the Jones' down the street.

Supporting Friends in a Post-Cold War World

An additional motivation for undertaking civil society programmes is the desire to thwart particular groups or political agendas. The problem is that the end of the cold war has removed much of the publicly acceptable reasons to support political friends or deal with enemies. Sovereignty evidently still matters and intervention is problematic. The Leeds study found that,

> *If there is an emerging consensus in favour of human rights transcending national sovereignty in international law, there is considerably more disquiet about and objections to external intrusion in the democratization process. The donors' underlying assumption appears to be that the purpose (i.e. democratization) justifies the means. However, even if (almost everyone) is in favour of democracy, external intervention is by no means so readily accepted. In evaluating the legitimacy of the donors' interventions in terms of their infringement or not on sovereignty, it would appear that the* manner *of their practices and procedures is crucial.*
> (Crawford, 1996: xii)

There are a number of examples of this phenomenon in recent years. Donor promotion of the Kenyan Law Society, for example, continues to be one of the vehicles for harrying Daniel arap Moi's government and for engendering badly needed constitutional reform (see Chapter 5). CIDA (Canadian International Development Agency) funding of the South Africa Educational Trust Fund was one of the most effective tools against apartheid that Canada had in its minor arsenal (Grandea, 1995). In Eastern Europe, US support to the International Center for Not-for-Profit Law (ICNL) has been key in manoeuvering change along American lines in Hungarian regulation to allow more freedom to the non-profit sector (chapter 3 in this volume). This support via existing, or donor-created,

NGOs has sent powerful messages to states. Politics by proxy has increasingly taken (at least part of) the place of diplomacy.

WHO'S IN?

Inter-American Foundation: *'We don't use the term "civil society" too much because we are working closely with business sectors, and many business organizations consider themselves part of civil society. Therefore, I prefer to use the terms governmental, for-profit, and not-for-profit – the latter two are civil society.'*

Free-Marketeering: The Civil Private Sector

Another questionable use of the civil society debate has been to include private enterprise uncritically *within* the sphere of civil society. Beyond the Putnam principle, whereby associations in the civic realm are argued to support the quality of economic association, some analysts describe civil society as a synonym for business itself. Throughout the literature, and in common discourse, the debate on the role of civil society has been dissipated to justify, among other things, further support for the privatization of national industries or the liberalization of trade regimes. The argument is not whether private enterprise is a good thing for society, of course, but whether it is the *same* thing as civil society. Examples of this use of an already harried idea are easy to find. At a recent conference in Washington to debate the controversial Helms–Burton law, for instance, one association of exporters described its private sector development programmes as 'civil society strengthening efforts'.*

This interpretation, surprising for those who had absorbed a more conflictual definition of civil society, has political roots in the neo-liberal tradition, in which political and economic forms are mutually supportive (part of the Putnam principle, discussed earlier). The marketplace needs a particular kind of (democratic but minimalist) State in which to flourish, a link long made throughout donor literature. In 1989, for example, the then World Bank President, Barber Conable, wrote of the 'failure of public institutions' as the 'root cause of (Africa's) weak economic performance in the past' thus linking economic and political adjustment as *joint*-preconditions for the marketplace needed to ensure development (Hutchful and Schmitz, 1992: 21). The Leeds study also found a clear shift in donor policy in recent years toward linking democratic political forms with economic performance (Crawford, 1996), further spurring donor attention on the motors of democracy: civil society organizations.

What is not explored in donor policy, however, are the ways in which that politico-economic linking is seen in some countries to be profoundly anti-democratic:

---

* Personal communication (1997) with conference participant, Ottawa.

> *They (the international financial institutions/IFIs) think that*
> *political variables can simply be treated as engineering*
> *problems and 'factored in' to improve the effectiveness of*
> *their structural adjustment programs, and thus that they can*
> *avoid changing their overall approach to development ... .*
> *This is a dangerous error ... . In all cases, adjustment*
> *programs have been vigorously resisted by the public. To*
> *implement them, governments have been forced to resort to*
> *a large dose of coercion ... . The IFIs have collaborated*
> *enthusiastically in this political authoritarianism.* (Ake,
> 1991: 41–43, in Hutchful and Schmitz, 1992: 22)

The argument presented by Ake is that the involvement of African States
within a profoundly undemocratic world trading and economic system
cannot create more democratic outcomes. This clash highlights one of the
problems with the use of civil society in this controversial debate: what
does one do with a definition of civil society that promotes capital expansion when set against an 'anti-hegemonic' definition promoted by
indigenous organizations, particularly in Africa? As Joseph writes,

> *There is likely to be an increasing contradiction between the*
> *expanded voice of Africans in the formulation of their*
> *government's policies and the minimal voice that these same*
> *governments will enjoy in influencing the operation of the*
> *global economic system .... International agencies that are*
> *increasingly outspoken in their calls for democratization in*
> *Africa must urgently address such questions. They have*
> *recognized that the authoritarian nature of the African State*
> *is a central part of the problem. How will they respond to an*
> *African demos whose ideas about economic restructuring*
> *differ from those of the World Bank, the IMF (International*
> *Monetary Fund), and their affiliates?* (Joseph, 1992: 22, in
> Hutchful and Schmitz, 1992: 23)

Keeping Up with the Jones'

Civil society, like other terms that have floated to the top of development
discussions, can also be in danger of succumbing to a neighbourly 'if you
say that in your policy document, then I'll say this in mine' phenomenon.

What may have happened, however, is a rush to vocabulary rather than
a rush to comprehension. We are seeing committees set up or refurbished
(the Development Assistance Committee (DAC) ad hoc forum on governance, for example), new coding systems established (the DAC was to
report on 'civil society strengthening' from 1997) and a further homoge-
nization of language. How that change in language affects change in
behaviour is yet to be seen. We may only witness the pouring of old, and
perhaps suspect, wine into more popularly designed bottles.

WHAT IS THE AID SYSTEM DOING?

Mark Robinson

If the preceding pages present some hypotheses to explain why donors are interested in civil society, what are they actually doing on the ground? Does their programming reflect the philosophies presented in their policy statements? If so, what might be the implications for those on the receiving end of this specialized aid?

This analysis focuses on aid to organizations that promote political change, those CSOs involved in the 'political projects' identified in our definition. We are aware here, as elsewhere, that the corpus of civil society organizations is much broader than this population of organizations. From this starting point, this section examines donors' definitions and how these identify the types of organizations supported. We then examine overall patterns of expenditure to determine the amount spent by donors on civil society projects and the regional breakdown of these aid flows. The following section then addresses the varied ways donors seek to strengthen CSOs and the types of intermediaries with whom aid donors choose to work. In the concluding section we address a number of key policy issues that arise in donor funding of civil society.

There are four main types of donors that provide assistance to civil society organizations: bilateral donors like CIDA and USAID, multilateral agencies (such as the European Commission and the UNDP), foundations and Northern NGOs. Although the main focus of this section is on official aid donors, the principal source of support for CSOs engaged in democracy and governance activities, we also examine NGOs and foundations that have considerable funds at their disposal for civil society purposes and often act as intermediaries for bilateral agencies. If all forms of support for civil society are taken into account, including aid for more narrow development purposes, Northern NGOs emerge as a significant source of funding because they funnel large amounts to Southern grassroot development organizations and NGOs.

Definitions

As we have seen, official aid donors have a number of objectives in supporting civil society, both political and developmental. Although the objectives of such support are reasonably clear, few have produced rigorous definitions of what they understand by civil society and its constituent organizations, an omission that has implications for their funding strategies.

The most common approaches are to describe civil society as an associational realm – civil society as space – that makes up the expanse between the family and the State[*] and as a collective of the associations themselves.

---

[*] This approach has its roots in the pluralist tradition, where civil society is treated as an associational realm where organized interests interact and compete with each other for influence over public policy (Robinson, 1995).

DEFINITION DILEMMAS

Mott: 'We talked about civil society at the time we were trying to reorganize our overall programme mission. There were catch-all programmes so we came up with "civil society" as a term to capture the means to these various ends. ... We didn't spend weeks reading books, but thought that "civil society" cut across all of our interests in CEE/Russia, the US and South Africa. In the US, for example, race relations have become a very serious domestic civil society issue.'

Inter-American Foundation: 'The term is a bit amorphous, especially when talking about actual strategies. At a general level, we can talk about strengthening civil society and "spaces" of civil society, but then we can't talk about civil society and "the state" – it is too vague for actual strategizing. However, we can talk about regional government and community organizations, or municipalities or foundations. What we are really looking for when developing partnerships is who gives what and does what in a relationship. The term "civil society", therefore, loses its usefulness at practical/concrete level. At a general level, it is useful. In concrete terms, however, "civil society" is unwieldy, amorphous and laden with connotations'.

IRI: 'There is also a real danger of getting into semantics by imposing mutually exclusive definitions of Rule of Law, civil society and political parties'.

NDI: 'We are concerned that civil society is an overused term, especially if it is not defined. Discussions we are having on advocacy and on civic education are susceptible to the same problems – accusations of being trite or pat'.

USAID: 'The definition is still an outstanding issue. There is tension over the definition with American NGOs. Because we chose to concentrate on advocacy groups, NGOs have been arguing to expand the definition to community groups. We took an instrumentalist view (vs. a normative one): to encourage political reform. A stronger civil society doesn't necessarily mean greater democratization; indeed, stronger civil society can be destabilizing and reactionary. Moreover, we don't know how to support "civil society" writ large'.

Bradley: 'I think it is important that civil society means different things to different people. For us, it means the area of life that is outside government; others may include or exclude the free market. We see the idea as one way of getting at a fundamental discontentment with a life governed by government. Its vagueness is part of its appeal. Having to define all things is actually part of our problem; an over reliance on scientific categorization'.

CIDA, for example, employs the following definition: '...civil society refers broadly to organizations and associations of people, formed for social or political purposes, that are not created or mandated by government' (CIDA, 1995). The OECD puts forward this version in a recent document: 'Civil society denotes a public space between the State and individual citizens where the latter develops autonomous, organized and collective activities' (OECD, 1995: 1). It is rare to see any recognition in the policy literature (although practitioners have different stories) that civil society might comprise organizations that are either anti-democratic (such as ethnic associations or religious fundamentalist groups) or motivated by narrow self-interest and the pursuit of financial gain. This limited perspective runs the risk of encouraging donors to make funding decisions that may not necessarily be supportive of the development and democracy objectives.

Although there is a great deal of common ground around core definitions, there are important variations in emphasis among donors that stem from their overall approach to democracy and governance issues. The former British government, for example, tended to stress public sector reform and enhanced competence of government; SIDA is strongly supportive of a human rights agenda; whereas USAID places considerable emphasis on democratization. Such variations translate into differing priorities for the types of organizations supported. USAID treats civil society funding as an integral part of its democracy promotion work and targets those organizations engaged in such activities. Similarly, SIDA channels a substantial proportion of its funds to human rights groups. The British Department for International Development (DFID, formerly the ODA) has not been a major funder of civil society projects in the past, though this is beginning to change.

In line with a tendency to avoid precise definitions, few donors offer a typology of the organizations considered to form part of civil society. Some offer a simple listing of organizations deemed eligible for assistance. For example, in an early statement of what was included within civil society, USAID listed the following:

> ... *political parties through national professional organizations (such as legal, medical or business societies or societies of chartered accountants), to research institutes (universities, academics of think tanks) to associations of citizens (neighbourhood community organizations, labor unions, women's organizations or parent–teacher associations).*
> (USAID, 1991: 6)

Despite similarities between official policy documents on broad definitions, donors do not have a shared understanding of the specific types of organizations that constitute civil society. Moreover, there are often disagreements *within* donor agencies about the nature and composition of civil society. In USAID, for example, there is a major difference of perspective between those in the Global Center for Democracy, which focuses on advocacy-oriented civil society organizations (for which it has coined the term civic advocacy organizations), and the Africa Bureau, which tends to emphasize local membership organizations and self-help groups as the primary units in civil society (Fox, 1994; Hansen, 1996). Clearly, definitions and classifications do matter as they have implications for the choice of funding strategy and the identification of eligible recipients.

Counting Coins

Further complications arise when we try to quantify the resources flowing to civil society programmes. The high profile given by many aid donors to democracy and governance issues in their official policy statements suggests that this sector of activity should account for a significant share of total aid resources. As support for government agencies wanes, civil society organizations are gaining increased prominence and aid agencies are seeking new and innovative ways of funding such organizations. But to what extent are these trends reflected in data on actual aid?

The Big Picture

Quantitative information on aid flows to civil society organizations is sketchy and limited. There are no comprehensive surveys of donor assistance in the democracy and governance field and civil society rarely appears as a distinct sector in aid agency statistics. Moreover, aid to civil society organizations is not only confined to democracy and governance programmes, but also features in other sectors, most notably health, education and in co-financing for NGOs. Despite these limitations, some insights can be gleaned from data collected by independent researchers and from statistics compiled by the DAC and individual aid agencies.

One striking finding is the smallness of official aid flows for democracy and governance programmes in general and for civil society in particular. Although there has been a gradual increase in spending on good governance projects in the 1990s, total expenditure as a proportion of overall aid flows is still very low. According to recent DAC data, projects in the governance field amounted to US$4 billion in 1995, equivalent to 8.6 per cent of total official aid flows of US$46.5 billion.* Projects in the civil society category amounted to US$391 million in 1995, up from US$113 million in 1991, with an increase from 30 to 440 in the number of projects funded over this period. Despite their increased visibility, total allocations made in 1995 represented just 0.84 per cent of total aid flows for that year and 9 per

---

* In 1997, the DAC reclassified aid flows formerly under central government services and public administration into the following categories: government administration, central government services, economic and development planning, public sector financial management, legal and judicial development, strengthening civil society, post-conflict peace-building, elections, human rights, demobilization and the media. It is now possible to enumerate civil society strengthening projects for the 1980s and 1990s, although there are gaps in the data for particular donors and the system of classification is not very elaborate.

Table 2.1: Governance Aid by Category, 1995

	Amount (US$ '000s)	Percentage of governance aid	Percentage of total aid
Economic and development planning	2,754,588	68.37	5.92
Public sector financial management	75,505	1.87	0.16
Legal and judicial development	36,347	0.90	0.08
Government administration	186,132	4.62	0.40
Strengthening civil society	391,504	9.72	0.84
Post-conflict peace building (UN)	30,987	0.77	0.07
Elections	28,817	0.72	0.06
Human rights monitoring and education	39,002	0.97	0.08
Demobilization	8,771	0.22	0.02
Free flow of information	997	0.02	0.00
General government services	476,203	11.82	1.02
Total	4,028,853	100.00	8.65

Source: DAC Creditor Reporting System

cent of total governance spending, with central government services and economic planning accounting for the lion's share (see Table 2.1).

Two factors help to explain the relatively small size of aid flows for civil society projects, surprising in view of the current level of interest in civil society issues among aid donors. One is the relative newness of the governance and democracy agenda and the lead time required for funds to be disbursed to the intended recipients. Another factor is that projects in this area of activity do not absorb large amounts of money because they do not involve substantial amounts of capital expenditure.

This relative low cost, however, may not always hold true, as there have been major funding initiatives in Eastern Europe through the EU's PHARE (Poland and Hungary Assistance for Reconstructing Economies) and TACIS (an equivalent programme for countries in the former Soviet Union) for democracy programmes, which included large civil society components with disbursements in excess of US$1 million. Similarly, in 1995, USAID allocated US$30 million over three years for its Democracy Network, which was designed to provide grants, exchanges and training for NGOs and civic organizations in East and Central Europe (discussed in more detail in chapter 3). The DAC database indicates an average project size of US$890,000, although this figure appears to be an overestimate in view of the small size of many civil society projects supported by NGOs and other intermediaries. The average size of a human rights project funded by SIDA in 1993/94, for example, was US$140,000, whereas, in the case of the US, it was US$650,000 – small in terms of conventional aid projects but significant for recipient organizations.

Cutting Up the Pie

In practice, civil society projects have fallen within a few existing programme categories. Civil society projects designed to promote democratization mostly come under the good governance category, although other sectoral projects increasingly have civil society components where civic organizations are involved in service provisioning and mobilizing project beneficiaries. According to DAC, the United States is by far the largest funder of civil society projects, with 335 out of the 440 recorded projects in this category and 85 per cent of total civil society assistance. Other prominent donors active in this field are Canada, Denmark, France, Germany, Norway and Sweden, although their programmes in this field are small in comparison to the US.

Evidence from four major donors (European Union, Sweden, UK and US) provides some indication of the relative importance of civil society projects within their democracy and governance programmes. Data collected in the Leeds study reveal that aid to civil society organizations (human rights organizations, pro-democracy groups and civic advocacy groups) amounted to US$160 million over 1993 and 1994 combined, equivalent to just over 50 per cent of project expenditure by the four donors on political aid (covering democracy, governance and human rights). In line with the DAC data, the US emerges as the largest sponsor of civil society in this period, with expenditure over the two years amounting to just over US$100 million, equivalent to one-third of its political aid spending. The European Commission and Sweden channel half their expenditure on political aid to CSOs; by comparison, the UK spends relatively little on civil society projects, with the bulk of its funding targeted at the public sector.

Evidence from other sources demonstrates the same order of magnitude. As one of the more prominent donors in this field, Canada spent

---

USAID AND CIVIL SOCIETY

USAID. *The Tuesday Group of all USAID and State Department representatives working on democratization had spent most of its time on Rule of Law issues up to 1992. We focused on the best practices of US assistance and the lessons learned. Increasingly, we found that civil society demands were the key for Rule of Law reform. Currently, civil society spending is greatest in Russia, Eastern Europe, the Philippines, Egypt, Indonesia and Bangladesh; but uncertain in Sri Lanka. By 1990–91, civil society came on strong as a theme in all programmes, and now is an accepted component in programming. Although USAID had had relations with unions for over 30 years, civil society became a larger banner for inclusion of other actors. Indeed, up until the end of the cold war, we feared that supporting non-governmental groups would destabilize friendly governments.*

Table 2.2: *Governance Aid by Region, 1995*

Region	Number	Amount (US$ '000s)	Percentage of total
Europe	162	593,144	15
North Africa and Middle East	110	2,016,946	50
Africa	456	379,482	9
Central America and Caribbean	245	208,057	5
South America	168	122,849	3
South Asia	68	55,179	1
East Asia	121	493,376	12
Pacific	28	9,158	0
Unspecified	106	150,662	4
Total	1,464	4,028,853	100

Source: DAC Creditor Reporting System, final column totals are rounded to 100

CA$49 million on democracy, governance and human rights projects in the period 1993–5. Electoral assistance and police training accounted for over half the total with much of the remainder going to various types of CSOs, especially human rights NGOs and women's groups, which between them received CA$13.5 million (Robinson, 1996: 18–19). Denmark is also a significant supporter of civil society projects, in that two-thirds of its expenditure of Dkr338 (roughly US$50 million) on democracy, governance and human rights projects in 1994 was allocated to CSOs. Germany has long been an important source of funding for civil society projects (especially for trade unions), with much of this channeled through the political foundations, although it is difficult to estimate the proportion of its assistance allocated for this purpose.[*]

There are also interesting differences among regions. As Table 2.2 illustrates, North Africa and the Middle East receives the largest share of total governance assistance, accounting for 50 per cent of the total in 1995. The picture for the smaller subset of civil society projects is somewhat different, with Central America and the Caribbean, Africa, North Africa and the Middle East each accounting for about one-fifth of total spending (Figure 2.3). Data for the European Union (EU), Sweden, the UK and the US for 1993–4 indicate that half the assistance to human rights organizations goes to Latin America, whereas two-thirds of the assistance in the pro-democracy and governance categories is channeled to organizations in Asia and Africa. Although these differences of emphasis reflect the policy preferences and regional biases of the major aid donors, Africa is the major focus for governance activity in general and for a large proportion of civil society projects.

---

[*] Germany does not figure in the DAC data for this category of assistance. This is a surprising omission; Germany channels a considerable amount of aid through the political foundations and church-based NGOs, much of which is designed to strengthen CSOs.

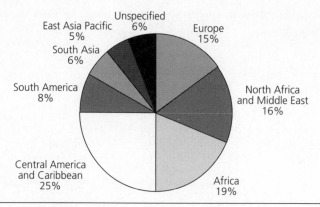

Source: DAC Creditor Reporting System

Figure 2.3: *Aid for Strengthening Civil Society by Region, 1995*

The Who and the How

The Role of Intermediaries

Most of the assistance provided by official aid donors is channeled through intermediary organizations rather than through direct funding to local organizations. In the case of human rights groups, nearly half the projects funded by the EU, Sweden, UK and US are implemented by Northern and international NGOs, whereas governance and democracy projects are largely undertaken by local organizations. This channeling may reflect the existence of established human rights NGOs that have a good track record at the international level (such as the International Ombuds Institute, the International Commission of Jurists and the International Press Institute), whereas fewer comparable organizations engaged in governance and democracy work have a record outside their home countries.

Some donors, notably Germany and the US, channel a significant proportion of their assistance to CSOs through specialized party-affiliated foundations such as the Friedrich Ebert Foundation (FES) and the International Republican Institute (IRI). These foundations, which represent the different political currents in the mixed parliaments of the two countries, have themselves grown out of beliefs about the role of civil society in shaping politics. Over time and through their field presence, the political foundations have earned a good reputation with civic and political actors such as trade unions, business associations and political parties. The German foundations have specific programmes aimed at strengthening civil society organizations and have accumulated considerable experience in this field. FES, for example, funded 48 trade union development programmes in developing and transitional countries in 1994 through a network of specialist consultants. In the US, there is a view that the American political foundations are also more flexible and effective than their official counterpart in providing grants to a large number of small democracy-promotion projects, and have greater latitude than USAID in supporting opposition groups and civic associations (Diamond, 1995: 30).

Alongside the political foundations are a number of independent foundations, many based in North America, which have an established track record in the civil society arena and specialized programmes of assistance targeted at specific types of CSOs. These include the Ford, Carnegie, Rockefeller and Soros Foundations in the US, the Westminster Foundation in the UK and the International Centre for Human Rights and Democratic Development (ICHRDD) in Canada. The former largely rely on endowment income and corporate philanthropy, but others such as ICHRDD receive considerable resources from government. The volume of foundation spending on civil society can easily dwarf contributions from other sources. Spending by the Soros Foundation's affiliate in Hungary, for example, was US$1.6 million in 1995.

Aid donors also channel funds to trade unions through a number of international organizations. The International Confederation of Free Trade Unions (ICFTU) based in Brussels is one such body. It facilitates the coordination of trade union development efforts among its 20 affiliates, which include trade union federations and international organizations such as the International Labour Organization and the Commonwealth Trade Union Council. Several donors have their own trade union funding programs (such as the US Free Trade Union Institute) and allocate resources to national trade union federations and sectoral unions for development projects in developing countries. But the resources allocated to trade unions are only a small proportion of overall flows to CSOs in developing countries, amounting to some US$70 million in 1994.

Northern NGOs are a favoured conduit for channeling donor resources to CSOs, especially those working in the human rights field, since a minimum average of 5 per cent of DAC aid flows (not including multilateral flows and funding through private donations) are channeled through such organizations (Overseas Development Institute, 1994). In the Swedish case, two-thirds of the budgetary allocation for human rights work is earmarked for Swedish NGOs and their counterparts in developing countries. The Dutch government channels most of its support for civil society through the four co-financing agencies. Similarly, the US New Partnerships Initiative aims to shift considerable resources into civil society activities by fostering partnerships between governments, business and civic organizations.

Northern NGOs are also a major donor source of funding for civil society organizations in their own right. A significant proportion of their funding for development projects includes institutional strengthening components designed to build up the organizational capacity of southern NGOs and membership organizations. It is less common for NGOs to support trade unions and business associations, or organizations not directly involved in development activity, which tend to be the focus for direct funding efforts by official donors and the political foundations (Clayton, 1996).

Support Mechanisms

If the previous paragraphs give a flavour of the kind of organizations involved in assisting CSOs, this section focuses on the mechanisms of that involvement and the types of organizations targeted for support.

Most donor assistance programmes focus on building up the organizational capacity of civil society groups, and use a variety of instruments to achieve this objective. CIDA, for example, supports initiatives designed to 'strengthen the advocacy role of organizations in civil society, including building the capacity for independent social, economic and political analysis, through training, technical assistance, participation in conferences and international networking' (CIDA, 1995). Not all donors are as explicit as CIDA about their approach or what they mean by capacity-building. For the most part, donor efforts aim to 'enhance the capacity of recipient organizations to mobilize resources, strengthen internal management and financial accountability, deliver services more efficiently, influence policy and network more effectively' (Robinson, 1996: 10). There is heavy emphasis on the provision of grants and technical assistance directed towards the following types of activities: training, workshops and conferences, study visits, office equipment and infrastructure, publications and information dissemination and research and policy work.

WHAT TO DO?

German Marshall Fund: *'Our thinking is constantly evolving. At the outset, our plan was to "let 1000 flowers bloom," in the hope that some would become trees. As some organizations have become more sophisticated, our grantmaking has had to change. Some organizations that are no longer relevant have dissolved. Our grantmaking now has begun to involve policy makers and to target the political elite.'*

UNDP: *'The bottlenecks are (1) the complexity of our policies and programs and (2) the lack of sufficient, and sufficiently senior, staff members and adequate funding to enact new simplified policies.'*

NDI: *'We are good at doing (election support), but not in creating sustainable organizations after elections are over. What have we left out of the organizational creation process? We are now trying to develop longer term sustainability in the groups we support. We need to know better at the outset where an organization is at in society and what unintended outcomes may follow from our support.'*

CIDA: *'We have had a chance to review our programs in the Ukraine at least. The evaluation found that we need to have primary stakeholders explore how "civil society" can best be defined; what capacities NGOs need to strengthen civil society in an independent, democratic and market-oriented state; what is the most effective role of outside helpers; and what special resources Canada has to apply to these tasks.'*

USAID: *'Financial sustainability is an issue: how long do we have to be involved? Also, there are now more delicate situations when working with NGOs in other countries; a factor which has meant building stronger relationships with policy staff within US missions. Now we have in-country US federal teams to coordinate activity, especially on civil society issues, and especially where the situation is delicate.'*

Mott: *'We will continue to put many of our major priorities on strengthening the non-profit sector: (1) supporting infrastructure (law, research, leadership training, information networking, financial resources), and (2) supporting governmental support of the sector (always the biggest support of funding to non-profits, of course; a fact too often overlooked). Further, in order to insure that the non-profit sector is always revitalized from the bottom, we will continue to give "fertilizer money" to exciting efforts. (...) Beyond the non-profit focus in the future, we will focus on race and ethnic relations and on advancing citizens' rights and responsibilities.'*

MacArthur: *'We are interested in strengthening civil society organizations in the sense of leadership and financial position, but also in terms of standards, transparency, and accountability. In many cases, issues of standards and transparency haven't been applied to civil society organizations as they have with governments. We certainly plan to continue to work with civil society and remain very vigorously involved.'*

Aid donors tend to fund particular categories of organizations but few provide comprehensive information about the range of organizations targeted for support (see Table 2.3). Among the most prominent organizations in receipt of this assistance are labour unions, business and professional associations (lawyers, journalists, etc.), church and religious organizations, women's groups and federations, human rights organizations, indigenous community organizations and the media. Data on the EU, OFID, SIDA and USAID indicate that human rights organizations (human rights NGOs, advocacy groups, legal assistance organizations) are the most popular, followed by pro-democracy groups, the media, civic education groups and women's organizations. Here again there is variation by donor: Sweden and the EU channel a large proportion of their assistance to human rights groups; more than half of US assistance in the civil society category goes to pro-democracy groups, whereas governance and civic advocacy are

Table 2.3: *Civil Society Assistance by Recipient Organizations Total EU, Sweden, UK and US, 1993 and 1994*

Type of organization	Number of projects	Expenditure (US$ '000s)	Percentage of total
Trade union rights	7	6,136	4
Pro-democracy	34	8,063	5
Civic advocacy	39	21,915	14
Legal reform	5	854	1
Human rights (general)	71	47,425	29
Protection of human rights	87	22,521	14
Promotion of human rights	220	53,122	33
Others	12	886	1
Total	475	160,922	100

Source: Political aid database compiled by the Centre for Democratization Studies, University of Leeds. Final column is rounded to 100.

the largest category for the UK, although the total number of projects is very small.

It is also important to note, however, that support to civil society is not solely a matter of spending money. Other mechanisms are also in play, including diplomatic support, sanctions and other political tools. Both positive and negative sanctions have been applied by international agencies and foreign donors to promote democratization in other countries with a view to creating an environment more conducive to the growth and development of CSOs. This enabling environment work can entail efforts to influence legislation governing the activities of NGOs, or to reform tax regulations to the advantage of the non-profit sector. Indeed, one of the main thrusts of UNDP's evolving programme for supporting civil society is facilitating the introduction of appropriate legal and financial frameworks for CSOs (UNDP, 1997).

Key Issues

These observations on definitions, funding, intermediaries and instruments offer a number of pointers on donor policies and programmes in the civil society arena. Most donors share a common understanding of civil society: like-minded civic organizations, and the sphere in which they form, that foster democratic political values and help to consolidate fledgling democracies. All too often, aid donors equate civil society with the development NGOs they already know, sidelining other types of civic organizations that may well be more legitimate and politically effective. Individual donors exhibit preferences about particular types of organizations they choose to fund, although few have yet developed a strategic approach based on careful analysis and clearly articulated definitions. The trickle of expenditure may indicate caution in the move to supporting the work of different kinds of CSOs. More work remains to be done at the fundamental level of concepts and country aid strategies.

Existing data on aid flows in support of civil society are still incomplete and often inconsistent. There is clearly a pressing need to refine the categories used to quantify assistance before we can capture their full significance. Moreover, several factors come into play that make it difficult to distinguish and quantify aid channeled to CSOs for democracy and development purposes as opposed to efforts on the part of donors to strengthen the enabling environment for all non-State actors. It could be argued that donor assistance for elections, legal reforms and public sector management potentially strengthens the enabling environment for CSOs, but there is no adequate method for categorizing and quantifying such assistance. Although some projects explicitly aim to promote reform in the legal and fiscal environment that shapes the activities of CSOs, these cannot be separated and probably constitute only a tiny proportion of donor assistance. Furthermore, there is no way of distinguishing aid flows for this type of activity from aid to civil society actors as implementers of other activities, as is the case for many NGO projects.

As noted at the outset, the quantitative significance of funding to civil society organizations seems small in aggregate, certainly when compared to total aid flows. The data suggest that such funding accounts for perhaps less than one per cent of the total, amounting to a few hundred million US dollars. Nevertheless, the amount of aid allocated for such purposes continues to grow rapidly as more donors become involved. Although the actual volumes are small, the funds can be of considerable importance for recipient organizations that are not be accustomed to handling large quantities of money. When donor assistance is concentrated on a few prominent organizations that expand rapidly, CSOs may encounter problems of dependency and sustainability that are all too familiar in the world of development NGOs.

The final issue here concerns the intermediary organizations and the range of instruments deployed. In practice, most assistance for civil society purposes is channeled through NGOs and various types of foundations perceived to have a field presence and established procedures for working with local organizations. Although a number of intermediary organizations (such as the German political foundations) have a track record, 'civil society strengthening' is a new field of activity for many Northern NGOs. Although many have a proven capacity to work effectively with smaller and more localized organizations, they may not be well placed to work with organizations seeking political change and policy reform at the national level. Other types of intermediaries and forms of assistance may be required in a context of limited organizational capacity and political uncertainty, for example, in the form of endowments and trust funds administered by a representative group of civic organizations, government officials and aid donors.* The types of support mechanisms favoured by aid donors will continue to revolve around a fairly conventional package of technical cooperation measures centred on training, workshops and study visits. Many organizations outside the traditional domain of development NGOs could benefit from assistance geared towards organizational development and building the institutional requirements for longer term sustainability, as a means of avoiding problems of aid dependence and the organizational weaknesses that have often beset the NGOs sector.

WHAT NEXT?

Alison Van Rooy

The discussion in this chapter has suggested the obvious: that donors (and others) do not always have a clear idea of what they are doing when they enter the civil society debate. But that assessment does not always make donors wrong, nor should it suggest they are foolish in their 'rush towards civil society'. The ideas inherent in the debate *are* important for social change, yet the corpus of theory is complex and contradictory, and the policy implications drawn from it are by no means straightforward.

Having thus made things more difficult on a theoretical and general level, the following four chapters make things more difficult on a specific level. The last section of this chapter, therefore, suggests ways in which the cases may be most usefully read by policymakers, by activists and by academics and students. The conclusion will pull many of these threads together and to suggest how policy, and theory, might be reshaped in light of the lessons learned.

What definition of civil society is used?

All the authors have agreed on a minimum definition: civil society encompasses both the observable reality of social organization (the population of groups working mainly outside the State and marketplace), as well as the normative assessment that having a 'civil society' is a good and important thing. Overlaid on those empirical and normative pediments, however, are clear country-specific and country-relevant emphases. Patrón, for example, pointedly indicates the sphere of the family when she describes the forces of survival that propel Peruvian shantytown women to organize, Saravanamuttu draws in the churches and temples for consideration in his discussion of Sri Lankan sectarian politics, Wachira debates the crucial inclusion of ascriptive (i.e. non-voluntary) organizations in shaping social change in Kenya and, Miszlivetz and Ertsey interrogate the legacy of the political party and its sometime reincarnation as 'civil society' in Hungary.

---

* See, for example, the proposal elaborated by Goran Hyden (1997) for a tripartite fund along these lines.

How healthy is the civil society they describe?

All authors also undertake to map the civil sphere they are examining; the forces that have brought into being both organizations and the projects they espouse. Each examines the indigenous characteristics of the landscape: how sustainable, in terms of financial and other resources, are those groups? From what sources is its leadership drawn? Are CSOs tied tightly to State or donor strings? Are they well networked? Are there serious conflicts over the political agenda? How are they resolved? Such questions are critical to policy, of course, for they lay the groundwork for what intervention is possible; but they are also important for theory. Civil society must be empirically portrayed in all its conflictual, relational aspects before we can make judgements about its relationship to either development or democracy.

What impediments exist to its health?
Who benefits from change or from the status quo?

These questions focus on the dynamics of power – the theme that underlies the whole of this volume. Civil organization is but one consequence of the distribution of power. Those dispossessed by a particular regime or policy may organize to overturn it (sometimes violently, as with the Shining Path in Peru and the Tamil Tigers in Sri Lanka). Those who stand to lose from changes in the economic order may manoeuvre impediments to social organization (as Fujimori has been accused of doing). Many may simply disengage from the formal process altogether and thereby have detrimental effects on the cohesiveness of the system writ large (as Maina explains in his discussion of 'active non-co-operation').

What role have donors played?

Against these country-specific dynamics, each author has then sketched the work donors have undertaken specifically to 'strengthen civil society'. Most interesting in each case is the discussion of the donor community's own dynamics and how policy incentives from headquarters have been interpreted on the ground. In Sri Lanka, for example, Canada's emphasis on conflict resolution through roundtables and networking highlights its own low-key approach and nestles in with the tone of Norwegian policies. In Peru, the donor community is divided by some of the same things that divide the country itself: support for grassroots programmes that have risen in response to the very economic reforms supported by many donors themselves, at the same time that economic support to Fujimori is tempered with concern for his trampling of constitutional due process. Maina's discussion of the Kenyan case is strikingly similar to the Peruvian in this instance: donor conflict over economic and political carrots and sticks, combined with fragmentation in political opposition, has probably sustained Moi in power longer than forecast. In Hungary, the donor stampede to buttress post-communist social organization is quickly reversing as economic development speeds up, even if the 'democratization' of the polity is still half accomplished.

What interventions seem to have strengthened civil society?

The work described in each country has, none the less, produced some spectacular successes: the Mott Foundation in Hungary has supported important resource centres; support to the Kenyan Commission of Jurists has kept open the space for civic opposition; in Peru, external support for the Glass of Milk programme has not only provided immediate aid to children, but also helped solidify a vast women's network of grassroots organizations in the provision of healthcare; and, in Sri Lanka, long-term support to the Sarvodaya network, despite recent conflict, has created a sustainable, indigenous, powerful rural self-help network. These examples are explored in the chapters in the hope of understanding why they are considered successful examples of a strengthened civil society. Are there general lessons that can be applied to policy? Are there general conclusions that can be applied to theory? The themes explored in these pages suggest there are.

3 HUNGARY: CIVIL SOCIETY IN THE POST-SOCIALIST WORLD

Ferenc Miszlivetz and Katalin Ertsey[*]

THE METAMORPHOSIS OF CIVIL SOCIETY

Ferenc Miszlivetz

Today's Hungary is not entirely what it seems. As economic and political transition unfolds and new institutions are created, we are witnessing a new democracy in name but not yet in the day-to-day practice of its people. Uncertainty, anxiety, old patterns of behaviour and ambitious (and sometimes corrupt) use of the new system have deeply affected, and sometimes perverted, the political project of civil society – the yearning for democratization *within* society. The non-profit organizations and CSOs that are filling the space left by the retreat of the socialist State are, there-fore, not all part of the civil society project, even as their organizational forms take on that shape. This section introduces the discussion on donor roles in this complex landscape by looking back at the renaissance of civil society in East Central Europe and at how donors have deeply affected Hungary's political and social future.

* This chapter is the product of a joint effort between Dr Ferenc Miszlivetz, a noted scholar in the Hungarian Academy of Sciences, and Katalin Ertsey, an activist, NGO development consultant and researcher. Miszlivetz's introduction situates Ertsey's detailed discussion of donor involvement in the political context of a rapidly changing Hungary. All text boxes are by Ertsey; all tables and figures are gathered by Miszlivetz.

The Tumultuous Century of Hungarian Civil Society

The communist absorption of Hungary after World War II deeply affected the character of Hungarian society. Driven by a curious missionary spirit, communist parties throughout East Central Europe pointedly cut the fibres of civil society to realign loyalties towards the central State. Intertwined with the Communist Party, the Hungarian State, and those of its neighbours, was engaged in demobilizing society by many different means: dismantling of democratic and social actors, monopolizing trade unions, liquidating the Constitutional Court and other means.

The most effective form of demobilization was the dissolution of civil society organizations (CSOs). Before the Nazi invasion in 1944 and subsequent Soviet domination, there were over 13,000 registered clubs and associations in Hungary. With the growing authoritarianism of the Hungarian State, the numbers of groups dropped dramatically (see Figure 3.1). This tragic process continued after the end of the war and reached its lowest point (about 100 organizations) in 1951 at the height of the Communist dictatorship.

This destruction of social networks and associations also led to the destruction of social identities and value systems. This exercise of power created a constant state of fear and uncertainty in society. Day-to-day life became marked with political indifference, the living of permanent lies and the total loss of individuals' sense of responsibility for public welfare. People were told that they had little or nothing to contribute to decision-making processes; at the same time, however, they wanted to believe (or truly believed) that their interests were taken into consideration by the 'gods' above. Citizens came to expect that the State would provide all; reinforcing the 'without us, but for us' syndrome.

The liquidation of civil society was fortunately only partial. Social networks survived in semi-latency and semi-legitimacy. After the brutal repression of the failed Hungarian revolution in 1956, the regime tolerated a certain degree of liberalization and a good number of non-political associations (mainly sports and hobby clubs) were established. The lesson of the revolutions in both Hungary and Poland had taught independent-minded East Europeans to look for alternative methods to democratize their regimes. They had to build up more autonomy and political, social and cultural freedom within the still stable framework of the bipolar world order. It was romantic, but hopeless, for small nations to consider upheaval and revolutionary war against the Yalta system, maintained and supported by the super powers. The first alternative, therefore, was the introduction of economic reforms and a cautious, still state-controlled opening towards the world economy.

This gradual opening was again curtailed by the political backlash that followed the economic reform in the 1970s. The initial success of the New Economic Mechanism, significantly exaggerated by the Western media, provided Hungary with the reputation as the 'most cheerful barrack of the camp'.

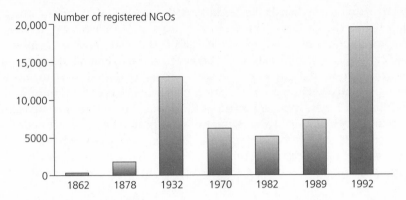

Source: Miszlivetz, 1997: 40

Figure 3.1: *CSOs in Hungary, 1862–1992*

By the early 1980s, the artificially maintained image of the country as an economic success story had become untenable. The economic crisis in turn triggered a political crisis, itself inspired by the success of the Polish Solidarity. This was the historic turning point for Hungarian society. The culture of silence was replaced step-by-step with more open dialogues among formerly isolated circles of independent-minded intellectuals, and as the media cautiously got involved in the new critical discourse, the long list of taboo themes started to shrink. Accelerating after 1989, but begun early in the decade, there was a sudden trebling of CSO numbers to over 19,000. In other words, a new public arena emerged to discuss social, environmental, cultural and even (in a restricted way) political issues. A modern critical discourse of dialogue was born in Hungary.

Solidarity was key in the transformation. This alternative, non-communist trade union of shipyard workers in Gdansk became, within a few months, a nationwide self-supporting political, cultural, social and economic network and a metaphor for an emerging civil society that could contain and partly control official authorities. The political philosophers behind the movement deliberately built their strategy on non-violent actions, involving the party-State and their local authorities in a dialogue with the representatives of the movement. The enforcement of dialogue, in the form of systematic negotiations, and radical demands were tempered at the same time with a readiness to compromise. The reborn adjective 'civil' was supposed to refer to the movement's characteristics of non-violence and solidarity, but 'civil' also came to mean autonomous, independent, non-military and non-official.

The very existence and pervasive success of Solidarity proved throughout the Eastern bloc that there was a chance for a peaceful challenge *from below* to authoritarian regimes and their apparatus. Naturally, the forms of civil movements differed from country to country according to historical traditions, the nature of the dictatorship, political culture and social structure. In Hungary, which lacked a large and strong independent moral authority like the Catholic Church in Poland, a wide variety of civil initiatives, movements and associations emerged at the beginning of the 1980s. At the early stage of their existence, however, the movements throughout Hungary shared Solidarity's co-operative and solidarity ethos. They drew from a particularly Hungarian tradition of political thought, building on the writing of István Bibó, a prominent independent political writer and historian, who introduced the metaphor of the 'small circles of freedom' in one of his essays written after the war. This concept was used and developed by the emerging student movement, environmental and peace groups, populist writers and the first independent trade union, established in 1988.

There was often an overlap between the apolitical objectives of some of the new organizations and the deeply political ramifications of their work. Many, like the environmental *Danube Circle* (see Box 3.1) or the *Dialogue* peace movement, presented themselves as West European-type, one-issue 'new social movements' and insisted on the non-political, 'professional' character of their activity, even in moments when their political role was obvious. This apolitical face made the new social movements less vulnerable to officialdom at the same time it hindered the crystallization of a new value system and an ethical base for the emerging civil society.

These changes in social consciousness led to a stunning growth in organization. By 1992, there were 30,507 registered NGOs, mainly in the fields of culture, ecology, science and research, human rights, interest-defence and sports and hobby clubs. The aggregate revenue of these voluntary organizations added up to US$1 billion in each of 1992 and 1993, or 3.1 per cent of GDP. By the end of the century, the face of civil society had indeed changed.

There was a broad mobilization of popular social and political attitudes, for example, especially among citizens in larger cities. This growing discontent reached the middle-rank leadership of mass organizations such as the National Assembly of Trade Unions or the People's Patriotic Front that had been previously controlled by the party and the secret police. Reform stretched deep into the organizational fibre of these key organizations,

---

BOX 3.1: THE DANUBE CIRCLE

The Danube Circle, an environmental CSO formed in 1984, opposed the Danube dam planned to be built by Hungary with the then Czechoslovakian government. The plan would have caused irreversible damage to the environment and to the water supply in Hungary. The movement created such enormous pressure on the government that it eventually broke the contract with its brotherly Czechoslovakian government as a gesture of peace toward the Hungarian people. The pressure generated from environmental protest had been too great to dissipate, lending strength to the outbreak of a peaceful revolution in other parts of Hungarian civil society.

reaching its climax when the Communist Party's reform-oriented members started to organize their own internal 'reform circles' against the will of the more conservative majority. In the autumn of 1987, the Hungarian Democratic Forum was launched by populist-nationalistic writers and intelligentsia in the presence of Imre Pozsgay, then the most reform-minded member of the Central Committee of the Communist Party.*

As the traditional, centrally directed organizations struggled with reform, other more innovative forms of civil organizing were evolving. The most innovative was the Network of Free Initiatives. Organized mostly by independent intellectuals and activists excluded from the Democratic Forum (because of their 'urban' radicalism or cosmopolitan attitudes), the Network worked as an umbrella organization with the clear mission to offer shelter and moral and political support for other grassroots initiatives. This fresh approach had been completely missing from the arsenal of Hungarian political tradition. In fact, the organizers of the Network were themselves uncertain about their own undertaking, yet, within a few weeks, thousands joined. This initiative was unable to avoid the fate of other new organizations, however, and a small but influential faction of its elected leadership turned it into one of the liberal, political parties at a time when Hungary was being swept by post-communist party-building fever. Although the Network died, the idea of horizontal co-operation among independent actors survived.

Another innovative and promising initiative was regular cooperation among East Central European social movements. This unprecedented and risky enterprise bore fruit, including a growing Central European awareness about shared identity and a strengthened need for solidarity. Co-operation occurred not only among the main democratic oppositional movements, such as Charter 77 in Czechoslovakia, Solidarity in Poland and the Hungarian Democratic Opposition, but also among smaller movements and groups, like the environmentalists, peace groups and professional associations. To protect this emerging civil society and its social movements throughout East Central Europe, Vaclav Havel, then the spokesman for Charter 77, suggested setting up an alternative European Parliament for social movements. Multilateral discussions about the proposal in Prague were constantly interrupted by the police, and it was only after the collapse of the old regime that the initiative could materialize. The Helsinki Citizens' Assembly, an international institution of CSOs established in 1990 in Prague, is continuing to protect human rights and support local grassroots initiatives for democratization.

Yet the project of building a new, autonomous civil society rapidly succumbed to a fever of party-building prior to the first free elections. An overwhelming majority of former civil society activists became members of the new political elite and occupied the highest positions in the new

---

* The quasi-independent character of the movement and the fact that some radical representatives of the Democratic Opposition were not invited to the opening ceremony provoked a fatal cleavage in the opposition, however.

leadership. In their new positions, their perception of the civil society–State relationship changed dramatically. The new political elite claimed, even before the first elections, that the time for social movements was over. They argued that continued grassroots mobilization was unnecessary, if not dangerous, to the new democracy; and that the well-articulated field of political parties provided an efficient arena for the competition of ideas. The new elite argued that the everyday political involvement of citizens was unnecessary and should be limited to maintaining the new institutions and to legitimizing the regime by giving their votes every four years.

The emergence of new parties, at the final stage of collapse of the one-party system, is the latest phase of the institutionalization of social movements. Alan Fowler, a well-known author on CSO issues, says that, 'civil society is the place where interest groups turn themselves into political parties, competing to become the ruling regime' (Fowler, personal communication).

The Implications of Transformation: the New Faces of Civil Society

Civil society has to be seen as an *ad hoc* melting pot and battleground of diverse interests and actors. This public arena is never homogenous; constituting itself as a permanent regrouping and renegotiating process. Its complex fabric and interwoven interdependencies are built on the voluntary will of individuals taking part in social and political affairs. This special social space *assumes* citizens' participation in social processes as well as a strong sense of citizenship. The uninterrupted social need for civil society throughout the world in turn stems from democratic deficiencies: the whole project of civil society is, therefore, an intensely political one. Mary Kaldor writes that 'the advantage of the language of civil society is precisely its *political* content, its implications for participation and citizenship' (Kaldor, 1997: 52) . Jørgensen formulated this precisely:

> *There are some risks in taking on civil society. It is of course perfectly legitimate for CSOs not to be openly political or to take sides in whatever constellation of parties or factions which is forming at a given moment, but they must recognize that their work has political aspects and relate to the authority of the State and to the political development of their society.* (Jørgensen, 1996: 52)

This political focus means that nothing is mechanically identifiable in civil society; the presence of organizations alone does not equal 'civil society' in its fuller sense. In East Central Europe, following the half-successful velvet revolutions, many NGOs declared themselves advocates and embodiments of civil society. Yet the impressive density of today's civil sector

Table 3.1: *Registered Hungarian CSOs by Activity, 1992*

	%		%
Sports	20.7	Foundations, associations	1.9
Hobby and leisure clubs	15.6	Professional, employers' and	
Political organizations	12.4	employee's organizations	1.9
Culture	9.1	Religion	1.4
Education	7.7	Others	1.4
Social provision	7.1	Economic and entrepreneurial	
Civil defense	4.2	development	1.3
Settlement development, housing	3.4	Legal defense	1.3
Health care	2.9	Crime prevention	1.3
Scientific research	2.4	International relations	1.0
Ecology	1.9		

Source: Mislivetz, 1997: 40.

does not necessarily mean that real participation in political decision-making has increased – and not only because 36 per cent of associations operate in the fields of sports and leisure activities (see Table 3.1). As Rueschemeyer puts it:

> *The dominant claim that widespread participation in strong intermediary associations and organizations is conducive to and supportive of democracy must be qualified. Organizational density of civil society as such does not guarantee favourable conditions for democracy.* (Rueschemeyer et al., 1998)

A large part of the problem is the 'artificial' nature of many CSOs, which is caused by a range of factors. The most insidious is the practice by political parties and official authorities of creating their own organizations dedicated to human rights, education, women or environmental issues to extend their influence to social spheres otherwise unavailable to them. Other factors are more commonplace: many organizations, for example, are formed simply as contracting bodies to replace retreating State services – part of the 'fictitious' economy that Patrón describes in her chapter on Peru. In still other cases, organizations that are registered nonetheless lie dormant because of a lack of skills and resources to implement the goals that brought them into being. Of the thousands of organizations registered in Hungary today, perhaps only a very few are active in pointedly pursuing the expansion of democracy and development in the nation.

The argument here is that CSOs *can* play an important role in strengthening democratic values, mobilizing participation, contributing to a culture of decision-making and dialogue and strengthening each others' bargaining capacities with authorities on the local, national and international level, yet that role is not inevitable. A number of impediments stand in the way of its potential.

The first impediment is a new dependency between Western donors and Eastern CSOs. Donors sometimes superimpose their values, however inadvertently, on recipients who in turn become dependent agents rather than genuine actors in their local civil sphere. It is also often the case that Western donors are unable or reluctant to analyse local social, political and cultural conditions and are, therefore, unable to select the most appropriate candidates. In most cases, those who are getting internal financial support are those who are in the circle of a global CSO elite. This elite is fortified with networking capital, the necessary skills of English, the Internet and application-writing and the ability to speak the most trendy CSO language and use the most fashionable buzzwords. This strange institutionalization of the initial impetus for social change has contributed to the image of a civil society intermediary class speaking for the masses, 'talking civil society', displaying the right liberal values, but divorced from their reality. Because of the scarcity of domestic resources, a growing dependency on State support, an uneven relationship with Western donors and growing rivalry (rather than solidarity) among CSOs, the very vision of civil society in Hungary may fade away.

A second impediment is the use of CSOs by government as a means to solicit donor funding. Certain political parties (like the ruling Hungarian Socialist Party) actually work through existing civil organizations (or create new ones) to solicit external support. The leadership of favoured organizations is recruited mostly from the politicians or marginalized officials of the *ancien régime*, although ambitious younger activists are also involved. Even though the country's history of dictatorship and authoritarian rule has made Hungarian society highly suspicious about officially sponsored institutions, this skepticism has not extended far beyond its borders.

The strongest link to the State, however, occurs with quangos, (quasi-NGOs), and the many umbrella groups that also thrive on State support. Many of the new parties realized after their *Sturm und Drang* years that they still needed regular contacts with the 'civil' world and that their civilian support base had been seriously eroded. The response has been to cozy up to existing organizations such as the National Federation of Large Families, the Society of Those Living below the Subsistence Level and the Association of Hungarian Women to curry the favour of their membership. In other cases, umbrella organizations, such as the Federation of Civil Associations, the Civil Parliament or the Civil Roundtable, have been staffed with one-time government officials and directly funded by State resources, even in instances where their programming has not warranted such degrees of support (see Box 3.2). Critics argue that such organizations provide an opportunity for pre–1989 apparatchiks to regain legitimacy in the domestic and international arena, but in so doing, discredit the whole of the 'civil' element in civil society organizing.

Although it is possible to find examples of genuinely inspired CSOs, neither their numbers nor their influence on the political sphere seems to be strong enough to change the picture in the short run. One outstanding exception is the Hungarian Foundation for Self-Reliance. The Foundation's

---

BOX 3.2: CONTINUING STATE POWER THROUGH CSOS

Noteworthy examples of State-directed CSOs are MSZOSZ and TESZ. MSZOSZ is the largest trade union and the successor of the official and only trade union of the *ancien régime*. It was the most unpopular of the organizations controlled by the State (according to 1989 opinion polls) yet, despite its unpopularity, it won over the new independent trade unions, such as the Workers' Councils and the League of Democratic Trade Unions. TESZ is the legal successor of the *People's Patriotic Front*, a front organization of the previous regime.

---

major concern is the development of Hungary's most marginalized social and ethnic group, the Roma community, derogatorily called 'gypsies'. They provide credit for those Roma groups that have a plan for income generation and the responsibility necessary to realize their plans. The Foundation is exceptional in its international recognition, thanks to its founder, András Biró. From the very beginning, it was heavily supported by the big American foundations such as Ford and the Rockefeller Brothers. Among the human rights advocacy groups, the Legal Defense Bureau for National and Ethnic Minorities, the Martin Luther King Association, the Raul Wallenberg Society and the Hungarian Human Rights Center are the most effective and best recognized. The Legal Defense Bureau, backed by the Otherness Foundation, concentrates on the violation of the Roma community's rights and is engaged in fact-finding, visiting clients, collecting documents, providing legal advice and initiating legal procedures. The Martin Luther King Association and the Hungarian Human Rights Center protect the rights of foreigners living and studying in Hungary who are victims of ethnic or religious discrimination. They provide legal help, advocacy with the bureaucracy, and daily life services.

Searching for Alternatives

In the post-Cold War period, one of the greatest challenges for civil society and its institutions is globalization. To respond to this challenge, CSOs in Hungary and elsewhere in East Central Europe have to link and integrate their domestic activity into a global context. Coming out of the parochial framework and political climate in which they are trapped today, they need to find those donors able to co-operate as partners and as equals.

The combination of local, regional and global activities is necessary because domestic governments are constrained by transnational financial institutions, multinational companies and other agents of the globalized world market and are becoming less able to solve burning social, environmental and human rights issues alone.

Certainly, the newly democratic leadership in the region has not been able to offer alternatives to the kind of globalization we are witnessing. Political leaders of the former communist regime who are now coming back to power as social democratic politicians, talk about the lack of alternatives of global capitalism. Not so long ago, this 'lack of alternative discourse' was targeted as a problem of the socialist world order. The overlap of opposing ideologies expressed by the same actors is not surprising; it is based on the same world view of the same power-holders. Their message is today just as it was before 1989: 'We are not responsible for anything, it is the Soviet Union (yesterday) and the World Bank (today) who decides, we try to do our best for you but you have to see: there are no alternatives.'

If the emerging CSO world in Hungary is about strengthening democracy and civil society, they have to offer alternatives themselves. This is possible if they act as independent and autonomous agents of our chaotic world.

MAPPING DONOR INTERVENTIONS: DO THEY MATTER IN THE BIG PICTURE?

*Katalin Ertsey**

Against this background of tumultuous social and political change, Western support organizations began to arrive in Hungary in the late 1980s. What has their intervention meant?

---

* Ertsey's research included interviews and documentation review from the following sources:
- Interviews with local representatives of: USAID, the European Commission, the Hungarian Foundation for Self-Reliance/PHARE Democracy Program Micro Projects, British Know-How Fund, Canadian Technical Cooperation Program, Friedrich Naumann Stiftung, Soros Foundation Hungary, Friedrich Ebert Stiftung, National Forum Foundation, United Way International/Democracy Network Hungary.
- Information collected and analysed, including annual reports, strategic policy documents from local offices or other sources on the organizations listed in the foregoing and on: Ashoka, Regional Environmental Center Public Participation Program, PHARE LIEN Program, PHARE Democracy Programme Macro Projects, PHARE Partnership Programme, the Belgian, Danish, Israeli, Japanese, Norwegian, Dutch governments/embassies, United States Information Service, Charles Stewart Mott Foundation, Rockefeller Brothers Fund, Ford Foundation, German Marshall Fund of the United States, Westminster Foundation for Democracy, International Center for Not-for-Profit Law (ICNL), Johns Hopkins University Institute for Policy Studies Third Sector Project, World Bank, Peace Corps, Partners Hungary, United Nations Development Programme, Civic Education Program, Civil Society Development Foundation, Foundation for a Civil Society, League of Woman Voters, Nonprofit Information and Training Center, Chamber of Nonprofit Human Services, CIVICUS, European Foundation Centre Orpheus Program Civil Society Project, Canada World Youth, National Endowment for Democracy, Directory of Social Change, Charities Aid Foundation, Charity Know-How Fund, Sasakawa Peace Foundation, Pew Charitable Trusts, Joyce Mertz-Gilmore Foundation, Trust for Mutual Understanding, Organization for Security and Cooperation in Europe, Joint Eastern Europe Center for Democratic Education and Governance, Environmental Partnership Program for Central and Eastern Europe.
- Conferences, including the European Foundation Centre's Funding East Workshop's 'funders only' meeting, a pre-Annual General Assembly Workshop on Funding East, including a special session on Western Funding for Civil Society in CEE in Paris, November, 1996; and 'Assessing the contribution of the EU to the development of civil society in former communist countries' in Budapest, 4–5 April 1997.
- Contacts with a range of embassies. Of those, no information was available from the French, Finnish, Australian, Austrian, Swedish and New Zealand embassies.

Hungary is a particularly interesting case study because the very idea of civil society as an element in development and democracy was 'discovered' by the outside world at about the same time as Central and Eastern Europe opened. From the very beginning, donors talked about the importance of strengthening civil society and poured vast resources into its organizations. Unlike other countries, the emphasis on civil society in Hungary was not, as the saying goes, old wine in new bottles: all of the interactions and relationships were new. Hungarians, sipping tiny amounts of that wine of support, in turn got tipsy drinking wines from Washington, New York, London, Brussels, Ottawa, The Hague and Bonn. It was a bitter awakening when the cheerful days of the velvet revolution were over and those who had talked about civil society also started talking about shutting off the taps. The Hungarian hope, is to learn to produce our own 'solution' ourselves. It is possible, if done with the same passion winemakers have for their work. But it must be understood as an investment and a learning process, not as a short night of over indulgence followed by the inevitable hangover.

This section reviews the history of the arrival of international donor support before exploring today's actors, issues and agendas, instruments, trends and concerns and returning to the larger implications of their work. This overview also forecasts prospects for long-term change in Hungary and discusses the dynamics of power and foreign intervention in any country's civil society.

A Bit of History

Until 1990, apart from scholarly and cultural exchanges, study trips, conferences and seminars on a relatively small scale, Central and Eastern Europe had not received particular attention from the international donor community. A few private donors and some governments began underground programmes in Hungary early in the 1980s by supporting individuals and informal groups in opposition to the socialist government, but these were small scale and secretive. Some support went through West European movements like the East–West Dialogue that was promoting increased citizen participation in public discussions on both sides of the Berlin wall and was active in small circles of the intelligentsia. Although these kinds of citizens' organizations received some funding from foreign sources at the outset, 'civil society' per se did not feature in the objectives of incoming donors (with the important exception of the Soros Foundation, see Box 3.3). Only after four or five years past transition did donors pointedly focus on the development of the CSO community, leaving a relatively large gap between 1989 and 1994–5. In a region where civil society is largely held to be the driving force of the transition to democracy, this gap is remarkable indeed.

• Outside the Democracy Programme, but within the framework of the overall national PHARE programmes, there are also some projects that contribute to the support of civil society. The complex nature and size of the programme, however, makes it extremely difficult to discern their scope and impact on civil society.

BOX 3.3: THE SOROS FOUNDATION

The Soros Foundation in Hungary was the only legal vehicle for substantial foreign support to enter the closed socialist society before the turnover in 1989. The Foundation was established in 1984 by expatriate Hungarian millionaire George Soros through a special agreement with the Hungarian government, long before the political transition had started in any visible way. The Foundation played a crucial part in further softening the already weak dictatorship and opening up the closed society. The Foundation initially funded scholarly and professional exchanges, as well as direct grants to organizations, thus helping to awaken the intelligentsia by exposing individuals and groups to other cultures and new experiences such as democratic and professional practices of partner organizations in the West.

Through subtle ways, that support reached the underground democratic movement. Copying machines, books, all sorts of material and immaterial support was made available through the Foundation, although much of the support went to a relatively small circle of beneficiaries. Some beneficiaries became more and more involved with the Foundation and, by the late 1980s and early 1990s, many of the significant political and public figures in liberal circles were, in one way or another, associated with the Foundation.

In 1995 alone, the Foundation committed roughly US$1.6 million to its civil society programmes, including the East–East programme, the Roma programme, the ethnicity and minorities programme and the new social initiatives programme. This figure is striking, even though the objectives of the CSO programmes are undefined and direct support to organizations is often random and improvised.

Since the mid 1990s, however, 'civil society' has gained in prominence as support organizations began projects on CSO institution building, training and research to help the growth and development of the non-profit sector. These programmes were mostly initiated by North American private foundations and implemented by foreign CSOs, and a few government programmes, like the SEED (Support to Eastern European Democracies) programme of the US government, which have provided these areas with small amounts (see Box 3.4). This new Western approach to programming was initially much appreciated. Most donors realized early on that there was not much need for such basic civic education programmes as 'introducing democracy' to Central Europeans. Although they had only limited experience with democracy, the people of Poland, Czechoslovakia and Hungary were surprisingly well prepared for the change of the regimes. They were aware of their basic responsibilities and rights as voters, although not quite yet as citizens. Donor emphasis was thus placed on enhancing the legal and fiscal environment of the CSO sector and to help the development of a healthy civil society (see Box 3.5 for the interesting example of the International Center for Not-for-Profit Law (ICNL)).

Other kinds of programs followed. In 1995, USAID started the Democracy Network programme with a grant of $30 million over three years to provide small grants, exchanges and training for East Central

BOX 3.4: THE BILATERALS

According to the 1996 edition of the UNDP directory on official democracy, human rights, governance and participation programmes, Hungary received US$42.9 million from OECD sources from 1990 to 1993, or some 3 per cent of all assistance arriving to the whole region, including the former Soviet Union. The overwhelming majority of funding for democracy, governance and participation came from the US and the European Union. The US contribution of US$20.3 million makes up 48 per cent of all support, the EU funding of US$17.3 million makes up 40 per cent and all others account for the remaining 12 per cent. Besides the two major donors, Belgium, Germany, Japan, the Netherlands, Switzerland and the UK committed significant amounts (5 per cent or more) of the total contributions.

- *The Netherlands* The Dutch Embassy Small Project programme (KAP) offers financial support up to 15,000 guilders (NLG) (about US$8,000) to individual, interest group and community organization projects aimed at strengthening the protection and guarantees afforded by law and improving public consultation procedures; seminars and publications on human rights, free elections, the environment and other issues of the reform process. In fiscal year 1994, the programme budget was 2 million NLG (about US$1 million).
- *Canada* The Canadian Cooperation Fund was launched in 1989 to fund local activities of community, minority and civic groups to organize, raise awareness, reach out to community members in the areas of human rights and minorities, women's issues and the environment and to support local initiatives arising from the large-scale Canadian technical cooperation projects. The grant is up to CAD$5,000 (about US$3,800) per group. During the 1996/97 fiscal year, the total support was CAD$100,000 (US$76,000).
- *UK* The British government allocates around GBP3.5 million a year for its entire support programme to Hungary, not on a government to government basis, but through individual projects. There is no amount within that budget that is specifically devoted to strengthening civil society, but the Charity Know-How Fund, funded equally by the British Know-How Fund and a group of British charitable trusts, is aimed at skill transfer and the development of the voluntary sector in Hungary through British–Hungarian linking projects. There are also occasional British–Hungarian partnerships supported in the area of environment and culture, and the British Council supports individual artists and cultural groups.
- *US* The US government supports civil society through its democracy programmes. The Democratic Governance programme of USAID, focused on improving the political process and increasing pluralism, accounted for 9 per cent of all the assistance (US$240 million in the SEED programme) during the period 1991–95. The strategic objective of the 1996–99 period is to help 'Better informed citizens increase their participation in decision-making at the local level', which includes the sub-goal of enhancing a 'more active and responsive civil society'. The amount devoted to this area within an annually decreasing total budget of US$3.4 million, is again around 9 per cent of the US$39 million total assistance. The other major effort supported by the US government through USAID is the Democracy Network programme, which spent US$2.5 million over three years through small grants, training and other activities to develop the CSO sector. Besides these programmes, the United States Information Service (USIS) runs a small grant fund to support cultural and civic initiatives, likely to remain in operation after the USAID assistance is over in 1999.

**BOX 3.5: THE INTERNATIONAL CENTER FOR
NOT-FOR-PROFIT LAW**

The International Center for Not-for-Profit Law (ICNL) launched a series of regional conferences in 1994 on 'Regulating Civil Society'. The series involved lawyers, CSO leaders and government officials in the discussion on enabling environments for non-profits in the region. In 1995, in Tallinn, Estonia and then in Budapest, dozens of CSO regulation experts emerged through these discussions, and new, talented and devoted lawyers debated the enhancement of the legal environment for the sector. Considered by both the CSO community and the donors alike to be one of the most successful civil society programmes in the region, ICNL was awarded the regional legal programme contract of the USAID DemNet programme. ICNL, however, plays a controversial role by aggressively and successfully promoting North American models of not-for-profit regulation in the region. These models, substantially different from the existing German legal tradition, will need major adaptation to serve as working models for actual legislation. Also, the American model may promote, rather than downplay, the contract-based service delivery tendency within the CSO community, further weakening its advocacy functions in shaping public policy.

European CSOs. The PHARE Democracy Programme of the European Union (Poland and Hungary Aid for Reconstructing the Economy) (see Box 3.6) had also started to support CSOs in the region at two levels: the macro programmes provide funds for cooperation between CSOs in European Union (EU) countries and Central and Eastern Europe (CEE) countries, while the micro programmes provide funds for local CSOs to run their democracy development programmes.

It has not always been easy. Some donors found it difficult to adapt techniques learned in other developing regions to the very different situation in the CEE countries. One of the reasons is the strange 'mixed' state of development in Hungary. It is neither the First World nor the Third World. Literacy, divorce, child mortality and fertility figures are similar to those of the most industrialized countries, and the diseases typical of the North (heart disease, stress-related disorders, cancer) are among the major causes of death. Indeed, the most recent World Development Report of the World Bank, which measures poor countries to more-developed countries, ranks Hungary quite high at 100, alongside upper middle-income economies like Malaysia, Brazil, South Africa and Mexico. Within the region, the Czech Republic, Slovenia, Croatia and Greece are in the same group.

At the same time, the infrastructure and practice of democracy were in chaos at the time of transition. 'Development' is certainly Hungary's largest challenge, but programmes designed for developing countries with different economic, cultural and political practices could not accommodate the post-communist model, where the formal features of democracy were quickly adopted (rule of law, separation of powers, free and fair elections

---

BOX 3.6: PHARE DEMOCRACY PROGRAMME

The three instruments of the Democracy Programme regionally are the macro-projects (ECU6 million), micro projects (ECU2 million) and ad hoc measures.

- The macro grants of up to ECU200,000 (about US$220,000) are awarded to joint projects of CSOs of EU member and non-member countries, or all non-member countries.
- Locally awarded micro grants finance small local projects with ECU3,000–10,000 (about US$3,400–11,000).
- For the ad hoc measures, one million ECUs are allocated to finance unforeseen needs or multi-country projects on cross border issues like minority rights.

---

and freedom of expression and association), but the substantive elements remain painfully missing (guarding human and minority rights, or an enabling environment for a healthy and strong civil society) (Kaldor and Vejvoda, 1996). These challenges doggedly remain.

The response, detailed in the remaining sections of the chapter, has been to focus on CSOs as the route to democratization. Piled on top of the massive investments in economic reform, this focus was designed to shape the environment in which the economy (and polity) could prosper under the watchful eye of the citizenry. The outcome, as we shall see, has been a strange combination of innovative programmes, quick fixes and rapid exit.

The Donor Landscape

Who are the major foreign actors in this picture? What are they doing, and how are they doing their work in supporting civil society in Hungary? In this section, a summary of bilateral, multilateral, Western NGO and foundation work is followed by a discussion of the instruments they wield to accomplish their work. This background sets the scene for a discussion of issues, agendas, trends and concerns that stretch well beyond Hungarian borders.

We begin then with the bilaterals. Among the government support programmes, the Dutch, Canadian, British and US governments play the most important roles, along with the Danish, the Israelis and the Swiss, who run some programmes in certain selected areas. Yet all the amounts involved are very small, and the message sent by their presence plays a larger part in civil society development than the impact of their funding.

The Dutch and Canadian governments run small, embassy-based grant programmes for Hungarian CSOs, whereas the British use the mechanism of the British Know-How Fund and the Charity Know How Fund combined with a small special gift fund of the Ambassador. The US government channels funds through its USIS (United States Information Service) small grants programme, the USAID mission's Democratic Governance programme and the Democracy Network Program, which is managed by the local chapter of an international NGO. These locally-based programmes all rely on local experts to some extent in their decision-making. Some components, especially ones involving foreign partners, exchanges and trips, are decided in the home countries, but decisions on support to local civil society is always taken by local embassy staff or local partners or both. Most of these programmes are launched with the specific aim to provide speedy and flexible funding to local groups who have no capacity or interest in going through the complex and time-consuming mechanisms of larger government-to-government programmes.

Among multilaterals, the single largest and most significant programme supporting civil society in Hungary and throughout the region is the European Union PHARE Democracy Programme, with macro, micro and ad hoc project facilities (personal communication, Patrick Egan, programme officer of the USAID mission in Budapest). The current programme runs from 1997 through 2000, with a budget of ECU10 million for 13 countries of the region with the aim of strengthening the rule of law, respect for human rights and fundamental freedoms. Within these broad goals, there are thematic and geographic priorities, such as the 'training of cross-party groups of parliamentarians and staff; the strengthening of non-governmental bodies and associations which by their vocation and specific activities can make a contribution to the promotion of pluralistic democratic society; and the transfer of skills and expertise of democratic practices and the rule of law to professional groups and associations' (PHARE Democracy Programme objectives, EU document 1997). Priorities include 'issues where governments are not or should not be active, and the most needy areas, i.e. the difficult or unpopular aspects of human rights, the development of the CSOs and representative structures; supporting independent, pluralistic and responsible media; and promoting and monitoring human rights' (PHARE Democracy Programme objectives, EU document, 1997).

Indeed, the major disadvantage Hungary suffers in comparison to the other 12 PHARE countries is that the Hungarian government, not seeing the importance of a healthy civil society in democratization and the European integration process, failed to request from Brussels the launch of the Civil Society Development programme (not to be confused with the American private initiative under the same name), which is successfully working in Bulgaria, the Czech Republic, Poland, Romania, Slovakia and Lithuania. The programme in those countries is a rare example of a locally managed, significant resource programme that moves beyond the mere small grants programmes governments and other donors usually undertake under the label of civil society development. It provides funding and capacity development programmes for CSOs but, in addition, it also works on enabling environment issues, involving the government and the private sector and fostering the advocacy functions of civil society.

NGOs from Western countries have also played a vital role in the development of civil society. The most important are the legal programmes of the Washington-based ICNL; the exchange programmes of the regional DemNet coordinator, the National Forum Foundation; the youth exchange programme of Canada World Youth (CWY); and the networking efforts of the Charities Aid Foundation along with some other, smaller UK charities. The most grounded foreign NGO that has adapted to the local circumstances is the United Way, whose local branches are successfully tapping community and private resources to support the needy, primarily in social care at the grassroots level.

Canada World Youth (CWY) is important because it promotes voluntarism among youth (a rare objective in civil society programmes) involving a neglected but key group – future leaders, not a typical target group of civil society programmes. A primarily CIDA-funded NGO, CWY started its programme in Hungary in 1994, bringing together young Hungarians and Canadians to work as volunteers and to study and live together for four months in small, rural host communities in each country. The programme combines the promotion of voluntarism, collective effort, co-operation and understanding between different cultures, while providing the opportunity for young Hungarians to experience the daily realities of a well-established market economy and consolidated democracy.

The ICNL, whose current major activity in the region is the coordination of the AID-funded regional programme, has gained considerable experience through working with legal experts, CSO leaders and researchers during their conference series on 'Regulating Civil Society'. ICNL has played a somewhat controversial role in the region's future legislation on non-profits by aggressively promoting the American model. Nevertheless, the organization has accumulated knowledge, facilitated regional discussion and debates, reinforced the usefulness of regional comparisons between concepts and drafts and promoted co-operation among legal experts of various countries. They also 'discovered' experts who may play a future role in shaping their countries' legislation for non-profits. Only time will tell whether the experts unearthed by ICNL can be really useful and influence government policies in the right direction. In some countries, such as Slovakia, civil society activists reacted forcefully to attempts by the government to reduce benefits legally guaranteed for foundations. Without ICNL's activities in the region, this reaction would have been weaker.

Another important American NGO involved in the implementation of the DemNet programme is the National Forum Foundation, which recently united with Freedom House. Their experience in the region had been limited to organizing US internships for CEE individuals to work in the US with various institutions of the media, government and congress, business firms or CSOs. They are responsible for coordinating the 11 DemNet national programmes and fostering communication and cooperation between CSOs in these countries. They continue to offer the US internships in the DemNet framework and implement a regional exchange and a newsletter. The major value added in their programmes is the regional exchange programme that enables CEE individuals from various CSOs to spend a period of up to three months in another CEE country, learning by working with a host CSO active on the same field. United Way International – Hungary is the CSO implementing the Hungarian component of the DemNet programme. The programme spends US$2.5 million over three years through small grants, training and so-called special projects supporting the development of CSOs, overseen by the local USAID mission.

Overall, it is the major US private foundation community that has played the most important role in the development of civil society. Of the foundations, the most significant are the Ford Foundation, the Rockefeller Brothers Fund (RBF), the Charles Stewart Mott Foundation and the Soros Foundation/Open Society Institute. The government-funded foundations like the German Marshall Fund of the United States or the German political foundations (Friedrich Naumann Stiftung, Friedrich Ebert Stiftung, Konrad Adenauer Stiftung) have complemented this work by supporting their particular areas of interest.

What distinguishes the most effective foundations is their openness to local concerns and their care in developing relationships with reliable and knowledgeable partners. Among the foundations, Mott has gained significant and well-deserved popularity for its work with CSO resource centres and other grantees. The foundation supports non-profit support centres in 11 countries in the region and, in all, $2.6 million has been invested since 1993. In Hungary alone, it has invested more than $1.5 million between 1993 and 1996 including all grants. Despite reluctance on the part of Hungarian umbrella organizations to form coalitions on issues such as the comprehensive legislation on non-profits, Mott has committed to this work for an extended period so that hopefully the centres can eventually take on more active roles in advocacy for civil society as a whole.

The Ford Foundation and the Soros Foundation have also devoted significant amounts in recent years to develop civil society organizing and joined in co-funding other projects. The Ford Foundation has committed US$1.558 million to Hungary to date, out of which US$1.050 million went to the Hungarian Foundation for Self-Reliance to support their 'grant and loan' programme helping the Roma community in Hungary.

The Rockefeller Brothers Fund and the German Marshall Fund are other good examples of donors who have concentrated on regional partnerships. Their example is particularly noteworthy because neither have long-term plans to remain in Hungary, nor have either established a local presence, but they remain committed to the notion of partnership. Their work has concentrated on the environment and civil society and is important because of their flexibility and understanding of the local realities. The Rockefeller Brothers Fund has committed in the range of US$0.5 million for the years of 1990 through 1995 to Hungary, most of it to the Hungarian Foundation for Self-Reliance, whereas the German Marshall Fund has granted well over a million US dollars to the Environmental Partnership Programme for Central and Eastern Europe in the same period.

Another important element is the informal co-operation among all the major American private foundations: they co-operatively support organizations like the resource centres, intermediary organizations like the Hungarian Foundation for Self-Reliance, environmental programmes such as the Partnership Programme and most recently community foundations, which are a new way to involve various local stakeholders in funding community needs. Private foundations such as the Ford Foundation, the Rockefeller Brothers Fund and Soros have joined in and supported ideas that work in addition to running their own programmes in related areas. In total, foundations spent an estimated US$400 million on various democracy assistance projects (including civil society programming) in the whole of the region between 1989 and 1994 (Quigley, 1996: 109); comparable to the amount allocated by official donors but distributed with a greater level of flexibility and less bureaucracy. They also played a role in attracting other sources and brokering joint efforts.

The means used by this wide variety of donors are similarly broad. The practice of giving direct grants, however, is widespread and appreciated by locals, so is the more exceptional instrument of giving general-purpose grants in contrast to project funding, the exclusive instrument of EU donors, general purpose grants help established organizations to plan ahead.

In terms of approach, apart from the relatively clear difference between official and private donors in flexibility, speed and political orientation, the most interesting differences exist between European and American donors. The American approach is flexible in its attitude towards supporting civil society, and US private foundations have been by far the most popular with Central and Eastern European partners for their flexibility and understanding of the CSO sector. This understanding is particularly important for service-oriented CSOs, aspiring to the American model of a vast, non-profit-operated social service and education sector. This general pro-American sentiment has had an impact on the legal development of the Hungarian CSO sector as well, as ICNL proposals for reforming non-profit legislation are promoted by CSOs in contrast to the German model proposed by the Hungarian Ministry of Justice. Europeans, however, tend to do project funding only, which makes it difficult for organizations to stay afloat in between projects. Also, the European ideas of voluntarism and philanthropy are quite different from the American and mean that CEE organizations have a difficult choice in deciding which models to follow.

Even as we praise the American foundations for their relative understanding and flexibility, we should remember that foundations must invest in their information base and knowledge of trends within the third sector or they may slowly lose sight of potential programme areas worthy of support. Distant from the region in which they work, donors find it extremely difficult to measure impact on an ongoing basis. This is not to say that expensive regional offices should be set up by anyone who ever devoted a dollar to civil society development in Central and Eastern Europe, nor does it assume that regional or local offices might not be as isolated as those in New York. Whether done from headquarters or from local offices, the labour-intensive work of identifying more reliable, effective, innovative projects in a region in constant transition cannot be eliminated. Furthermore, if the basic system of reporting is not sufficient to measure the results of the project, an honest examination must take place to ensure that lessons will be learned. Simply hiring 'someone local' does not guarantee the needed knowledge, and the lack of understanding of professional standards compounds the problem.

Differences in approach are not only reflected in the presence of local offices, but also in the actual programmes and instruments wielded. Current programmes typically concentrate on two related areas: supporting the 'bricks' of civil society through training and direct grants to specific organizations, and, in much smaller measure, supporting the enabling environment in which CSOs and other organizations work. Almost all donors take on the brick-building roles of supporting individual organizations and their work: the PHARE Democracy Programme Micro Projects; PHARE Link Inter European NGOs (LIEN) Micro Projects; USAID DemNet; small embassy grant programmes of the US, Canada, the UK, and the Netherlands; grant programmes by the Mott Foundation, the Rockefeller Brothers Fund, the Ford Foundation, the Soros Foundation and the German Marshall Fund and many others. Only a few, like the ICNL legal environment programme and the regional networking programmes of DemNet have broadened their programme priorities to examine the legal, social, economic and political environment in which those organizations prosper or fail.

What is interesting about most brick-building initiatives is the presumed link between supporting individual organizations and strengthening a larger civil society. When donors are asked to think about the gaps between objectives and instruments, they often acknowledge that merely training and providing small grants to registered (often service-provision) CSOs will not necessarily contribute to the development of civil society. The very nature of funding through direct grants, however, makes it easy to slip into the same solution: give them money to do what they do best, and that will eventually serve the development of civil society. The fact that only registered, institutionalized organizations can receive grants makes it difficult to fund processes. It is also very difficult to tell how the actual work of support organizations, even if done in a professional manner, contributes to the development of civil society. Simply using the evocative expression 'capacity building' when in fact all what is happening is plain staff training does not help either. A more holistic approach to organizational development as well as a sector-wide approach in helping coalition building efforts is needed to contribute in a meaningful way to the development of civil society and its actors.

Grant making is certainly the most prominent instrument of support, varying in tone across donors. Direct core grants to existing organizations are typical of private foundations that have the necessary flexibility, and trust, to provide general-purpose grants to local CSOs. Less flexible project support (with or without overhead costs) is common with larger, official donors. Funds given to be re-granted locally are very rare, and endowments are virtually unknown. Self-initiated, headquarters-designed programming is characteristic of the German political foundations, whose unique policy restricts them to running their own programmes such as round-table talks, seminars and publications.

With the rarity of flexible, core-supporting grants, training has become the preferred vehicle for both grant seeking and grant making. The dangers of this emphasis, however, are at least twofold. One is the danger that without quality control, the sea of training can become a dangerous swamp land; in Hungary today, anybody can claim to be a trainer. A group of former rural cultural centre staff, laid off due to downsizing, may now enter the market as trainers after completing a couple of quick courses on communication and management skills. This way many support organizations become mechanic training centres providing factories. Although training can be very useful for organizations up to a certain level of development, more holistic capacity-building efforts can enhance an entire organization. Training that just develops one person's skills is not necessarily the answer to strengthening civil society writ large. Some donors are willing to make grants towards more comprehensive organizational development processes. Just one example of this is the Hungarian Foundation for Self-Reliance, which used parts of their general grant to undergo a capacity-building process using outside consultants who clarified the grey areas in the management of the office, sorted out conflicting job responsibilities and authorities and helped the entire organization as a team to grow over an extended period of time. They were encouraged and supported by their funders, the Ford Foundation, Mott and RBF to go though this process. Recently, more well-established organizations applied for and received PHARE Democracy funding to go through this process.

The second danger of an emphasis on training is irrelevance. By 1994, many of those who had regularly participated in foreign-sponsored training and who were first- and second-rank CSO leaders became disappointed by Western training styles. Experts flew in and out, trying over a weekend to teach Central and Eastern Europeans how to do things in a market economy and a democracy. These experts, the 'Marriott Brigades' as they are called in Poland, often left recipients disappointed because of their lack of knowledge about the local context, but the experience also inspired locals to find new ways of implementing foreign aid, especially technical assistance (see Box 3.7).

Non-material support is another instrument used by donors to influence civil society in Hungary. Financial restrictions can limit donors in actually transferring funds to informal groupings of civil society, even though they are often the most active players in mobilizing for certain causes. Linking such groups with one another and helping them with information, non-material resources and connections is a very useful, but often undervalued, way of support. There are certainly programmes that support networking among well-established organizations, such as the Civil Society Project of the European Foundation Centre, which works very well, or the

---

BOX 3.7: THE CIVIL SOCIETY DEVELOPMENT PROGRAM (CSDP)

One prime example of alternative training is an idea formulated in the Rebirth of Civil Society, a 1992 study funded by the Rockefeller Brothers Fund and written by Jenny Yancey and Daniel Siegel. Among their recommendations, an important idea emerged responding to the criticisms of Western methods. This idea was then taken on by many funders: a new Civil Society Development Program (CSDP) started 'training of trainers' courses, producing teams of well-trained CSO activists in Poland and Hungary to carry on the work of Western trainers but with a thorough knowledge of the local reality. These programmes are considered by both donors and local civil society leaders to be some of the most effective new means of developing the non-profit sector in Central and Eastern Europe. Parallel with the CSDP, the Johns Hopkins University's Institute of Policy Studies started their own Training of Trainers programme, building on their experience of in-depth non-profit research and workshops on CSO management held in the region.

Although some programme components were not fulfilled, useful lessons can be learned from the experiences of both programmes. In the CSDP, where newcomers to the sector were recruited and trained to become full-time trainers, push-and-pull factors decimated the number of final qualified trainers. Because many were newcomers, attracted to the programme by relatively high salaries and the opportunity to travel and study in the US, the group included some who were not fully committed to civil society. Only two of the original eight are still with the organization and, among those who left, only a few stayed in the CSO community as trainers or in other capacities. The Johns Hopkins programme, which selected a group of six young people already committed to the non-profit sector, had better success. Although leaving some of its promises unfulfilled, the programme left behind a good team of four out of the six originally trained, working in a loose but supportive professional cooperation around NIOK, the Nonprofit Information and Training Center.

East–East Program of the Soros Foundation. They link resource centres and national foundation offices and support them in developing joint projects. Despite the best of intentions, however, unregistered informal groups and movements are largely left out. This gap further reinforces the neglect of informal actors of civil society, those ad hoc movements that have played at times the most important roles in advocating key issues of human rights, free expression and anti-racism. It is this sector, unreachable by brick-building activities, in which civil society will continue to bloom.

Strong on training and project-by-project grant making, donors in Hungary have made a powerful impact on CSOs. That impact, however, is undermined by weaknesses in the very enabling environment in which organizations accomplish their civil tasks. The following section examines some of those weaknesses and the implications for donors.

Issues, Agendas, Trends, Concerns

The devolution of service provision, the impoverishment of political advocacy and the difference in the development of environmental groups and the rest of civil society are today's key issues and will affect how donors shape their agendas in days to come.

First among contemporary issues is the State's rush to hand over service provision to private companies. Movements like the Democratic Charter, the Danube Circle and other CSOs focused on large-scale social and political reform have become marginalized amid the rush to hand over social, health care and other services to local service organizations. Local governments, no longer able to finance services at the level required by law, contract CSOs hoping that, miraculously, they will do a better job. Such an arrangement can imperil local organizations and inhibit the development of a true civil society when the State only provides up to 60 per cent of the actual costs of the service and forces the non-profits to rely heavily on other (often foreign) sources of funding, which is not a sustainable scheme. Involving volunteers does help to a certain degree, but expecting people to work full time as volunteers is not viable. The need for advocacy on behalf of social service providers so that the State increases its support to an acceptable level of funding is obvious.

If funders support this service-substitution track, they may easily make CSOs dependent on foreign money. After all, foreign support began to reach CSOs during a period when the privatization of social services had become the number one challenge facing the State and non-profits alike. This dependency is one of the most dangerous new trends. Furthermore, although CSOs appear to be aware of this danger, there is little they can do about it. Often they are simply happy to have any State support for activities they undertake from their own initiative. They do not realize that the State is using them to deliver cheap services. Even donors have trouble avoiding the service trap. With the best intentions, donors intent on supporting the public policy process sometimes end up paying for social services; programmes that clearly state the objective of 'strengthening public policy-oriented NGOs' often end up providing training and small grants to service-oriented local CSOs. Part of the reason for this inadvertent focus is the very complexity of regional programming. Donors face tremendous challenges when dealing with many different countries, particularly if they focus on finding common objectives for countries as diverse as Poland and Albania. The outcome of both domestic and international forces has been that, step by step, CSOs in Hungary have become increasingly responsible for providing basic services.

Such problems surrounding service-oriented CSOs stand in stark contrast to the problems facing advocacy CSOs working in an extremely difficult political situation. Funded almost exclusively by scarce outside sources, and unlikely to receive government support, they are most vulnerable to collapse. There is very little support within Hungary for the work of CSOs to create mechanisms to channel public opinion and popular will to influence and check government actions. Similarly, little is heard in domestic circles about strategies to involve government in the support of civil society. The highly political division among leading groups of civil society, especially since the return to power of the ex-communists, is a long-standing problem that has led to a standstill in the development of this aspect of civil society. Former Communist Party officials masquerading as civil society activists are successful in attaining uncontrolled State funding under the current legislation. Using the most demagogical arguments, they were also behind the successful efforts in circumventing the creation of new, transparent mechanisms to control government funding for civil society.

For donors, the response to domestic ambivalence and the challenge of advocacy has been mixed. Funders with good intentions but lacking in-country knowledge sometimes choose implementing agencies unequipped with advocacy strategies. When the results fail to show up, another response is to avoid advocacy altogether on the grounds that advocacy groups are too urban or not sufficiently needy when measured against basic human needs criteria. 'You simply do not have public policy-oriented NGOs at the local level in Hungary', said one programme officer, 'There are academics and intellectuals in the capital city. Is that the most needy area'? (personal communication, Patrick Egan, programme officer of the USAID mission in Budapest). Still another way of avoiding support to advocacy groups has been to argue that as long as service providers are involved in the redistribution of resources and participate in the decision-making of a public policy issue, then public policy needs are being addressed. Any group of citizens who organize around an issue, even if they simply want to provide care for the elderly, become part of a public policy issue. As the same government support programme officer explained, trying to defend the failure of their local implementing partner in doing what the programme set out to do, namely supporting public policy-oriented NGOs: 'It is not fair to say that if you do not support public policy-oriented NGOs you are not supporting civil society in any meaning-ful way. Civil society includes many different animals which are just as important' (personal communication, participant at the European Foundation Center Annual General Assembly in Paris, November 1996).

One notable exception has been the nurturing of the advocacy functions of the CSO resource centres which have been at the core of some donors' attention for many years. The CS Mott Foundation is a devoted supporter and has helped independent centres get off the ground to serve as service centres for the CSO community. The centres' strategy, however, on whether to remain simply as service centres or to take on advocacy roles as well, is as yet unclear. Some say it is not wise to mix representa-tional functions with providing support services or grants to CSOs. In reality, it is rather the political position of donors such as the Soros Foundation in Hungary that prevents their resource centre from taking on advocacy functions.

A third issue within Hungarian civil society is the strength of the environmental sector. The quality of the environment is a local issue: clear, hot, pressing, tangible and popular. Also, it is both a regional and a global issue, and green CSOs have had great results organizing communities at all levels. Its roots are in the movements of the 1980s, which played a key role in bringing down the last reform-communist government, and throughout that history environmental issues have been the most successful in attracting significant outside resources from organizations such as the Environmental Partnership Program for Central and Eastern Europe (funded and coordinated by a consortium of donors led by the German Marshall Fund, the US government-funded Regional Environmental Center and various private foundations, including the Rockefeller Brothers Fund). The success of the environmental sector means that for the rest of civil society and other foreign donors in Hungary there is an uneven development throughout the CSO community. Environmentalist groups tend to form their own exclusive clubs, so they are a little isolated from the process of civil society now that they are well-established and professional. Unlike in the 1980s, when they had an effect on the entire political process through being able to mobilize popular protest, now they would not be able to do so, despite their individual successes as groups. Donors also tend to use them as vehicles for making safe bets: successful programmes tackling very visible, hot issues. If this tendency continues, the more painstaking work of helping the coalition-building, mobilizing and advocacy processes that only civil society can achieve will be further ignored and the very process of citizen participation and democracy will suffer.

Although these three sectors – service provision, advocacy, and environmental activism – are the focus of domestic and foreign support, no significant assistance has gone to other areas of civil society development, despite a clear need. In a country where corruption is overwhelming in the public service, there is a vast grey economy. Issues of transparency are not targeted by cross-sectoral groups, and there is virtually no independent investigative journalism, public control of government activities or watchdog organizations. These critical areas, perhaps lumped under the heading of 'enabling environment' features, have received almost no attention from the outside world.

Donors must retrofit their agendas to these domestic forces at the same time as they examine how existing emphases may need to be reshaped. Most important are concerns about the political affiliations that brought many funders to Hungary in the first place. Initially, funders did not have to concern themselves with the political affiliation of individual CSOs. In 1990, it seemed that only those CSOs that had former (often personal) ties with Western support organizations were funded. Many organizations, such as the Hungarian Foundation for Self-Reliance, were established with foreign money in the first place. Later on, when the former Communist Party won the 1994 elections and brought once discredited allies back into important positions in society, funders had to face the issue of political alliance. It was, of course, politically embarrassing to be caught cooperating with people or organizations that had shady histories or close ties with the pre-1989 Communist government. Anecdotal evidence suggests that donors have chosen the least risky solution: instead of trying to untangle the authenticity of organizations and their leadership, many funders have adopted a least-controversial 'don't ask, don't tell' policy, which has meant not asking where an organization is coming from but where it is going.

This approach may end up as a misdirected investment, however. Although one might imagine that those with questionable political affiliations would be scrupulously transparent in managing their newly-established organizations, it is striking to see how slow some leaders are in adapting to new standards in management, financial reporting and transparency in the use of funds. All this happens in a country where corruption is high in the public service, and the CSO sector is largely understood as a smart vehicle for laundering money. Fraud remains a serious problem for Hungarian civil society agencies. Of course, involvement in any local political scandal can be uncomfortable for diplomatic missions or multilateral agencies. The result has been reluctance to publicize fraud, thinking that it is better to avoid scandal in favour of blacklisting dubious organizations. The outcome, however, has not been to shake loose questionable, 'inauthentic' agencies, but merely to ignore them once the damage is done. The difficult political decisions remain unanswered, and the continuing presence of fraudulent organizations, downplayed by donors, undermines public faith in the whole of civil society.

Some of the lessons learned in the first half of the 1990s, however, have affected the menu of new interests expressed by donors in Hungary. By mid-decade, a number of elements were in place: a focus on supporting particular kinds of CSOs, an underground wariness of political matters, a switch to service provision, the development of resource centres and basic training in CSO management. What new emphases have arisen since? The rest of this section looks at some of these new trends: a switch to East–East exchanges, a growing emphasis on sustainability and a focus on 'sexy' issues.

A promising new type of programming has recently emerged. East–East and East–South networking is becoming a successful and relatively cheaper means of skill transfer than West–East exchanges. Funding Central European consultants to go to Southern or Eastern countries is often more effective and always cheaper then sending someone from the West. As one participant of the European Foundation Center Civil Society Mutual Support Programme reported, 'as a Lithuanian, I can learn so much more from a Pole than say, a German. It is incomparable' (personal communication, Peter Wiebler, Deputy Regional Director of the National Forum Foundation). Exchanges, twinning projects and mentoring projects between organizations in East–East, East–South, South–South relations are growing in popularity, including the National Forum Foundation (NFF)-run Regional DemNet Program of USAID. As Peter Wiebler of NFF points out, however, it can take quite some time to make the benefits of these programmes more obvious and tangible (radio interview, undersecretary of the Hungarian Ministry of Education and Culture).

Another definite interest among support organizations is the strengthening of sustainable institutions and procedures, even though discussions are at the earliest stage. Recently, funding agencies that have announced their exit dates have shown a clear interest in creating mechanisms for leveraging local support while they pull out quietly. USAID, for example, has suddenly become very active in coordinating with funders, organizing donor meetings and talking to European funding agencies more intensively. Funders have also started to back programmes that promote corporate citizenship among prosperous companies, attempting to build a sustainable resource base for CSOs after major foreign funders are phased out. It is always the civil society side of the potential corporate–non-profit partnership, however, that takes the initiative.

Another trend has been the introduction of unfamiliar issues on to the Hungarian social and political agenda. Ironically, what foreign donors find most pressing are the areas that are often the least popular among locals: human rights, women's rights and the Roma and other minorities; conflict management; multi-culturalism; and tolerance. These issues, with a clearly Western set of ideas behind them, are not always in the forefront of civil society debates in Central and Eastern European societies, and their local financial support is negligible. Although these priorities are certainly valid, donors will face resistance from local voices that resent foreign agenda making. There are simply certain issues over which Hungarian organizations cannot absorb the enthusiasm of donors.

The record in Hungary, for example, is that projects concerning women are likely to be funded by foreign organizations even if the local CSO is far from sincere. This Western enthusiasm, despite inappropriate or insincere local support, has meant that funding has been granted to groups such as the former communist ally, the Hungarian Women's Alliance, which cannot be said to be working on behalf of Hungarian women. The lesson is clear. Foreign programmes meant to address 'women's issues' must first address consciousness raising in a country-specific manner. Hungary's situation is unusual because, under the past regime, women gained many of the 'rights' that Western women are still fighting for. Yet women's status is far from equal as they continue to be expected to perform housework in addition to underpaid and undervalued wage labour. It is perhaps ironic that Hungarian organizations that promote a traditional role for women are the ones that represent an alternative approach: the right to choose between career and home. Such a choice is simply not realistic in today's economically vulnerable Hungary.

The resistance to new issues is not always the case, however. For example, the rights of the Roma people, almost universally discriminated against in Eastern Europe, have been of keen interest to Western funders. The Roma face racism and extreme discrimination in addition to official and unofficial persecution, and the protection of their rights has become topical both in Hungary and among foreign donors, and that joint interest has recently created models for programmes funded by the Hungarian government. Growing in-country support is thus a potential success story because commitment shown by Western donors has raised awareness and encouraged the local authorities to act as well.

What donors have *not* done is to look at the appropriate roles of government. They do not push governments hard enough to regard CSOs as anything other than alternative contractors. Recently, a government official in Hungary clearly voiced the political goal of the government on passing the legislation on non-profits: 'Yes, it is kind of a business deal, if you will. We want them to take over social services that the State will not provide in the future. We even provide part of the costs. In exchange, we want to know how they spend the money' (personal communication, participant at European Foundation Centre Annual General Assembly in Paris, November 1996). No sweet talk here on working with civil society to shape the future of our country and create a better world. Hungarian government officials talk about the importance of democratic institutions, procedures and practices in public life as if they were no more than empty slogans. The membership criteria of the European Union should make governments start thinking about how they are going to ensure the stability and proper functioning of democratic institutions that are guarding human rights, as it is prescribed in the Copenhagen documents. Sadly, however, this is not the case. Indeed, after a short, initial period of a relatively liberal and enabling legal environment, the government tightened its policies on the regulation of CSOs almost to the point of hostility. Because a number of cases of fraud had occurred as a consequence of earlier liberal regulations, the State was quick to reduce benefits instead of more strictly enforcing an enabling regulatory framework that would have weeded out abuses but not punished the whole of the CSO community. As we await the passing of the new legislation, the real danger is not the introduction of hostile regulations, but of a vision that regards civil society as a contractor for service provision, rather than as an ally to shape State policies and to enforce human, minority and other civil rights that are guaranteed on paper only.

Relationships of Power

The last part of this chapter stands back from the mechanics of the relationship between donors and CSOs in Hungary and examines the power dimensions of their dealings. Power dynamics between civil society and the donor community, between civil society and the national government and between the government and the donor community all pass under the microscope in an effort to see the potential of a strong civil society emerging from these seemingly divergent efforts.

First among concerns for practitioners in the field is the locus of decision-making for programmes and projects destined for Hungary. Information from interviews suggests that the majority of programmes are devised either in agency headquarters or, in the case of government programmes, at even higher policy levels. The USAID Democracy Network

Program, for example, was originally designed by the National Security Council, whereas the basic idea of the PHARE Democracy Programme was initiated by a British Euro-MP.

The concern is rooted in the long-term viability of civil projects in the country. Activists and others are troubled by the extent to which donors depend on foreigners rather than use local resources, including staff. At the outset, most donors chose not to work with locals at all, and some continue this practice even today. Some prefer to deal with a foreigner who may or may not be familiar with the region rather than risk handing the management of an expensive programme to an unknown local. A typical experience is described by a participant at a recent European Foundation Centre Funding East Workshop:

> *For a long period of time in the beginning of a project, when foreign experts come to teach locals, the real learning is happening on the part of the foreign experts who come in, get familiarized with the local circumstances and learn about the needs. In the case of a two- to three-year long programme, just by the time the programme finishes, will they really understand how things work here.* (personal communication, participant at the European Foundation Centre Annual General Assembly in Paris, November 1996)

Another important concern is the rigid requirement to focus on legally registered entities at the expense of unformalized groupings. It is important to underscore that almost all donor activity involves transferring funds from one legal entity to another. Only established, registered organizations with annual budgets, ongoing activities and staff are potential recipients of material support. Even though informal movements such as the Democratic Charter and the Danube Circle have played a major role in pushing political transition, they received little attention from foreign bodies. Ineligible for funding as informal groups, movements are either pushed towards formalization, which often leads to a loss of momentum, or are marginalized in the 'formal' CSO world occupied by funders. This observation is not made to blame funders required by law or internal regulations to support formal groups, nor is it to say that support to formal groups is in vain. Indeed, much of that support was needed, timely and relatively well-targeted. The point here is that formal organizations are only one part of a larger civil society in Hungary.

Another key problem is the focus on elites. Since support often does not go beyond the capital (with some exceptions, see Box 3.8), cross-sectoral alliances are hard to find other than in the alliance of urban elites. With former communists returning to power, new elites are forming and, in some cases, old elites are reappearing. In the early years of transition, the old elites were professionally less developed, didn't talk the civil society talk, didn't chant the democracy mantra, and were, therefore, not chosen as partners by donors. Now, with some years of experience in the

---

Box 3.8: Carpathian Euroregion Project

One important example for regional cooperation outside the capital cities is the Mott Foundation-funded Carpathian Euroregion project. The project is unusual because it not only moves away from the usual grantee groups in urban areas, but it also goes to the most isolated, poorest areas of five countries in Central and Eastern Europe. The innovative idea of directly connecting marginalized regions into globalization and fostering local community development will certainly provide some important lessons, especially about the power relations between civil society, government and donors.

CSO sector and extensive experience in local bureaucracy, many have re-found their voices, realizing that skills continue to work within the new power structure. Gaining confidence in the domestic political arena, they have all the reason in the world to push for international recognition. The new generation that did not collaborate with the former regime has little means to stop that re-emergence, other than to promote more professional work and more genuine approaches. But the younger generation is also part of elite; they are simply a new elite, trained abroad, and cosmopolitan in their outlook. For donors, it may take a while to discern what is really behind today's alliances and leading organizations.

A further issue is the threat of dependency and the lack of sustainability. The major problem is that donors that arrived in 1990 or later started talking about phasing out almost immediately, without first devoting programmes to address sustainability. Donors helped to set up institutions, strengthened them by funding, but did not do more for their sustainability than to urge them to find local sources, simplistically advising them to 'be businesslike, wear a tie, be precise, be professional'. The problems, of course, centre not only on a lack of fundraising skills, but also on the neglect from the public sector and the crucial absence of a philanthropic tradition among formerly State-run companies or small, new private businesses. Without local philanthropy, endowments, domestic government support or foreign funding, the reality is that many key organizations created by foreign donors will simply cease to exist. The most vulnerable are umbrella organizations, re-granting agencies and advocacy groups and those dealing with difficult or unpopular issues, like support to the Roma. Those that continue will be sub-contracting organizations of the government, living partly from client fees. If representative bodies, advocacy groups and public policy-oriented CSOs are treated as service organizations, the preservation of an alternative voice will be left to the mercy of local or national governments. Touchy political issues will not be represented in this country if independent sources outside government, business and politics do not act in the public interest.

How will donors eventually find ways to help the transition between their phase-out and the rise of local supporters? That question is still unanswered. The truth is that they do not have any experience to draw upon; they haven't pulled out from any major geographic area in the history of aid intervention. If Central and Eastern Europe is to be the first witness of withdrawal in the history of international development, plenty of careful consideration and planning must be part of the exit strategy.

In time, however, sustainability is certainly viable. The Johns Hopkins team's comparative third sector research surprised us recently by showing that Hungary has proportionally the highest private giving among industrialized countries (US, UK, France, Germany, Sweden, Italy, Hungary, Japan) (Anheier and Salamon, 1996) and one of the lowest in State support. Of all CSO sources of income, about 60 per cent comes from earned income (selling services), 20 per cent from the State and 20 per cent from private sources (the seven-country average is around 50, 40 and 10 per cent, respectively). In Germany, the State accounts for 68 per cent of all income, and even in the US, where philanthropy is considered to be the most developed in the world, only 19 per cent comes from private sources (Kuti, 1996). These findings suggest that domestic contributions may play an even greater role in supporting CSOs as the country's economy grows. It will be decades, however, before domestic contributions are significant enough to match foreign support, and this generosity cannot make up for the current trends in State funding.

Impact to Date

It is hard to determine the overall impact of donors on the development of a rooted, active civil society. In the first instance, it is important to underline that the amount donors devoted to civil society development in the region is insignificant. The total support to programmes that contribute in any meaningful way to the development of civil society is markedly low compared to the amounts devoted to all other programmes supporting reforms. Perhaps only 5 to 10 per cent of all support is targeted at civil endeavours, an estimate that partly depends on an ever-changing classification of projects. Whether a typical 'civil society development project' is listed under 'democracy', 'non-profit sector', 'community development', 'human rights' or even 'media' programme categories defines where the amounts devoted to that programme will end up in financial reports and statistics.

The creation of strong key organizations and a broader civil elite, however, is certainly an outcome of donor activity. Foreign support has created and strengthened a small number of strong organizations now establishing roots in the local culture while maintaining and promoting professional and democratic standards in their everyday activities. The civil elite, funded by foreign sources, is not only able to formulate good proposals but also has, by now, years of experience in spending foreign donations responsibly and with formal accountability. Although that example may be valuable to the rest of civil society in Hungary, there remains none the less a huge gap between the handful of elite members and the struggling tens of thousands; recent militant waves of anti-elitist opinion against organizations supported by international sources are a warning sign.

Furthermore, the impact of foreign funding on civil society beyond the institutionalization of CSOs is unclear. The work of CSOs affects the lives of many, but the link between those activities and a stronger overall civil society, in its incarnation as a political process, it is not easy to discern. Indeed, how can one measure the intangible goals of awareness-raising, coalition-building and mobilizing around common issues? Sub-sectors of civil society, however, seem to have gained confidence and have organized around concrete issues such as the human rights of ethnic minorities, the disabled, equal opportunities for all types of educational institutions, children's rights, environmental concerns and other such issues. In each area of activity, there are numerous service-providing organizations and one or two advocacy groups. The survival of those advocacy groups in particular is an important element in the development of a society-wide 'mechanism' that will eventually bring more particular and common concerns to public policymakers.

What conclusions can we then make about donor work in Hungary? Certainly, the major challenge that lies ahead for donors and their partners is analyzing current trends and deciding what lines of action they should take. Although EU membership is on the horizon for most countries in the region, serious divisions within societies, growing inequalities and a general disenchantment with democracy remains. Central and Eastern Europe has a long way to go towards a stable and prosperous democracy and an even longer way to travel towards a cooperative, active and vocal civil society – perhaps a lot longer then anyone expected.

The recognition of the need for a long-term approach is more visible in circles of both donors and recipients. Some donors, for example, may need to reconsider their decision on phasing out. The donors who decide to stay in the region also need to decide whether they want to contribute to the growth of the CSO sector in a quantitative sense, supporting new organizations that are more and more service oriented, or whether they want to take on the more time-consuming and labour-intensive work of strengthening civil society in qualitative ways as well by focusing on larger enabling environment factors.

If they choose this larger and more difficult task, they will find partners in the region but they will need to undertake that search carefully. In each and every sector, there is at least one relatively stable, highly experienced, often voluntary group doing advocacy work. If donors want to increase the potential of civil society to enact sustainable social and political change, they need to make the difficult political choices in supporting advocacy groups rather than their service-provision counterparts alone. Furthermore, it is important to complement this approach with direct work with the government, pushing for active public service co-operation with civil society. Other crucial functions are also in need of support: single-issue pressure groups serve as important watchdogs working closely with independent journalists to monitor government, investigate corruption in privatization or uncover abuses of power. The media is another area in need of independent assistance. Journalists in Hungary are under-educated and improperly trained, and societal respect for their work is low because many are considered to be among the prime collaborators of the former authoritarian regime. Self-censorship has always been a factor, and with the changes in the ownership of the media, the old habits of self-imposed censorship are reappearing; this time, in the service of the new media owners and Western media consortia. Improving the legal environment for CSOs has also been a pressing issue for a long time and great efforts were made by donors to help in drafting a new, comprehensive non-profit law in Hungary. Much of that investment, however, was recently wasted when major components of the law were altered through political battles between the socialist and liberal governing parties. The very idea of a transparent system for scrutinizing non-profits was unacceptable for those who still use the old boys' network to receive government funds for their organizations.

Donors must, therefore, look again at the question of supporting broader policy alliances in the CSO sector. That move may mean nurturing one-issue organizations or umbrella organizations that go beyond serving their members to take on advocacy functions. According to many accounts, the experience to date in trying to create a representative umbrella organization to voice unified positions has been bitter. After many attempts, both issue-oriented umbrella organizations and donors gave up the idea. Without a representative coalition in place that could negotiate with government, the potential scenarios for civil society and government relations are not very encouraging.

What scenarios can be forecast, then? In her excellent analysis on the future of CSO-government relations in Hungary, Éva Kuti draws up three story lines for the development of CSOs. The worst scenario would be the dismantling of existing cooperation between the government and CSOs, leaving the sector without any measure of public support. An even more confrontational relationship may develop, preventing the further evolution of the CSO community.

The second, more likely, scenario describes government use of CSOs simply as contractors to deliver services. In that vision, government support would be exclusively devoted to those who provide State-approved or ordered services, creating a small but professional financially stable non-profit sector as part of the market economy, while ignoring those that aim at influencing policy and decision-making on issues affecting society.

The third is an ideal scenario, in which government regards CSOs as partners in identifying and meeting social needs and in formulating and implementing social policy. The government would in that case cooperate with civil society and thus set an example in the opening regions of Central Asia, the former Soviet Union and the former Yugoslavia. Thus, the lessons learnt from the past decade of foreign support to civil society in Central and Eastern Europe may be more successfully applied in the brave new worlds of the Eastern bloc.

4 SRI LANKA: CIVIL SOCIETY, THE NATION AND THE STATE-BUILDING CHALLENGE

Paikiasothy Saravanamuttu

This chapter examines the debate on civil society in Sri Lanka. This debate is important because it is deeply enmeshed with the history of nation and statebuilding and the violence that has accompanied it. It highlights the asymmetries in power relationships between civil society organizations and the State. Consequently an underlying theme has been that civil society in Sri Lanka needs to be strengthened and to strengthen itself. Civil society organizations (CSOs) themselves must be more vigilant and conscious about preserving and expanding their democratic space. Donors have a role to play here and, in the case of both the civil society groups and the donors, the success or failure of their endeavours hinges on their appreciation of the political environment, of getting the big picture.

The chapter thus begins with a historical mapping of civil society before discussing the political context of today's debates, including the controversial NGO Commission. It is only against this political background that the work on the international donor community can be evaluated. One of the chapter's conclusions is that donors' professed commitment to democracy, human rights and governance sits very uncomfortably with claims of non-intervention in the affairs of a developing country. In Sri Lanka, a case for intervention – albeit cautious and careful and long-term – must surely be made.

MAPPING CIVIL SOCIETY

Understood as the voluntary and professional associations formed in response to the needs of society at large, civil society has been in existence since pre-colonial times in Sri Lanka. It has been associated with religion, the economy and modes of production and with the fostering of civic virtues. It is with the growth of the centralizing tendencies of the State, both colonial and post-colonial, that the spread of these organizations at the grass roots has been checked and weakened. As the coordination of land, irrigation and food production, as well as village administration, have been taken over by central government agencies, the functional *raison d'être* of these local organizations has been affected accordingly.

Historically, as this state domination affected the economic sphere, local organizations were restricted to the religious and cultural spheres. Here too, political and social developments conditioned their growth. In the nineteenth century, under colonial rule, Christian missionary organizations with patronage from the centre moved into the fields of education and social welfare. Christian organizations such as the Baptist Mission (1802), the Wesleyan Missionary Society (1814), the Church Missionary Society (1818), the Young Men's Christian Association and Young Women's Christian Association (1882) and the Salvation Army (1883) were established in this period.

The indigenous reaction to colonial rule and the dominance of these organizations in the fields of education, culture and social welfare led to a revival of Buddhist and Hindu organizations. The Buddhist Theosophical Society (1880), Mahabodhi Society (1890), Young Men's Buddhist Association (1897), Ramakrishna Mission (1899), Vivekananda Society (1902), All Ceylon Buddhist Congress (1918) and Muslim Education Society (1890) were all products of this revivalist and early nationalist movement in the late nineteenth and early twentieth centuries. The educational institutions they established were eventually included into the centrally managed school system as a result of effective lobbying. In the post-independence era, the extension of State patronage to religious-based organizations culminated in Buddhism, the religion of the majority Sinhalese community, giving the 'foremost' place in the constitution and in the creation of ministries for Buddhist, Hindu and Muslim affairs.

Interestingly, the relationship between the State and NGOs was a concern to the State in the immediate prelude to independence in 1948. In 1946, a Social Services Commission was set up. On the basis of its recommendations, in 1948 a Department of Social Services was established, with responsibility for the provision of social welfare services to women, children, elders, paupers and wage labour, with a Central Council of Social Services (CCSS) to coordinate all voluntary social service organizations in the non-governmental sector.

It is clear, therefore, that the need to lay down an asymmetrical relationship between the NGOs and the State in favour of the latter was embedded in the attitudes of the ruling elite from the outset of independence. It was justified on the grounds of the need to ensure accountability and transparency in the internal management of the NGOs. The argument appears to have been that 'if any organizations are given complete freedom without any State intervention they tend to overstep the limits that they have to observe... They must also be protected from mis-appropriation of funds (from either local or foreign donors) by their employees or others. Therefore any right-thinking person would agree that there must be a mechanism to control and supervise these activities' (de Silva, 1981: 29).

As the post-colonial State entered the developmental field, there was a mushrooming of State-managed co-operative, rural development and thrift and credit societies. They developed alongside independent grassroots organizations such as the Federation of Thrift and Credit Societies (SANAJA). The demands of development, however, especially the increasing financial costs involved and the greater role for money in the process, led to a diminution in the role of the voluntary organizations, an increasing role for the State and the advent of foreign donor assistance.

Internationally too, by the 1950s, with the rise of the People's Republic of China and the Indochinese and Korean wars, the cold war had come to Asia to stay. By the 1960s, the battle was joined for the 'hearts and minds' of the peoples of the world, the majority of whom were in the developing world.

At the same time as governments in the developing world were pulled into the vortex of superpower competition and rivalry, at home the challenge of nation and State-building was in full swing. This meant that the sovereign nation-State, assumed at the point of the transfer of power, had to be created now that the transfer had been effected.

Better described as 'state–nation' rather than nation–state as far as the principal organ of collective political organization was concerned, the State had to create the 'nation' as well as live up to its pretensions as the defender against external attack and the provider of the welfare and well-being of its citizens. Paradoxically, however, all this had to be accomplished at a time when it was more and more difficult for any State, least of all a developing one, to do so.

Moreover, neither fully independent, nor sovereign, nor a nation, the State had to project itself as protector and provider at the same time as the global ideological rivalry was being grafted upon the nation- and state-building challenge. By the 1970s, international interdependence, the easing in cold war tensions and the expansion of the market contributed to exposing the widening disjunction between the pretensions and performance of the State. As the State could not admit to the limits of its competence, it moved from protector and provider to predator.

The Context of Civil Society

It is pertinent at this point to give an overview of the political and socio-economic developments in Sri Lanka so that the arguments about civil society in the first three decades of independence can be put into context. By the 1980s, the relationship between civil society and the State had come to be recognized as essentially adversarial for those elements of civil society that resolutely refused to be co-opted by it.

The perception of Sri Lanka as a textbook liberal democracy with high quality of life indices and literacy, a multi-party system and regular elections with universal franchise granted as far back as 1931 has been replaced by that of a country torn apart by civil strife and ethnic conflict. Sri Lanka still boasts an adult literacy rate of 90 per cent, a human index development value of 0.698, an infant mortality rate of 17 per 1,000 live births and life expectancy at birth of 72 years. On the basis of life expectancy, education and income, Sri Lanka is ranked 89th out of 174 countries in the 1996 United Nations Development Programme (UNDP) Human Development Index. Yet the country has neither sustained the image of its textbook description or fulfilled the economic potential endowed it at independence.

A number of arguments have been advanced in explanation. What is relevant, however, for the purposes of this chapter, is to outline those events that have undermined pluralism and democracy and have encroached upon the space occupied by civil society and the space available for its development. It is important to understand the State in understanding civil society.

There are two major issues that dominate the discussion on Sri Lanka: the composition of the nation, as exemplified by the ethnic conflict, and the nature of the State in its ongoing process of constitutional reform. These two issues, along with the evolution of the market economy on which there is currently a societal consensus, structure the context in which civil society has to operate.

At independence in 1948, power in Sri Lanka was passed on to an Anglicized successor elite drawn from all ethnic communities; not as a result of a mass independence struggle. And when adult universal franchise was granted in 1931, it was the first Afro-Asian colony to be so favoured. Although there were manifestations of ethnic tension in this period up to independence, they were managed within the framework of the liberal democratic and parliamentary ethos of the Anglicized elite.

The demands of the principal minority ethnic community, the Tamils, for communal representation in the legislature were rejected by the colonial authorities. Tamil leaders adopted a strategy of parliamentary support to and participation in majority Sinhalese governments in exchange for measures safeguarding minority interests. Political accommodation, although subscribed to in principle, was not fully reflected in practice by government policy. Despite setbacks, the constitutionalist and parliamentary consensus to survived until the 1970s when it finally eroded.

The year 1956 was a watershed year in Sri Lanka's political development and its repercussions are still being felt. In 1956, a centre-left coalition of Sinhalese populist forces led by SWRD Bandaranaike swept to power having won overwhelmingly in the south of the country. In the Tamil north, the Federal Party, committed to a Sri Lankan State along those lines, was similarly favoured by that electorate.

The significance of this election was that it facilitated the first major challenge to the elite consensus and to the strategy of political accommodation. Ethnic populism was exploited for partisan advantage and, until a bipartisan accord signed by the President and the Leader of the Opposition in 1997, explicit identification with ethnic populism has been seen as crucial to electoral success. Accordingly, older and more divisive identities were acknowledged as the ultimate sources of political power, and the inability of the elite consensus to mould them into a durable national identity was exposed.

The 1956 government made Sinhala, the language of the majority community, the official language of the country, and embarked upon a programme of nationalization. Meant to strike at the heart of the Anglicized elite's monopoly of power, the official language policy sparked off communal riots and open ethnic conflict. Tamil fears were aroused that this would institutionalize the hegemony of the majority community and block minority access to social mobility through education and employment. Attempts by the government to mitigate the effects of its language policy through a measure of devolution to regional councils were abandoned in the face of opposition mounted by chauvinist elements in the south. During the next two decades, ethnic relations deteriorated and the residual vitality of the elite consensus proved inadequate to pre-empt or prevent a slide towards the Tamil secessionist demand backed up with armed force.

By the 1970s, the elite consensus on parliamentary democracy collapsed and violence came to be enshrined as the effective arbiter of political grievance. Although two governments enjoyed landslide electoral wins in this decade, the first in 1970 with a two-thirds majority and the second in 1977 with a five-sixths majority and two autochthonous constitutions were promulgated in 1972 and 1978, the 1970s also witnessed the armed challenge to the State and to the idea of the nation. The first was represented by the southern youth insurgency and the second, the armed challenge to the idea of a nation underpinned by majoritarian democracy in a unitary State, was expressed by secessionism in the Tamil north, spearheaded again by the youth.

As authoritarianism became the order of the day in the 1970s with increased bureaucratization and centralization in the name of the people, the State encroached more and more upon the space inhabited by civil society. Majoritarian democracy was enshrined in the constitution with provisions ensuring pre-eminence for both the religion and the language of the majority community. Professing to socialism, the first government of this decade the United Front (UF) left and centre left coalition, extended State control over the economy, paralleling the authoritarianism in the polity.

The first youth insurgency in the south, headed by the leftist Janata Vimukthi Peramuna (JVP) or People's Liberation Front, was squashed by a preponderance of force in 1971. The government recovered and embarked upon a series of radical statist reforms in an effort to re-establish its ideological credentials and secure its hold on power. It also arbitrarily extended its term in office, and if 1956 had meant the capture of power on behalf of the majority community, 1970 was to represent the capture of power on behalf of the party.

With control over economic resources and access to them, party affiliation and allegiance came to be institutionalized and ranked higher than merit in attaining employment. Partisan politicization of society became the accepted *modus operandi* of the regime in power, except for a few notable pockets of resistance in civil society, of which the Civil Rights Movement (CRM), formed in 1971, is the oldest and most notable.

In 1977, the voters overwhelmingly rejected the experiment with socialism and the right wing United National Party (UNP) government was elected with a huge five-sixths majority. Under the UNP, the relegation of parliament to the role of a rubber stamp legislature, begun by the previous government, was completed and authoritarianism of the crudest variety allowed to run rampant. With the second autochthonous constitution of 1978, which ushered in an executive presidency on the grounds that economic development demanded a strong and stable executive, the checks and balances that characterize a parliamentary democracy and are vital to its health and strength were progressively eroded.

The former Prime Minister was deprived of her civic rights through a highly questionable procedure, judges' houses were stoned and the fines of police officers found guilty of offences were paid by the government and the officers were promoted. A series of constitutional amendments were enacted, the effect of which was to consolidate the ruling party's hold on power. Most notorious was the use of a referendum marred by violence and malpractice, to postpone a general election and extend the ruling party's hold on power to 11 years.

The acceptance of the cynical and undemocratic practices of the UNP regime was attributable to a considerably discredited and enfeebled opposition, the deterrent effect of creeping authoritarianism and the allure of the market economy that this government ushered in. There was money to be made, the depoliticization of society engineered by the regime to secure its hold on power was made easier by this. The shift was effected from a welfare-oriented economic development strategy to a growth-oriented strategy.

Democracy was to be secured by the market economy and the trickling down of its largesse to the mass of society. A 1992 study by the International Fund for Agricultural Development (IFAD) on 'The State of Rural Poverty' concluded that Sri Lanka had the most marked increase in rural poverty in the years 1965–88 among the 114 countries in the study. The World Bank's World Development Report of the same year found that income disparities in Sri Lanka had reached a point only below that of Brazil.

The increasing incivility of society and the regime's avowed goal of consolidating its stranglehold on power, was seriously shaken by open, armed ethnic conflict in 1983 and youth insurgency in the 1987–1989 period. The anti-democratic nature of the regime, the apparent callousness of its attitude towards the disadvantaged in society, coupled with unwillingness and inability to heed growing minority community grievances resulted in civil war on two fronts.

The insurgency in the south was ruthlessly crushed by counter-terror operations, deemed to be terrorism, nothing more or less and the attitude to ethnic conflict was not very much different. A temporary respite in the ethnic conflict was obtained through the intervention of India and the induction of an Indian Peacekeeping Force (IPKF) in July 1987.

The result was a measure of devolution at the provincial level, the expropriation of nationalist credentials on behalf of the majority community by the insurgents in the south in opposition to Indian intervention and further conflict in the north between the Indian forces and Tamil guerrillas. Without democratic space to vent their grievances, the youth experienced increasing anomie and alienation. When confronted with the sealing off of access to the sources of political and economic power, the youth took up arms – the ballot box and the parliamentary floor were not available to them.

In any event, the mediation of societal grievance through non-violent and parliamentary channels had become discredited by the inability of the elite consensus to live up to its pretensions and erect a system that facilitated the pursuit of the good life for all. Interestingly, the challengers to the State, the JVP, both in its 1971 ultra-left incarnation as well as in its role as the champion of Sinhala chauvinism in 1987–89 and the Liberation Tigers of Tamil Eelam (LTTE), were totally statist and even fascist in their ideology, method and orientation. This is still true of the LTTE. The JVP has entered the democratic mainstream and now holds a seat in the current Parliament.

Under the second UNP regime (1988/9–1993), the challenge to nation and State was at its height. The LTTE were at war with the Indian forces in the north and south, and the JVP laid siege to the political establishment on the grounds of its being undemocratic and traitorous for allowing direct Indian intervention in the nation-building exercise.

Ranasinghe Premadasa, who was elected to the presidency by the narrowest of margins in the 1988 presidential election, which was framed by widespread violence, was the first chief executive to come from outside the Anglicized elite, that had produced Sri Lanka's leaders since 1948. Ironically, the task of saving the political establishment fell on his shoulders.

The JVP insurgency was crushed in a massive counter-terror operation in which tens of thousands disappeared and perished. (The UN Working Group on Enforced and Involuntary Disappearances in its 1991 report stated that the number of disappearances in Sri Lanka between 1988 and 1990 relating to the JVP insurgency and its suppression was the highest recorded by the group up to that date.) A tactical alliance with the LTTE to get rid of the Indian forces succeeded in the short term, but did not prevent a resumption of hostilities between them and the Sri Lankan state by June 1990.

President Premadasa's formula for rule was a mixture of ruthlessness, nationalism and populism stemming both from the suspicion, paranoia and insecurity of the outsider as well as the conviction and commitment to succeed associated with that position. Invariably, he became the *bête noir* of human rights organizations and democracy activists who were as appalled by his methods as he was contemptuous of their concerns and convinced of their inability to share in his vision for the country.

The climate of fear and control engendered by the Premadasa regime and the brutality it presided over constitutes a key phase in the maturing of civil society as check and balance upon the State and of its ability to overcome the attempts by a repressive State to destroy it. The lines were drawn at the same time as they were blurred. Civil society was explicitly politicized in partisan terms.

In the economic development and welfare field, the Poverty Alleviation or Janasaviya Programme of the Premadasa regime ensured the marginal-ization of the NGOs in that arena. As one analyst observed, 'In effect, the NGOs were squeezed out of their main business (poverty alleviation). By the end of 1990 the NGOs had no particular role to play except in assisting the State' (Wanigaratne, 1997: 225).

During this 17-year period of UNP rule, a number of actions were taken by government to control the NGOs. In 1980, a Voluntary Social Service Organizations (Registration and Supervision) law was passed under which all social services organizations had to register with the Department of Social Services. The CCSS was enhanced to function as a umbrella body for NGOs and grassroots organizations under the aegis of the State and, in 1981, development NGOs set up the National NGO Council (NNGOC) for village-level NGOs and their affiliates (Wanigaratne, 1997: 223–4). In 1991, the Premadasa regime appointed an NGO Commission, which submitted its recommendations in 1993.

The Evolution of Civil Society: From Confrontation to Co-option ?

The content of these controls and their significance will be discussed in a later section of this chapter. Relevant sections of the Commission Report provide an insight into the concerns of the government and political estab-lishment regarding the relationship between the State and civil society at a point at which this relationship was characterized by antagonism and hostility.

Although the Commission was largely concerned with developmental NGOs, its deliberations and findings, nonetheless, encompass the entirety of the State – civil society relationship. It is clear that these concerns relate to the political role of civil society – the extent to which civil society action that arises out of a relationship with foreign agencies, and donor agencies in particular, constitutes a threat to national sovereignty and culture as interpreted by the government of the day. Included in this threat is the regime's concern for its own security and longevity.

Accordingly, the report emanated from a mindset critical and suspicious of NGOs as potentially unpatriotic and even subversive actors, when not inefficient and corrupt. The Commission clearly favoured a partnership between the State and civil society in the development arena and one in which the *raison d'être* was pre-eminent. It conceded a role to civil society as check and balance vis-à-vis the exercise of State power, but cautioned against an expansive interpretation of this as both unrealistic and dangerous.

The Commission agreed that the majority of the NGO community was above reproach and that 'we owe a certain amount of necessary development at the periphery to them'. It is the few that have 'transgressed their proper limitations' in areas of vital importance to the country such as political stability that are of concern (NGO Commission, 1993: 104). The Commission considered civil society as a Western concept:

> *It means that society is counter-posed to the Nation–State or State–Nation. It is claimed that Civil Society at one time embraced the whole of society and was co-terminus with it. Civil Society in its plenitude of powers and activity 'was the arena for organizing governance, material activities and intellectual, moral and cultural aspects of communities'. It is said that in the course of time and with the rise of the Nation–State, the State progressively delegitimized or destroyed the material base of Civil Society, constituted by voluntary organizations and has to a great extent appropriated even the ideological base of Civil Society by State control of education and the media, etc.* (NGO Commission, 1993: 118)

Despite the argument that civil society is a Western concept, the Commission saw 'affinities' between Eastern and Western models. Elaborating on the Gandhian distinction between the Lok Neeti (civil society) and the Raj Neeti (the State), it quoted Chandra de Fonseka:

> *Fundamentally, Lok Neeti's concern is with the issues of Right, Power, the dissolution (not the seizure) of centralized Raj Neeti (State Power) into Local Forums of Lok Neeti (People's Power) among the myriad small, human scale, primary scale communities in each society with the mobilization of these local forms of Lok Neeti as the building blocks of societal powers through flexible federal organization, to achieve the critical mass that would establish and maintain mastery over Raj Neeti.* (NGO commission, 1993: 119)

The Commission argument is that the existing NGOs, particularly the international development NGOs, do not conform to the Lok Neeti idea of civil society because they are not grassroots organizations (GROs) but dispensable secondary or intermediary organizations. Their true function should be to augment these primary organizations and by doing so remove the need for NGOs.

The Commission also called for regional linkages between NGOs that would not carry the dangers to national sovereignty and security as could be the case with Northern NGOs. The Commission agreed that 'authentic' GROs would be the ideal. It cautioned, however, against the manipulation of these organizations, which, it stated, it knew occurred. Funding was acceptable as long as it was not tantamount to control and alien influence and was achieved with transparency and equal respect. There was a role for the 'moderate notion' of civil society in Sri Lanka according to the Commission, and the role of NGOs within it was to work towards participatory democracy at the grassroots (NGO Commission, 1993: 128).

In doing so, the Commission opined, NGOs could 'cooperate on reasonable terms' with the State. They should at all times maintain their integrity and not become 'a mere extension service of the Government.' However,

> *...their main usefulness may lie elsewhere... it would be more profitable if the immediate attention is turned to ensure that the democratic system functions without distortion and the people exercise their franchise with understanding and a sense of maturity and a due sense of responsibility. This calls for moral regeneration ....* (NGO Commission, 1993: 128)

Approvingly, the Commission noted a programme along these lines in Thailand entitled 'Land of Dharma, Land of Gold and Prosperity'. It was, the Commission noted, a government initiative with an emphasis on the moral element.

The innate conservatism and nationalism of the Commission was revealed in its discussion of the explicitly political role of NGOs. NGOs had a duty to play their role in constructively criticizing the government, but not 'indiscriminately'. This required them to be wary of 'larger international forces' exploiting the Third World. Indeed:

> *There would be occasions when silence is an option. There would be occasions where the destructive or even constructive criticism may burden or weaken the State which may be placed at odds battling devious and designing powerful international forces.* (NGO Commission, 1993: 139)

The Commission also stated that if governments wanted to avoid the risk of aid being tied to human rights and even cut as a consequence of NGO criticism of the government's record in this field, it was incumbent upon governments to improve their record. At this point it is pertinent to address the overall evolution of civil society in the context of challenge and confrontation by an increasingly authoritarian State. One analyst notes that:

> *Sri Lankan society is structured upon a monolithic political base. It is monolithic to the extent that all institutions and interests outside political society (i.e., those that should strictly belong to the civil society) draw their power, usually to a greater and sometimes lesser extent, not from their own social bases but from political society itself. Civil society organizations and formations deriving the bulk of their power from sources independent of political society are by and large not a feature of the Sri Lankan social scene. Religious organizations provide the only possible exception.*
> (Fernando, 1997: 2)

Fernando's further point is valid in that given the extent of the partisan politicization of civil society, CSOs pursue and attain their interests by exploiting the competition within political society as well as through it. As a consequence, there is a thin line between civil society groups being political and being politically partisan. The notion of civil society organizations formed around issues is lost when they become more concerned with the impact upon their partisan political allegiance and its source.

As a result of what happened in the 1970s and the ensuing 17 years of right-wing UNP rule, a number of changes occurred. Although the trade union movement, which in any event was aligned to the left in political parties, was considerably weakened, a number of chambers of commerce and private sector organizations were established. With the dismantling of the welfare State and the introduction of structural adjustment conditionality in the economy, a number of NGOs sprang up to avail themselves of foreign funds to fill the gap in the provision of welfare services previously provided by the State.

When the second UNP regime (1989–93), more populist and repressive than its predecessor, embarked upon its Poverty Alleviation or Janasaviya Programme, however, a number of these NGOs were absorbed within it. As the chapters on Kenya and Peru attest, this is not an uncommon occurrence in the developing world. Even large, well-established organizations were affected, although not absorbed, by the tide of populism, coinciding in this case with the eagerness of the World Bank to meet its commitments to a poverty agenda. The experience of SANASA is illustrative.

In 1985, SANASA became the rural delivery mechanism for the USAID funded Million Houses Programme (MHP) implemented by the National Housing Development Authority (NHDA). The programme was a pet project of Prime Minister and later President Premadasa, and political pressure played its part in obtaining SANASA involvement. Once initiated, a number of problems arose.

Many new societies were formed to obtain subsidised credit, poor villagers were excluded, political interference impeded the disbursement of loans and SANASA staff were exposed to death threats from the JVP for participating in a government programme. Moreover, before the 1988 presidential election, the government announced that 'poor people' would not have to pay the instalments on their MHP loans.

One analysis notes that, as a consequence, SANASA experienced an immediate decrease in repayments and widespread default, leaving it 'wary' of involvement in financial arrangements with the government (Hulme et al., 1994: 8). This analysis goes on to argue that, as a result of this experience, SANASA was reluctant to work with the Janasaviya Trust Fund (JTF). As the fund bypassed SANASA, it also threatened to undermine its federal structure, which had facilitated the expansion of thrift and credit cooperatives. The analysis notes that 'in effect the World Bank is financing institutional destruction' (Hulme et al., 1994: 63–64).

The persistence of armed ethnic conflict in turn spawned CSOs engaged in relief and rehabilitation work with refugees and the internally displaced. Aspersions were invariably cast on the credibility of some. From the mid 1980s and up to the present, in addition to partisan political affiliation, sympathy for either side of the ethnic divide is both an inhibiting factor in the growth of civil society as well as a handy reference point for impugning its integrity.

It was during the 1980s that many CSOs committed to a human rights, ethnic reconciliation and democratic governance came into being. Some of them were predominantly research organizations and others were predominantly activist in orientation. Patrón notes a similar development with respect to Peru.

While the CRM had been established in 1971, the Social Scientists Association (SSA), the Marga Institute, the Law and Society Trust (LST) and the International Centre for Ethnic Studies (ICES) were established in the 1980s. They were intended to be academic institutions that nevertheless contributed to the democracy and ethnic diversity struggle and debate through the dissemination of the ideas generated by their research.

The more activist organizations set up were the Movement for Inter Racial Justice and Equality (MIRJE), the Movement for the Defence of Democratic Rights (MDDR), the Information Monitor of Human Rights (INFORM), the Dharmavedi Institute for Communication and Peace, the National Christian Council, the People's Action for Free and Fair Elections (PAFFREL), the Movement for Free and Fair Elections (MFFE), the Free Media Movement (FMM) and the National Peace Council. The focus of their activism is clear from their names.

The decade between the mid 1970s and 1980s also saw a proliferation of women's organizations. The more welfare-oriented groups took on issues of women and development and empowerment. In this respect, they focused mainly on gender discrimination in education, employment and the media, domestic violence and the forced use of contraception (Abeysekera, 1995: 448). With the advent of civil war on two fronts, however, the role of women in society was transformed accordingly. Issues such as internal displacement, enforced and involuntary disappearances of persons, extra-judicial killings, trauma and the treatment of women detainees had to be addressed and the ambit of human rights concerns expanded.

A number of organizations were formed to meet this challenge. The Mother's Front and the Organization of Family Members of the Disappeared were formed to deal with the issues relating to disappearances. Women For Peace, Women in Need, the Family Services Centre, the Family Rehabilitation Centre and a number of rural self-help groups were set up around the issues of economic and psychological needs. The SURIYA Women's Development Centre helps displaced women, and a coalition named the Mothers and Daughters of Lanka has been formed to campaign against the war and the detrimental effects of conflict on democracy (Abeysekera, 1995: 453).

There has also been organization around the impact of the market economy on the rural agricultural sector and its linkage to societal conflict. The Movement for National Land and Agricultural Reforms (MONLAR) formed in 1991 is based on such a critique of the consequences of the post-1977 economic orthodoxy of structural adjustment conditionality.

Emerging from the Peasant Information Centre formed in 1987, MONLAR has concentrated on building a solid base among the rural poor. At its second National Congress in January 1993, a policy statement was adopted and some 124 organizations ranging from farmers and environmental groups to organizations in the field of human rights, fisheries and plantation sectors obtained membership. In its programme of activities, MONLAR has focused campaigns on specific economic and environmental issues and on influencing national economic development policy.

That these organizations came into being in a climate of growing repression and survived its worst excesses is a testimony to their resilience and commitment. Yet many have had to defend themselves constantly against attack from other elements within civil society who have viewed them as anti-national and subversive. They have also had to be vigilant against the attempts of the State to stifle or co-opt them.

The University Teacher's Human Rights (UTHR) group, formed by four academics from the University of Jaffna, is acknowledged as a source of information of the highest integrity on human rights and the plight of civilians in the wartorn north of Sri Lanka. Their fearless reporting continues despite considerable risk to their lives. One of the group, Dr Rajani Thiranagama, was murdered by the LTTE in 1989.

At the end of the 17 years of UNP rule and the advent of a new government of left and centre-left parties constituting the People's Alliance (PA), the need to defend and to be vigilant persists. Currently, the challenge is to resist the relaxation of vigilance because of a relatively more congenial environment, political sympathies and loyalties. While the opposition party lay largely dormant for 17 years because of organizational weakness and internal division, it was these civil society groups that mounted the resistance and voiced criticism against authoritarianism. This protest benefited the opposition by facilitating the change of regime.

In this respect, civil society groups directly and indirectly worked to put the opposition in power, even to the extent of framing its manifesto in the case of some leading individuals. There is a strong element of vested interest, therefore, on the part of some civil society groups in the success of the current government in furthering national reconciliation and democratic governance and in being seen to do so. This hope invariably dilutes and inhibits their criticism.

To get a better understanding of this interplay between the State and the civil society groups that are to act as its checks and balances, we need to return to the statement of political society and the nation and State-building exercise in its current phase. The General Election of August 1994 that ended almost two decades of UNP rule brought into government the nine-party PA coalition headed by Chandrika Bandaranaike Kumaratunge. The coalition was subsequently overwhelmingly endorsed by all sections of the population in a presidential election three months later. She received 62 per cent of the total votes cast. Ms Kumaratunge had never before held national office and, although her victory was attributable to the great desire for change, her substantive appeal in policy terms rested on her promise to resolve the ethnic conflict and restore democratic governance.

The UNP had come to be associated with corruption and terror and the new dispensation promised an end to it. The UNP had also never moved beyond innate chauvinism and defence of the unitary State in the face of ethnic conflict, while the new government made constitutional reform and conflict resolution its flagship policies. It was to be judged by its ability to achieve a lasting peace through a political settlement and the restoration of parliamentary democracy by abolishing the executive presidency.

Neither a lasting peace or the abolishment of the executive presidency has yet happened, and the prognosis on both accounts is by no means clear or unequivocally hopeful. In keeping with its promise and the hopes vested in it, the new government began direct negotiations with the LTTE. Within six months the talks collapsed and war had broken out once more. The government is now in possession of the major part of territory held and claimed by the LTTE as the traditional Tamil homeland. As the government concedes, however, there is no military solution to the conflict, and further negotiations with the LTTE have not been ruled out. Both sides have laid down conditions for the resumption of talks. What is of special interest in the PA government's negotiations with the LTTE in the 1994–95 period is the extent to which it has relied on civil society to provide the expertise and personnel for this task.

Government delegations did not contain politicians. Instead they were made up of persons close to the President and even included the head of the Anglican Church in Sri Lanka. Furthermore, the government has continued to rely on the expertise of CSOs to canvass popular support for its devolution package – an unprecedented, controversial and flawed set of proposals for a political solution through a measure of regional autonomy.

This practice has been attributed to the close association of civil society with the President and her victory. A further element is the extent to which the President was at variance with her party, the Sri Lanka Freedom Party (SLFP), which headed the PA coalition, on a number of issues. It was the SLFP under her father that pioneered the official language policy and ushered in the legislation that imperilled ethnic harmony. Over the years, the party has come to be seen even as the party of Sinhala chauvinism. The ideological affinity of the government and the civil society democracy and ethnic harmony activists notwithstanding, this government too is not beyond moving to control NGOs or to allowing the use of force against civil society groups that disagree with it, regardless of their earlier camaraderie.

War with the LTTE began again in April 1995 and, by December 1995, government forces had taken the northern capital and LTTE stronghold of Jaffna. A climate of triumph and jingoism was fostered. It was preceded by xenophobia reinforced by apprehension that information regarding the movement of the population and the possibility of a humanitarian crisis would galvanize enough international pressure to force the government to abandon its political and military objectives.

It was against this backdrop that the NGO Forum of Europe-based organizations and their Sri Lankan partners met in Colombo for an annual meeting. At the outset, there was a controversy between them and the government over whether the government had been informed of the meeting. Numerous newspaper articles insinuated that there was an international conspiracy to pre-empt a military defeat of the LTTE.

The meetings of the forum were disrupted by violent mobs believed to be associated with members of the ruling coalition. Accordingly, the venue had to be changed several times, and, on one occasion, the editor of a newspaper that had been a key supporter of the ruling coalition and involved in facilitating its ascent to power was beaten up. The assistance of a cabinet minister was obtained to prevent further disruption and violence.

Two years later, the Ministry of Ethnic Affairs and National Integration launched an initiative to 'establish civil society' through partnerships and a forum with NGOs. It seems that the catalyst was a Norwegian Agency for Development Cooperation (NORAD) programme. The invitation from the ministry to organizations to join the government in first 'establishing civil society' for this purpose is indicative of either the ignorance of the ministry on the process of civil society building, or of an attempt to co-opt civil society groups to fulfil its mandate. Patrón's phrase, 'the State summons civil society' in Peru is reminiscent of this event.

The ministry official chairing the discussion appeared to operate on the assumption that the NGO groups represented were primarily interested in the funds that the ministry would be able to disburse. The NGOs, however, were left with the impression that the ministry had no real strategy to fulfil its mandate and was eager to pass that responsibility on to them.

The debate on free media is an important example. In one instance, CSOs spearheaded by the FMM launched a campaign against a government bill to impose a government-controlled regulatory authority on the electronic media. Some 15 petitions were filed in the Supreme Court, and the bill was subsequently struck down by the Court as unconstitutional. In the face of media repression under its predecessor, the government promised to institute a regime of free media and on attaining office set up four committees for this purpose. The committees have submitted their reports but no action has been taken and the reports have not been officially released to the public. In another instance, on the question of a broadcasting authority, the government had promised the FMM that it would first publish a White Paper for public discussion. Instead, a bill was introduced on to the Order Paper of Parliament at the end of an emergency debate and just before the holiday season. The issue is still alive and the FMM is now launching a campaign on the basis of an alternative draft that resulted from a working group coordinated by the Centre for Policy Alternatives (CPA) and the FMM for this purpose.

With growing evidence of ruling party use of violence, especially in the context of elections, civil society groups have had to organize on the question of political violence as well. This is the topic of subsequent sections of the chapter.

Exploring Power Relationships Between Civil Society and the State

In these examples, it has been argued that there is a dialectical relationship between the State and civil society. Indeed the identity of one is also a function of the independence and integrity of the other; the State must not be captured by the dominant class in civil society, and civil society must not be eliminated or co-opted by the State. In Sri Lanka, this has been an asymmetrical relationship in which the State has attempted to control civil society, which, in turn, has run the risk of being politicized in partisan terms to either buttress the legitimacy of the State or check its excesses and effect a change of regime. In this section, the attempts by the State to exert control on civil society groups will be examined.

In 1980, the government proposed and passed the Voluntary Social Service Organizations (Registration and Supervision) Act. All organizations so defined were compelled to register under the Act and, in so doing, submit themselves to direct government control. It empowered government officials to enter and inspect the premises of an organization, convene an executive committee or general meeting to take place at a venue and time of their choosing and give directions to the executive committee. Provision in the Act for the dissolution of the executive committee of any organization and the appointment of a Board of Management until a new committee is chosen was later dropped. Such a board was to have been set up following an inquiry by a tribunal appointed by the minister if there was evidence of fraud and financial irregularities. The CRM condemned the Act as a 'gross and unprecedented violation of the freedom of association'. In its statement, it warned that 'a ruling party may well have prejudices against certain organizations; individual politicians too may for their own reasons be tempted to interfere' (CRM, 1980: February).

In 1995, following alleged financial misconduct in the Sri Lanka Red Cross Society, an amendment to the Act was proposed. It was to have retroactive effect, because an Interim Board of Management appointed by the minister had been declared invalid by the courts. The amendment, according to the CRM, compounded the original act by reintroducing the Board of Management by ministerial appointment (CRM, 1995: November). INFORM noted that 'this totally negates the concept of NGO autonomy' (INFORM, 1995). Both CRM and INFORM argued that the existing law should apply in instances where there was evidence of fraud and misappropriation of funds. The amendment has yet to be passed. The NGO Commission set up by the Premadasa regime in 1991 also recommended changes. These changes were not translated into proposed legislation. The Commission produced its report in 1993 after a change of regime had taken place following the assassination of President Premadasa in May of that year.

In a preceding section, the work of the Commission was discussed in terms of its understanding of the role and function of civil society in a developing State. This section will discuss the recommendations of the Commission and its proceedings in the context of the State–civil society relationship.

In May–June 1991, Dr Stephen Neff, on behalf of the International Commission of Jurists (ICJ), visited Sri Lanka to study the mandate and operation of the NGO Commission. His report was critical of the Commission in both respects and the ICJ, keen to discuss the matter with the Sri Lankan government, requested an opportunity for a second ICJ delegation that would include Dr Neff and Sir William Goodhart, QC.

Just before this delegation was to depart for Colombo, the Sri Lankan Permanent Representative to the United Nations in Geneva informed the ICJ that any critique of the Commission would be in violation of the principle of sub judice. The ICJ was asked to resubmit its request to send a delegation after the Commission had reported on its findings to the President. The ICJ disagreed with the sub-judice argument and reiterated that it did not want to publish its report without discussing it with the Sri Lankan government. Moreover, it was willing to modify any criticism contained in the report that was warranted by such discussion and asked the Sri Lankan government to accede to its request by 6 September. On receiving no response from the government, the ICJ published its report in November 1991.

The ICJ Report found a 'palpable fear of impending – and even of actual – victimization by the government' among the NGO community in general and heightened awareness on their part of vulnerability to easily aroused xenophobic sentiment and public hostility. The most exposed to this danger, according to the report, were those that had association with foreign groups and funders, invariably an elite group of the English-educated middle and upper middle classes. Human rights groups and activists were the most vulnerable.

The report made special mention of the treatment meted out to the Sarvodaya Shramadana Movement, the major NGO committed to community action and self-reliance and represented in a third of the villages in the country. The bulk of Sarvodya funds are from abroad and its president, Dr AT Ariyaratna, has been both a controversial and charismatic figure who has made pronouncements about the politics and governance of the country. The report noted that there was a strong feeling that Sarvodaya was being singled out for harassment by the government and that Dr Ariyaratna and his family had received death threats. According to the report, there was the 'aura of a trial' about the proceedings of the Commission, and the task of instructing the police unit attached to the Commission was performed by the State counsel. Police investigations were characterized as 'the single most disturbing element of the commission's functioning'.

The Presidential Commission presented its findings in 1993. It recommended a comprehensive policy declaration on NGOs by the government, which would allow them the space to pursue their interests legally and peacefully. Certain GROs and NGOs were to be exempt from incorporation or compulsory registration, to be tabulated on the basis of their annual income and assets. The Commission also recommended that the local NGOs should give every assistance to GROs and that they should 'try to become more democratic and representative of the community'. International NGO financial and other assistance was welcomed. The Commission 'expected' them in the future to move from Project Aid and, in their assistance to GROs, recommended collaboration with local NGOs rather than direct assistance.

The appointment of a commissioner for NGOs was called for, along with a secretariat. A new and comprehensive law was proposed to provide for the compulsory registration of NGOs other than those exempted, the formation of NGOs and supervisory powers over NGOs including the monitoring of foreign funding and the supervision of children's homes and homes for the aged, among others, run by NGOs.

An NGO fund solely to help 'needy and deserving' GROs and local NGOs was also proposed. It was to be supported from monies granted by the State, local and international NGOs and funds were to be disbursed on the basis of guidelines and strictures made by an NGO advisory council. Co-ordinating mechanisms were called for at all levels of NGO–government co-operation and the government was called upon to 'encourage and assist' the NGO sector to formulate a code of conduct, establish a research and training institute, information centre and data bank, develop the skills of the GROs and to set up their own representative organizations and networks to deal with the government.

It would seem that the Commission reflected the political climate in that its recommendations were not as draconian as feared. The change of regime in 1993 was accompanied by a growing sense of relaxation in the prevailing authoritarianism.

MAPPING DONORS

Between Civil Society and the Support Community: Dependency and Agenda-Setting

Set against this groundswell of internal political debate on the work of CSOs, the international donor community has played a pronounced role. This section will look at questions of dependency and agenda-setting that strike at the core of the debate and are often advanced to argue that the State–civil society relationship is an extension of the North–South relationship in international politics.

Civil society groups acting as check and balance on the State are reliant upon Northern donor assistance. Maina makes the same observation in his chapter on Kenya. In a written communication to the author, one European donor who stated that his future funding priority would be to groups that could contribute to a political settlement of the ongoing ethnic conflict, agreed:

> *Yes, some groups definitely seem to have become dependent on our financial resources. Here the element of sustainability comes in and, of course, we are first and foremost interested in sustainable development. Having said this, I do not see how some of those groups could survive without foreign funding and I personally have no major problems in continuing to support a programme over a number of years, provided of course that it is achieving its goals. (personal communication)*

Although this dependence means that CSOs may be seen as 'agents of a foreign power', depending on the political climate, it may be preferable to the potentially more damaging accusation of being funded by a local political party or vested political interest. That link would probably result in the unavailability of foreign funding. Local funding would show too that civil society is subject to control by the dominant class at a very basic and fundamental level.

In this respect, the post-cold war context of globalization intersects with the local context of partisan nation- and State-building at the point of the donor–grantee relationship. Support for democracy, governance and human rights civil society groups is contingent upon sufficient donor appreciation of this link, in addition to the oscillations in their funding priorities. For example, the latest World Bank *World Development Report*, entitled 'The State in a Changing World', marks a shift in Northern emphasis regarding the role of the State. From an ideological perspective that saw the State as part of the problem of governance and not its solution, there is now a focus on the role the State has to play in governance. This in turn leads to an interest in forging partnerships between the State and civil society groups.

The NORAD grant for ethnic reconciliation is an example of this emphasis. Another is the proposed Good Governance Project planned by the Canadian International Development Agency (CIDA), discussed below. In the design phase of the CIDA project (in which the author was involved), the Canadian consortium was concerned with ensuring the co-operation, participation and support of the Sri Lankan government at the outset. Although there were obvious reasons at the level of demonstrating goodwill and benign intent, the importance of forging partnerships between the State and civil society was also emphasized.

There is a clear logic to this link at a conceptual level. Neither ethnic reconciliation or good governance can be attained without the participation of the State. Furthermore, the interests of both civil society and the State are best served by realizing the opportunities for collaboration between them when necessary and where possible. The reality, however, is that the relationship between the State and civil society groups in Sri Lanka is asymmetrical and unequal. For this type of partnership to be meaningful and durable, the strengthening of civil society needs to be emphasized in programming or else it will be co-opted or subordinated.

A related aspect is that a fair proportion of the funding for democracy, human rights and governance issues comes out of official bilateral donor assistance, and funding has to be routed through the Department of External Resources and the Ministry of Policy Planning and Implementation. This administrative requirement serves to heighten donor susceptibility to government sensitivities. Such susceptibility could operate to deter a willingness to tackle directly the more vital issues of democratization and governance, which, invariably, are also the more controversial.

Another aspect of this financial dependence is donor fear about mismanagement, extravagance and potential embezzlement. Concerning suspicion of misuse of funds by NGOs, the 1991 ICJ report found that some at USAID saw no need for the government of Sri Lanka to 'police the use of funds' because the donors themselves have stringent monitoring systems. The same sources also said that some of the 'apparently reasonable government concerns' like extravagant NGO spending on overheads, administration and salaries could in fact be 'misconceived'. USAID had the opposite experience of too little being spent on this element, to the detriment of NGO's overall efficiency. The pendulum has now swung the other way, and the provision of infrastructural support is less forthcoming.

This swing is also tied to the 'results-based' approach to programme funding now in vogue in the aid community, favouring quantitative reports on outcomes commensurate with the level of investment made. In the field of democratization, this 'results-based' emphasis translates into a preoccupation with activities that can be clearly enumerated, even though the nature of democratization requires sustenance of *a process*. Democratization does not easily lend itself to the clear-cut production of a specific result over a limited period. Here again, donor sensitivities are understandable; tax dollars obviously must be spent for a clearly demonstrable purpose. Nevertheless, given the characteristics of the subject area, insistence upon a results-based approach runs the risk of facile conclusions based on glib assumptions equating correlation with causality.

This concern surfaced at a meeting at USAID in February 1998 between the agency and a consortium of partners to discuss a work programme on human rights. It was pointed out that, although the precise contribution of a project towards the realization of a general objective, such as the resolution of ethnic conflict, is difficult to identify, a general assumption that it contributed would likewise be difficult to disprove. Consequently, there is a circular logic to the exercise. The existence of the project itself is, in effect, an indicator of its success.

Are Donor Organizations Interested in Civil Society?

Recent examples

The USAID Citizens' Participation Project (CIPART) is a case in point. It was to last for six years (the projected completion date was the year 2000 and it was not to exceed US$7 million in grant funds). The government of Sri Lanka was to allocate the local currency equivalent of US$8 million, and the total project cost was estimated at US$16 million. The goal of the project was to:

> *provide the stable democratic government essential to achieve Sri Lanka's objective of becoming a democratic Newly-Industrialized Country (NIC). CIPART's project purpose is to strengthen democratic processes that enhance opportunities for ordinary citizens to address fundamental social, economic and political development needs.*

CIPART was to be 'people focused' and its results were to be obtained by empowering ordinary citizens to be self-reliant in problem solving. CIPART was to strengthen democratic institutions that could facilitate this empowerment. At the end of six years, CIPART was to have produced a more responsive local government, a more effective NGO movement and modernized legal systems, including greater respect for fundamental rights and a more professional media. CIPART was to also contribute to peace and nation building:

> *Although it would be presumptuous to say that the CIPART project will directly contribute to introducing democracy in the North, the democratic processes that are strengthened and the feeling of empowerment that is awakened by CIPART may contribute to changes in attitudes and practices that are prerequisites for sustainable conflict resolution on a national scale.*

It was to have four components: local government, participatory development, modernized legal systems and professional media. The local government and participatory components were to be awarded by competition to a single NGO or to a consortium of NGOs. Whichever was selected would have to work closely with the Ministry of Home Affairs and Provincial Councils, the Ministry of Social Welfare and Rehabilitation and the Ministry of Policy Planning and Implementation. The law and media components were awarded to the Asia Foundation (TAF), which had to work closely with the Ministry of Justice and the Ministry of Information.

The local government and participatory components of CIPART never materialized because the project was halted in its tracks. Although CIPART started in January 1996 and its law and media components began in August of that year, by December the project had been halted and two months later, terminated. According to USAID, the programme had to be revised and restructured because of financial constraints, leaving the Sri Lankan implementing agency to look elsewhere for funds to continue with the work. In the process of revision and restructuring, USAID funds may become available in 1998 and in the interest of programme sustainability salvaged.

Factors external to the situation in Sri Lanka appear to have determined the fate of CIPART. Budget cuts in the US and the shift of focus to Eastern Europe and to Africa, as well as the enduring commitment to the Middle East, no doubt played their part in terminating CIPART as originally envisaged. Although the civil society objectives and activities under the programme are to be 'revised and restructured,' USAID programmes in Sri Lanka focusing on the economy and the strength and viability of its open-market, liberalized orientation none the less continue.

The curtailing of the programme is important. In its short tenure, CIPART was able to fund a monitoring exercise of campaign-related violence in the recent local government elections – the first such exercise of its kind in Sri Lanka. Although USAID was able to support this exercise, it is uncertain that it could have otherwise been undertaken. Political violence reached a peak in the south of Sri Lanka between 1987 and 1989, and the use of violence as the key arbiter of societal grievance has not been eliminated in the face of terrorism in the North and the political culture in the South. Even under the PA government with its promises of greater freedom and democracy, violence has been employed as an instrument by which the party in power asserts and consolidates its rule.

Given the pivotal importance of peaceful political activism for democratic governance, and the possibility that the local elections would be used as a dress rehearsal or a testing of the water for further electoral contests, including a referendum on devolution, the CPA together with the FMM and the Campaign Against Political Violence (a coalition of grassroots organizations) established the Centre for Monitoring Election Violence (CMEV). The CMEV put out daily bulletins on campaign violence based on information sent into the centre and corroborated by the police and political parties, a monthly report and a final report. The bulletins and reports were widely disseminated through the print and electronic media.

Interestingly, despite the concern with democratic governance, participatory democracy and capacity building of civil society voiced by many donors, USAID assistance aside, most others found the issue too politically sensitive. One donor who expressed a verbal commitment to partial financing withdrew on this basis. This is not unlike the example of Transparencia, a non-partisan election monitoring organization, cited by Patrón in her chapter in Peru.

CIDA is also beginning a major Good Governance and Institutional Strengthening (GGIS) project for Sri Lanka. The design of the project has been awarded by competitive tender to a consortium of Canadian organizations composed of the Human Rights Research and Education Centre (University of Ottawa), the World University Service of Canada and the Institute of Governance. The GGIS project will involve representatives of the government of Sri Lanka as well as CSOs and it is intended to be participatory. It is underpinned by work financed directly by the Canadian High Commission through local mechanisms such as the Canada Fund, the Human Rights Fund and the Sri Lanka Canada Development Fund.

Another substantial commitment to ethnic harmony is symbolized by the NORAD project with the Ministry of Ethnic Affairs and National Integration mentioned earlier. The underlying rationale is to forge a partnership with that ministry, and the ministry in turn is to be encouraged to forge links and work with civil society groups. The objective of the programme is to gain acceptance of the multi-ethnic nature of Sri Lankan society and the need for power sharing and local democracy. Joined to these goals is the fairer distribution of developmental resources among communities throughout the island and the sustenance of a bureaucratic culture to both reflect and facilitate this distribution.

Given the centrality of constitutional reform to conflict resolution in the Sri Lankan nation- and State-building process and, in particular, the political controversy surrounding the government's devolution proposals, this programme attracted criticism at the outset. Critics denounced it in the media as interference in the domestic affairs of the country and a violation of Sri Lanka's sovereignty. The argument used was that the funding supported the political programme of the party in power and would not be spent to implement a national consensus, but rather to forge one in favour of the ruling party. These criticisms notwithstanding, the programme has begun and a National Integration Policy Unit has been established.

The General Context

The largest funders to civil society groups are CIDA (Canada) and NORAD (Norway). In each case, over the two-year period from 1993 to 1995, the bulk of overall funds (62 per cent) went for community development and services. Gender policy, research and development as an explicit focus accounted for 16 per cent of NORAD funding and 9 per cent of CIDA's. (In CIDA's case, 16 per cent of funding was expended on education and on training in general.) Human rights and governance issues follow with 8 per cent (CIDA) and 10 per cent (NORAD). NGOs are the recipients, on average, of just over a half of these overall funds from CIDA and two-thirds from NORAD; grassroots organizations receive a third in both cases. Some 18 per cent of NORAD and 7 per cent of CIDA funds were allocated to a single organization, Sarvodaya.

An important addition to this profile is the twenty-five per cent or so of British High Commission funding that falls under the human rights and governance category because of a large grant to the Human Rights Task Force and a similar proportion of SIDA (Swedish International Development Cooperation Agency) funding from grants made to the Centre for the Study of Human Rights at the University of Colombo and to the Council for Liberal Democracy.

Since 1992, the Canadian High Commission has established a Human Rights Fund of CA$500,000 to be disbursed to government and non-government institutions. As of the end of June 1997, 74 per cent of the fund has been disbursed to NGOs and 16 per cent to the government. The bulk of the remainder went to individuals for conference attendance and completion of higher degrees. Although the largest number of disburse-ments was for seminar and course attendance as well as for publications, 20 per cent of the funds disbursed went towards awareness of human rights issues, education and community reconciliation. The commissions set up to inquire into involuntary disappearances, as well as organizations of the families of the disappeared, received 16 per cent of the funds disbursed and the same proportion was allocated for research.

There is also a Peace Fund of CA$500,000 established in 1995 to promote a peaceful resolution of the ethnic conflict. (The funding profile of this channel varies from the Human Rights Fund, reflecting the current position in the two issue areas. The Peace Fund was established in April 1995; hostilities between the government and the LTTE began on the 19th of that month when the LTTE unilaterally broke off talks). By the end of June 1997, 94 per cent of the Peace Fund had been distributed to NGOs and 4 per cent to the government. The largest grant (CA$43,500) went to the Kalmunai Peace Foundation in the east of Sri Lanka to continue work on a two-year Community Reconciliation Programme among the three ethnic communities in the area. Previously funded by CIDA, this programme was followed by a grant of CA$30,000 to train facilitators of non-violent conflict resolution workshops and to develop networking among them across Sri Lanka. Another CA$25,000 has been granted to the Centre for Performing Arts, Jaffna, in the north of Sri Lanka, for its 'Promoting Peace Through Culture' island-wide campaign through the medium of the performing and visual arts.

The Asia Foundation is a non-governmental donor with a consistent interest in issues of governance and democratization. In its progamming category for the financial year 1997, entitled 'State and Society', out of a total of 32 projects, 22 are to be implemented by NGOs. Out of a total programming budget of US$882,700 from USAID for this financial year, the largest single component of US$455,000 is in the issue area of the law (the making of laws and their administration) spread over 13 projects. Of these, the improvement of formal and in-service legal education for lawyers and judges amounts to US$180,000 and increasing public awareness of legal rights and access to justice to US$275,000. Programming in this issue area includes human rights concerns and ranges from legal awareness projects in rural areas for families of victims of political violence, legal literacy clinics and workshops for citizens and lawyers in the provinces as well as assistance to the courts and the legal system.

The next largest issue area is the media acting as a force for greater accountability, augmenting public debate and improving citizen access to reliable information. A sum of US$242,000 has been allocated for this work with US$185,000 devoted to the encouragement of a 'more responsible' broadcast and print media and US$57,000 to increasing the free flow of information. Programming in this issue area includes support for community media, media monitoring and skills training for provincial media.

The Issues

There are a number of factors identified in the chapters on Kenya and Peru that also apply in the Sri Lankan case with regard to 'donor capture', the networks they access and the considerations they give weight to. There is no denying that in the democracy, human rights and governance area, funds are largely disbursed to urban middle-class organizations staffed by an English-speaking elite. Outreach to the rural areas is, therefore, also dependent upon these organizations' interest in the capacity-building of grassroots organizations.

The urban Anglicized bias is attributable to the problems of communication between donor and potential grantee, resource constraints in country-wide programming, donor confidence in the grantee's management skills and absorptive capacity. Furthermore, in a climate of proposed change at the institutional and structural level, as is the situation in Sri Lanka, policy reform is highlighted. Reform agendas serve to strengthen the links between the donors and the urban, Colombo-based organizations that, in turn, have positioned themselves, albeit not always effectively, in the policy-making process. The smallness and even incestuous nature of this group cannot be denied. Individuals are involved in more than one organization and more than one organization is often involved in a very similar activity in the same issue area. This smallness of community applies to the donors as well.

Programming in the issue areas of democratization, governance, ethnic reconciliation and human rights tend to revolve around a particular set of activities and institutions. Given the saliency of the issue, donors will gravitate towards those with the most visible role. Donor eagerness to assist the recently established Human Rights Commission is one example. Although the Commission could benefit from assistance, given its pivotal institutional position in the issue area of human rights, donors must be alert to the possibility that duplication rather than reinforcement could result from their eagerness to help. The sharing of information with respect to each other's activities is as important for donors as it is for grantees.

Individuals will often know donors at a personal level or through the cocktail circuit and as a consequence, reputation and name recognition has become important in gaining access to donors. In some instances, better known individuals will act as gatekeepers for donors in the consideration of proposals from organizations unfamiliar to donors. In the area of democracy and governance with its potential for controversy, this gatekeeping function also reflects donor need for reassurance through dealing with known individuals. This practice – defensible for many reasons – none the less opens organizations to the charge of perpetuating the elite.

A Debate on the Issues

This work by donors is important. It informs the local debate on the appropriate roles of the State, civil society actors, and other players in the nation- and State-building exercise.

A symposium on civil society in Sri Lanka organized by ICES in July 1996 gives an insight into current thinking in Sri Lanka on the nature and role of civil society. Issues raised in the chapter were echoed at the symposium.

Prof GL Peiris, former Vice-Chancellor of the University of Colombo and current Minister for Justice and Constitutional Affairs, Ethnic Affairs and National Integration, gave a presentation on the 'Five Requirements for Civil Society'. In it, he referred to the 'irreducible minimum elements for the establishment of civil society in our country'. The first requirement was empowerment, the second was participation, and he argued that the two are '...sides of the same coin. You empower people and then you encourage them to participate fully on the basis of that empowerment. I would define that as the cornerstone, the very pivot of civil society'. Next, he identified the problems with the durability of basic political and constitutional structures, identified on the basis of the inability in Sri Lanka to solve the ethnic conflict despite a tradition of democracy and a high rate of literacy. Finally, the minister identified compassion and goodwill as requirements.

Prof Savithri Goonasekera, Professor of Law at the University of Colombo, noted that empowerment and participation had been devalued in the Sri Lankan context by partisan politicization and that without incorporating a sound human rights basis, which in turn reflects the rich religious traditions in the country, a vital dimension of civil society would be lost. She noted that: 'the challenge seems to be to create a civil society where the government is empowered to govern and the people empowered to demand accountability in governance. The realization of Prof Peiris's "panchaseela" of good governance will require a commitment to democracy rather than populism.'

Charles Abeysekera, a leading civil society activist, President of MIRJE and Chairperson of the Official Languages Commission, began his presentation with Norberto Bobbio's argument 'to create through its own agency a State apparatus which would be efficient without being oppressive'. He believes that this is what Sri Lanka needs. Abeysekera elaborated this argument in the Sri Lankan context on the grounds that State power has been and is very likely to be abused. There is a need, therefore, to set limits to State power and as Bobbio advocated, to 'erect defences'. Abeysekera concluded that in Sri Lanka '…we have the trappings of democracy but not some of its essential features', illustrated by the origins and evolution of the ethnic conflict, infringements on the freedom of thought and expression and the 'ambivalent attitude creeping into government actions' with regard to human rights.

For Abeysekera 'the State is the arena of the political process; it therefore comprises all the State apparatus – the administrative, security and judicial. All else comprises civil society. This will include within civil society, economic relations and the social forms controlling them'. Yet he concedes that the differences are not always clear and the State and civil society have become 'increasingly intertwined'. Certain civil society groups advocate greater State intervention for the furtherance of their interests. Consequently, democratic control has also entailed greater State intervention: 'State and society are thus become separate but interdependent instances in modern society'. Abeysekera also made reference to the statist mentality of the bureaucracy as an additional complicating factor and to the 'ethical life of the community'. The latter he concludes is the most important feature of civil society.

Vijaya Samaraweera, a legal academic and Fulbright Scholar, disagreed that the State is the arena of the political process with civil society making up the rest or that in modern times the two have become increasingly intertwined. He stated that there is no known case in modern times that fits this bill and argues that it would be more productive to characterize the relationship as 'two polar opposites, with a continuum between them in which the great bulk of cases would be located'. At one pole, the State would be autonomous from civil society and, at the other, a social class would exert so much control that the State would be subservient to it. Somewhere between, however, there are boundaries between State and civil society. It is important to identify them and where they meet. For Samaraweera:

> *The nature and form of the boundaries between the State and civil society are just as much the function of the make-up of the respective entities as they are the function of the boundaries between them. It is in this sense, more than any other, that it could be said that the relationship between State and civil society is dialectical.* (International Centre for Ethnic Studies, 1997: 22)

Samaraweera raised a number of questions regarding the nature of the State and the nature of civil society. The nature of the State needs to be examined through questions about its historical origins, structural arrangements, and the sources of its material needs. For civil society, questions need to be asked about class formation, the relationship between the dominant class and foreign capital and the subordinate classes, as well as the relationships between the subordinate classes themselves. He acknowledged that ascertaining the nature of civil society through an analysis of social class will be in itself inadequate to understanding civil society in the developing world. There is also the need to take into account ethnicity and religion, the 'ethno-sectarian geography' of civil society.

Samaraweera proceeded to outline the Sri Lankan case. He contends that the autochthonous constitutions involved important 'departures' from the State that were inherited at independence in 1948. There are similarities too. The contemporary State is paternalistic, albeit with a different emphasis from its colonial predecessor. An important difference, he suggests, is that cohesiveness and integrity, the 'undoubted hallmarks of the British colonial State, have been lost, perhaps irretrievably'. Arguing that the post-colonial State has been weakened by political control and its own institutional expansion, Samaraweera suggests that the State has become vulnerable to encroachment by certain elements in civil society, and the coercive apparatuses of the State have become instruments of the controlling classes.

Samaraweera went on to say that Sri Lanka is a mixed economy in which the capitalist, middle and proletarian classes as well as the peasantry can be clearly identified. The class formation, however, is still evolving. This is a reflection of the instability and tenuousness of the modern sector of the economy. For a true picture, however, the ethnic and caste divisions must also be taken into account. For Samaraweera, the State 'is clearly under the assault of the dominant class in civil society, the capitalists; the role of the middle class, whether on its own or as a co-opted element of the dominant class, cannot be determined with precision as yet'.

The final presentation at the symposium was by Bradman Weerakoon, former secretary to six of the eight prime ministers of Sri Lanka and International Relations Advisor to President Premadasa. His talk was entitled 'An Alliance of Insiders and Outsiders'. Weerakoon's approach was to look at civil society by looking at the elements that could become 'incivil'. He identified three basic elements: the State, the market (or the corporate economy) and the system of political parties, seeing civil society as the 'countervailing power' to these elements when they operate in a manner different from what was intended when they were created.

Weerakoon argued that civil society can work best when it has contact with receptive and sensitive 'insiders'. To illustrate this notion of effective partnership, he cites the example of Justice Bhagwati of the Indian Supreme Court and the 'Social Action Litigation' pioneered there. In the Sri Lankan context, he cited the 'strategic alliance between those inside and those outside the establishment', which led to amendments in emergency regulations relating to arrest and detention during the government of President Premadasa 1988–93. He also referred to the Human Rights Task Force set up during this period. Initially, it was headed by Justice Soza who persevered in investigating a particularly shocking atrocity involving school children in Embilipitiya – an incident that was used very effectively against the last regime at the hustings in 1994.

Radhika Coomaraswamy, UN Special Rapporteur on Violence Against Women and a commentator at the meeting, quoted Neera Chandhoke's 'civil society is the site for the production of critical rational discourse which possesses the potential to interrogate the State'. In her comments, she provided an overview of the evolution of the concept culminating in Gail Omveldt's category of 'new social movements' and pointed out that 'the new appeal to civil society attempts to police and refashion the post-colonial State'. Alluding to the 'crisis of governability' in South Asia, she hailed the mobilization against repressive State power as a victory for civil society. Consequently, in South Asia in general and in Sri Lanka in particular, she argued that civil society is bound up with a rights-oriented discourse directed at limiting the excesses of the State.

She pointed out, however, that there are other groups involved and was critical of Weerakoon's exclusion of them from his presentation. These are groups that champion ethnicity, religion and nationalism and are, accordingly, excluded from civil society on the grounds that they do not fit into the liberal Marxist formulations of the concept emphasizing rational discourse and rights consciousness. They have been referred to by Indian scholars as 'counter-civil society movements'. Coomaraswamy posed the question as to whether this exclusion should be accepted, arguing that even though these organizations propagate values that are antithetical to rational discourse and rights consciousness, they too exert vigilance over an over-mighty State:

> *Once we acknowledge that these movements are creatures of civil society, then we can engage with civil society as a site of contestation and struggle. The real task before rights-based civil society organizations is to prevent the appropriation of the space created for civil society by ethnic and religious mobilization... Their appropriation of civil society space is the greatest threat to democracy in all South Asian societies.*
> (International Centre for Ethnic Studies, 1997: 35–6)

Where does this conversation leave us? What all these presentations have in common is the association of civil society with democratization and rights consciousness and its function as check and balance on the power of the State. Although this perspective does not capture the entirety of civil society, it focuses on the agendas that predominate in the Sri Lankan discourse today and in the hearts and minds of donors as well. The message is clear: the field is complex, there are problems with the depth of State encroachment on the civic sphere, civil society organizations themselves are not homogeneous or fully representative, and the potential for peace is still a long way off.

CONCLUSION

This chapter has taken as its central theme a particular notion of civil society, that of check and balance on the State. The debate in Sri Lanka is deeply entwined in this vision of State-civil society relations, and so the chapter has focused on the asymmetries in their power relationship.

An underlying theme has been that civil society in Sri Lanka needs to be strengthened and to strengthen itself. It must be more vigilant and conscious about preserving and expanding its democratic space. Donors have a role to play here and, in the case of both the civil society groups and the donors, the success or failure of their endeavours hinges on their appreciation of the political environment. Essentially, this means that they must have a clarity of purpose to help in identifying and assessing permissible limits of action.

None the less, there is an unreality about donors professing a commitment to democracy, human rights and governance at the same time as they proclaim their respect for non-intervention in the affairs of a developing country. Although donors are not the main actors in the nation- and state-building drama, they are actors nevertheless. They are not the audience nor, as they sometimes prefer to be known, are they the facilitators. The international donor community does, however, have a role in setting and realizing the peace agenda.

This focus is not to argue for an explicit political advocacy role for donors but to reinforce the point that the sophistry employed in certain cases is not helpful to civil society and the State. Pretence at neutrality also runs the risk of becoming a source of tension rather than amelioration. Donors eager to tread the thin line between provocative intervention and political non-intervention should shift the focus of funding from a preoccupation with programmes in which each line item is delineated, and move to funding a process in which there is agreement with recipients on the overall strategic objective, leaving them responsibility and tactical flexibility for its realization. Of course, there are no quick fixes or shortcuts and few immediately quantifiable results to be reported. Yet civil society came into being over time and it cannot be strengthened overnight.

5 KENYA: THE STATE, DONORS AND THE POLITICS OF DEMOCRATIZATION

Wachira Maina

There is a vast and growing literature on associational life in Africa (Mamdani and Wamba-dia-Wamba, 1995; Harbeson et al., 1994; Hyden and Bratton, 1992; Diamond, 1993; Rudebeck, 1992). Much of this literature is an important and seriously needed corrective to the afro-pessimism prevailing in policy circles in the West. Having despaired of revamping the supposedly derelict African State, researchers and some policy-makers have turned their attention to social movements and groups, optimistic that these, if re-invigorated, may organically lead to stronger and more democratic states in the continent (Bratton and van de Walle, 1997: 255, Diamond et al., 1997). On this conception, the movements and groups loosely termed civil society are both sanctuary and missionary. They not only nurture but are also the refuge and repositories of democratic forces in Africa. More crucially, they carry the evangelical mission of rescuing the African State from otherwise inevitable perdition.

This chapter accepts, as does most of the literature, that civil society is crucial to democratic deepening but it sounds a more skeptical note, deprecating the carnival air surrounding much of the recent discussion of civil society as the midwife of democracy. It argues that the complexities of associational life in Africa are less elegant and seamier than much of the literature cares to admit.

Part one of this study has two sections. The first explores some of the assumptions underlying most studies of African civil society. These assumptions are queried in the context of actual African realities and rejected as inadequate. The second section proposes two ways in which the concept of civil society could be expanded to accommodate the complexities of associational life in Africa, then draws the historical backdrop to the emergence of civil society in Kenya. It suggests that some of the structural strains and stresses that characterize Kenyan civil society are a carry-over from colonialism and the nature of the State as it has historically evolved. This section also discusses the ways in which the State shapes the context in ways that limit the choices available to civic organizations.

Part two uses recent survey data to test some of the propositions set out in the first part. Here we flag some institutional features of civil society in Kenya today and suggest some reasons for some of those features.

The third part maps donor intervention in civil society in Kenya: the first section describes the overall pattern of support by key donors, showing levels of support and programme areas selected for funding; the second shows the ways in which funding has affected the character of civil society in Kenya.

Part four brings the various strands together, exploring the dynamics of power and the issues that should be on the research and policy agenda.

Civil Society in Africa

Breaking the Conceptual Paralysis

There is a kind of catalepsy, or less polemically to use Mamdani's phrase, a 'paralysis of perspective' about civil society in Africa. We suggest that this paralysis is rooted in five untested assumptions frequently made about civil society generally and applied, *tout court*, to the specificities of Africa.

First, it is assumed that by definition civil society is primarily a counter-vailing power to the State. That assumption is moored to a fact true of Western society but hardly so of Africa: namely, that political resources are on the whole fairly distributed in society or, at any rate, that the rules for the distribution of such resources are even-handed. By this accounting, civic groups have roughly an equal chance of accessing these resources. That assumption rests in turn on a view of the State as a largely passive and generally indifferent bystander with limited adjudicatory functions. As groups slug it out in the civic arena, the State steers clear, coming in only to stem acrimony and adjust conflicts that get out of hand. This assumption ignores the fact that in Africa the assumed boundaries between State, political society and civil society are rather porous, often blurring into each other.

First, as a corollary, the hands-off State implicitly assumed by some of the literature is untenable. The State in Africa is neither indifferent nor passive (Ekeh, 1992). Historically, its political project has been domination and its *modus vivendi* the fragmentation of any opposition to that project. In analysing civil society in Africa, therefore, one must explore not only civil society's pluralizing potential but also the ways in which the State uses the civic sphere and some civic institutions as vehicles for its hegemonic project, shrinking the popular sectors of civil society and sundering and frustrating democratic deepening in the process.

Second, current civil society literature has fallen under the spell of formal civic institutions. The peril in this bedazzlement lies in its implicit assumption: namely, that formal institutions are representative of key social and political interests. This assumption often means that interests not articulated within these formal organizations are either given a dismissive nod or ignored. Thus, much of the less radical literature on civil society in Africa focuses on business associations, labour unions, women's groups, welfare associations, professional groups and the Church. The reason may be easy to guess. Organized groups are more amenable to empirical investigation. But focusing on them blinds investigators to the fact that much associational life in Africa takes place outside of formal groups. There is good political sense in this; formal groups are easier to target through licensing, criminal law, official slander, harassment or even prosecution of their leaders.

Third, much of the literature frequently overlooks the ways in which the larger conflicts in political society are reproduced in civil society. The orthodox belief that civil society is an arena for negotiating interests, itself a touchstone of democratic deepening, masks the point that civil society can and often does feed into and aggravate existing social and political cleavages. Put differently, this assumption *declasses* and *de-ethnicizes* civil society, thereby obscuring the ways in which the twin cleavages of class and ethnicity, seen by many as the bugbears of African politics, find voice and sustenance in civil society.

Fourth, the key assumptions made about the State in Africa are not tenable in the context of the actual reality. Generally seen as incompetent and often described as deinstitutionalized, neo-patrimonial and sultanist, the State in Africa has been written of as an artefact of research, a museum and period piece to be occasionally dusted off to surfeit the fancies of political archaeologists. This is rash. Much of the weakness of civil society in Africa has to do with the active role the State has played in fragmenting and dissipating the energies of those it distrusts. Behind its dour, turgid and seemingly lifeless aspect, the African State is alive and well.

Part of the skepticism about the future of the State in Africa rests, as Krasner points out, on the model against which the African State is judged. Set against the fluid, efficiency governed, adaptive State model of neo-classical economies, the African State is a shambles (Krasner, 1989: 74–80). Judged thus, it seems foredoomed by the challenges it faces. This proof by analogy, however, is bad social science: it assumes that what the liberal State does is the natural purpose of the State, any State. Seeing that the African State does not do these things, it is concluded that it is decrepit.

Finally, the assumption that civil society groups are only those that are self-organizing and relatively autonomous of the State is inapplicable to most civic organizations in Africa. African civil society's scope for self-organization and self-direction is often severely restricted by invasive NGOs and registration of societies laws. Groups distrusted by the State must torture language into euphemisms that the hatchet man from the Office of the President finds acceptable. A barrage of annual licensing requirements are often the occasion for chastising those who have not stuck to the mandate for which they were registered. Draconian powers of deregistration hang over all registered civic organizations. Those who forget that the government possesses such powers often find themselves proscribed or driven into expensive lawsuits.

In terms of funding, formal civil society institutions are even more dependent. The orthodox view is that middle-class forces will put their money into causes that they would like to advance. In Africa, however, much of the emergent middle class has come into its own with the help of the State. If they support causes that the government dislikes, their lifelines could be severed (Kennedy, 1994; Sahn and Sarris, 1994). Moreover, even those that have not been nurtured by the State know that the State's capacity to harm them is still considerable. Bereft of local financial support, local organizations largely depend on external funding, hence the key role of donors in Africa's redemocratization.

These propositions are put forward as flash-cards for the central thesis of this chapter: namely, that existing conceptions of civil society have limited explanatory power for the complexities of associational life in Africa. A first corrective step is a search for a more acceptable conception.

Expanding the Horizons: Beyond a Designer Concept of Civil Society

If, as we have suggested, civil society is a concept made to order for the political reality of Western society, should we use it at all in the study of African society? With great reservation, this chapter argues that it is still serviceable. But two amendments are first suggested.

The first amendment is that we propose a shift in perspective from a preoccupation with organizations and institutions to *an activity view* of civil society. Those who focus on organizational forms and institutions do a great injustice to civil society in Africa. Much that is both interesting and transformative in the continent occurs outside or at the periphery of formal organizational life. Spontaneous protests, laxity and lack of discipline and active non-cooperation with the State are important civic activities that take place outside of formal organizations. Spontaneous, non-confrontational methods such as these are safer ways of registering one's disagreement with the government than more robust public activities such as protest marches, placard-waving and burning effigies.

Moreover, an activity view of civil society also allows us to include within civil society activities that would otherwise be invisible. For instance, much that is articulated by ethnic and kinship groups (such as families and clans) is easy to ignore, dismissed as *not-civic-activity*. But even without treating ethnic groups as civic groups, we need to see that many of their activities engaging the State are civic activities. No account of African civil society is complete if it does not deal with this fact. The key corrective here is to alert students of African politics as to why clan and ethnic groups have remained so fundamental to African politics. Two reasons stand out.

Tribe and ethnic identity give groups a political language
As Lonsdale and Berman remind us, a political language 'unites people over what to argue about; it provides the images on which they can base their ideologies (and) ideologies mobilize political support around social divisions' (Lonsdale and Berman, 1992: 211). Moreover, in the context of an increasingly mobile and deracinated African professional class, ethnic identity provides social anchorage and orientation. Many urban-based professionals are members, if not senior officials, of their clan and tribal associations. If they intend to pursue a political career, clan and ethnic support may make the difference between failure and success.

People's histories and identities are encoded in their customs as are their philosophies of power, justice and entitlement
In those African countries where official histories have reworked the past to buttress predatory government, ethnic awareness and historiography, even if oral, may be the only effective counterweight to the State's hegemonic project. In this view, rather than see ethnicity as the rupturing force of African politics, we see it as the proper starting point for the study of African social movements and of civil society. One recognizes, thereby, the fact that democratization will not advance unless we explore 'the interior architecture of tribe' (Lonsdale and Berman, 1992: 210).

This exploration means explaining not only the 'social and moral codes of ethnicity' and kinship but also, crucially, investigating the ways in which these codes intersect with issues of class, gender and poverty (Lonsdale and Berman, 1992: 208–15). The point is to illuminate the intuitively felt but rarely expressed reality that in Africa class and tribe are not always opposed categories.* Ethnicity supplies the grammar and metaphor of African politics, even for the middle classes. It frames the political and social demands that they make on the State. The African middle class straddles the twilight zone between individualism and communitarianism. They are not just members of a class, they are also sons and daughters of the tribe. They are held up as icons of its progress and power, its emissaries at negotiations, and their exploits the stuff of which fireside tales are made.

As noted in the following, the violence of the colonial State nurtured civic resistance and, more importantly, led to substantial distrust of the State and other official institutions. Traditionally, high trust institutions, such as the family, clan and tribe, then became the site for political activity.

There is, thus, the second amendment. We propose to move away from preoccupation with rights and advocacy as the key features of civic action.

---

* In Kenyan politics, for instance, most of the young professionals (especially lawyers like Paul Muite, James Orengo, Kiraitu Murungi, Gitobu Imanyara, Kijana Wamalwa, George Kapten, Gervase Akhaabi and political scientists such as Prof Anyang Nyong'o and Dr Mukhisa Kituyi) who entered elective politics with the advent of multi parties fought for seats in their rural homes rather than in the urban areas in which they had built their professional practices and careers and where, presumably, one would expect that they had more contacts. This pattern is a salutary reminder that in their minds they see no contradiction between their class affiliation and their role as leaders of their tribes.

We argue that the focus on rights reveals a Western bias, excluding groups organized for economic ends from their rightful status as civic actors. This conception unfairly circumscribes what civil society means in Africa. Groups created to advance personal economic interests (such as farmers' cooperatives and associations, clan and tribal welfare organizations), are often the most active sites of State/society conflict. They help nurture an economic elite, especially in the rural areas, that is relatively independent of the State and that often incubates future political leadership. Before we put this analytical perspective in the context of the evidence, we will look back into history.

A Blighted Harvest:
The Foundations of Civic Polarization in Kenya

Writing in 1992, Njuguna Ng'ethe remarked that 'what is believed about NGOs (and civil society groups) frequently obscures what is known about them' (Ng'ethe, 1992). Five years later, much more is known about NGOs and civil society generally but, in some ways, there is, to quote Horowitz, 'too much knowledge and not enough understanding' (Horowitz, 1985: xi).* This truism has an especially sharp bite when applied to Kenya, a much-studied country; for all the attention it receives in the literature, the nature of its civil society remains obscure. Researchers remark on the vigour of its associational life, yet wonder why democracy has seemed so reluctant to take root here. The problem, we argue, is the dearth of historical insight into the nature of civil society in Kenya and of its problematic relationship with the State. The career of civil society and the State in Kenya begins in 1895.

Annexed that year as a protectorate of Britain, Kenya quickly acquired the accretions of a modern state. In less than a decade an administrative structure, complete with a legal framework for governance, taxation and policing were in place. In short order, massive settlement programmes were initiated and the most fertile African lands were appropriated for settler farmers from Britain.

With expanding colonial penetration came the bifurcation of Kenyan society. This was later to form the basis of a dual development policy that sharply demarcated a European economic and political sphere and an African one: the one, formal and served by a battery of administrators and organs of rule such as a judiciary and a legislative authority; the other, informal and managed by a bastardized corps of traditional chiefs dependent for their survival and material advancement on the State bureaucracy and the goodwill of a settler plantocracy.

The immediate impact of this colonial penetration was to change the foundation of African society. In traditional Kenyan society, as with many

* Horowitz is thinking of our understanding of ethnic conflict, not of civil society. See the introduction to his 1985 *Ethnic Groups in Conflict*.

pre-capitalist societies, communal and social activities were coordinated through custom, force of habit and shared moral codes. On these pre-capitalist institutional arrangements, colonialism foisted new coordination mechanisms: coercive police power, rationalized bureaucratic authority and a market system. But, given the fact that this system had not grown organically from the realities of the people, it could only be implanted by force and fraud.

There was both force and fraud galore. Between November 1893 and December 1911, Lonsdale and Berman record at least 27 military expeditions by the British expeditionary forces against different Kenyan groups (Lonsdale and Berman, 1992: 13–44). Taking advantage of the deleterious impact of the 1870 epidemics of pleuro-pneumonia, rinderpest and famine and of the subsequent (1890 and 1895) outbreaks of smallpox, the arrival of jiggers on cargo from Brazil and invasions by locusts, the British forces found a people toiling to restore depleted stocks and enervated by hunger and gangrene.

Deception was also not long in coming. In 1904, and again in 1911, for instance, the Maasai were duped into signing treaties with the British, which were later to cause them considerable hardship. The effect of these treaties was to move 11,000 Maasai and 11 million livestock to make room for 48 settlers. When the Maasai challenged these actions in court, they were told by Chief Justice Barth that the agreements they had signed were treaties between two sovereigns: the British crown and the Maasai paramount chief, Laibon Lenana. These agreements were, therefore, matters of international law that could not be adjudicated in domestic courts.

But the enormity of the violence and chicanery should not obscure the deeper logic at work. The violence was to stamp European authority on the Africans; the duplicity on the Maasai was a key plank in the campaign to free land for settlement and create an economy that could meet the fiscal goals of the imperial government. In the beginning, that goal was to make the new colony turn enough profit to pay for the 5.5 million pounds sterling sunk in railway building.

To realize settler objectives, further efforts were necessary. Africans had shown great reluctance to work for the settlers. Taxes payable in cash were introduced, driving scores of Africans into wage labour. Rules to govern the registration, identification and movement of Africans were enacted, forcing Africans to carry a *kipande* (a pass), somewhat dog-collar-like, around their neck. The *kipande* had to be signed by the settler who last employed an African, thus making it easy to identify and apprehend labour deserters. To ensure the efficient administration of this system, natives' reserves were created as reservoirs of cheap labour for the settlers. Local administrators, mostly chiefs, were given sweeping powers to enforce these labour laws (Ghai and MacAulsan, 1970; Van Zwanenberg, 1975). Set on marginal and environmentally fragile lands, the labour reserves became home to a growing African population, engendering increased land stress and open conflicts between the increasingly impoverished Africans and the settlers. These conflicts would eventually lead to the Mau Mau war.

Such, then, are the background events against which Kenyan civil society evolved. The State evolved instrumentally, generally to meet the demands of the settler economy. Promises made to Africans were only kept if they did not frustrate settler expectations. The State's key problem was the stabilization of this alien rule to meet the largely economic and strategic objectives of imperial imposition. The process of stabilizing and propping up this alien state was euphemistically termed the 'native question' (Mamdani, 1996: 4).

Civil society grew apace: settler and white interests were represented via an array of formal and informal institutions. The formal institutions ranged from farmers' associations to professional bodies (such as the Kenya Farmers Association (KFA) and the Law Society of Kenya (LSK)). Informally, many whites were members of exclusive country and sports clubs strewn all over the country. These clubs formed convivial conditions for settlers to lobby the mandarins of the colonial State for favourable policies and actions. Moreover, recruitment for the colony for settlers and the civil service alike favoured the upper classes. There was, in the main, a broad class understanding between the settlers and the formal bureaucracy. Although this understanding did not always imply agreement, it buttressed a consistent attitude to the native question. Additionally, the hands-off policy of Whitehall – trust the man on the ground – generally meant that the professional cadres in the field were given a free hand to forge their own links with the settler community. When the settler economy was in a shambles, these links could be both strong and important for settler survival – as they obviously were in the early 1930s.

In the social sphere, the Anglican Church was the established Church, its proximity to the State symbolized by the erection of the bishop's house next to the governor's residence. This contiguity in time and space created a perception among the Africans that the Church was itself an instrument for the buttressing colonial rule. This suspicion carried over into independent Kenya.

At the other extreme, popular African civic life emerged in the crucible of resistance. Much of the early associational life of the African populations was rooted in a two-fold desire: one to ameliorate the rigours of the colonial labour system on the one hand and, on the other, to preserve their imperiled traditions. On the labour question, the colonial administration would not relent. Although some of the earlier excesses of the settlers, such as Colonel Ewart Grogan's ruthless flogging of his Kikuyu workers outside a Nairobi courthouse, generally came to an end, the labour system was harsh. It comes as little surprise that some of the more radical associational activities in colonial times, African as well as Asian, involved trade unionism. Some of the famous names of Kenya's liberation movement (Bildad Kaggia, Fred Kubai, Kung'u Karumba, Makhan Singh and the exceptionally brilliant Tom Mboya) were children of the labour movement.

A second strand of Africans' associational life arose from their subnationalist attempts to preserve their traditions, often suppressed by the new missionary teaching. In some areas, this led to major schisms. Among the Kikuyu of Kiambu the break with the missionaries was total, eventually spawning the *Gikuyu Karing'a* ('Authentic Kikuyus', the false ones being those that had converted to the new Christian faith). A key area of the Kikuyu dispute with the missionaries centred on clitoridectomy, female circumcision, which they favoured and the missionaries deplored as barbaric. The *Gikuyu Karing'a* established the African Independent Church of Africa (AIPCA) and the Gikuyu Independent Schools, the first African-run schools. Although these schools taught formal Western education, in religion they preached a thorough-going Africaness. In Western Kenya, there was a similar schism, leading to *Dini ya Msambwa*, the Luhya equivalent of the AIPCA.

Later, these independent churches and schools were to play a crucial role in the liberation movement. The Gikuyu independent churches reworked Old Testament theology, infusing their own Kikuyu creation myths and religious beliefs with the prophetic and heraldic messages of the bible. Their hymns foretold the coming of a deliverer, secular rather than spiritual, and reminded the Gikuyus of the special divine ordination by which *Ngai*, their god, gave them their land and bid them never to surrender it. Recent recordings of Mau Mau songs illustrate dramatically the debt that the Mau Mau fighters owed to the theology of power churned out by these churches.[*]

Naturally, the colonial government grew nervous about these movements and imposed tighter controls on their organization, registration and rituals (such as oathing). With the shrinkage of this formal space for cultural and religious expression, informal social groups, of which there were many in Kenya, became even more important arenas for political activism. For example, all the key organizers of the Mau Mau oaths, later to be demonized in subsequent media coverage, were of the *Riika ria Forty* (the age group that got circumcised in 1940). Age groups were always important in African social life: among the Gikuyu, for instance, the duties that one owes the society, one's status and the political role one plays in clan are often non-optional and predetermined, generally (although not always) by one's age-set and clan. Key Kikuyu proverbs warn every potential truant that *Riika na muhiriga itiumagwo* (You can never opt out of your age-set or clan) and that *Kagutui ka mucii gatihakagwo ageni* (the oilskin of the home is not for rubbing visitors).[**] These are not just admonitions but clarion calls to close ranks if the age-set and clan are threatened by an external foe and to reserve tribal privileges, secrets and plans for one's kin.

Yet there was a third strand of associational life. The settlers and the resistant Africans represented the nodal points in the conflict that defined

---

[*] See, for example, Joseph Kamaru's *Nyimbo cia Mau Mau* 1and 2 (Mau Mau Songs, volume 1 and 2).
[**] The Kikuyus preserved castor-oil, a rubbing ointment as well as beauty product, in a pipe cut out of bamboo. A piece of animal skin, *kagutui*, was kept together with the oil, to be used to oil oneself when the oil ran out. It would hardly be prudent to share the *kagutui* with visitors, so it was preserved for those close to the family.

the emerging of Kenyan society under colonialism. In between the extremes, there were those who had made peace with the system. From early on, the government had bastardized some traditional authority structures, inventing a new realm of chieftaincies that, although using the idiom of the African traditional past, were, in fact, new structures of rule. These chieftaincies were crucial to the success of colonialism and, from our perspective, were key in shaping the character of Kenyan civil society.

For one thing, they nurtured an African bourgeoisie, made up of chiefs and headmen – outriders of the colonial administration – who were indebted because of the opportunities for accumulation and personal advancement that these positions offered. Some of the first Africans to be educated abroad were the sons of such chiefs. Most returned to Kenya on the eve of independence, leaders to whom the departing colonial government would hand over power.

In addition, these 'native authority' structures (Mamdani, 1996 calls them a system of 'decentralized despotism') ensured that bureaucratic violence was mediated by the Africans themselves. Orders to billet *askaris* (police) on natives were made by chiefs and executed by a retinue of administrative police attached to the chief's office. Conflict with the administration in colonial Kenya was, therefore, conflict between two faces of Africans (Berman, 1990); given that the police and army were generally recruited from ethnic communities considered dependable by the colonial government, the conflict inevitably deepened ethnic divisions.

Ethnic conflict and polarity was further aggravated by the reserve system and given an institutional base in provincial and district administrative boundaries that parcelled Kenya into insular ethnic enclaves. To move to another reserve or enter another administrative area was difficult: it was often necessary to have the permission of the administration or to report upon arrival to the chief or the district officer in the destination district or reserve. Some areas, especially marginal and pastoralist districts, were fenced off by special laws such as the Outlying and Contiguous Districts' Ordinance and the Special Districts' Administration Ordinance. This exclusionist system was used rather effectively in the government's war against nationwide political activity. In the early 1950s, people were allowed to organize only at the district level, and national political parties and organizations were banned. Much of the associational life that was later to flower into the drive for national independence, therefore, began in the family, the clan and the tribe.

Such are the antecedents. By independence, the defining cleavages of Kenyan associational life were in place.

First, there was a significant religious sector that was now less sharply split between the conservatives and the radicals. Most of the mainstream churches were gradually becoming the conscience of the nation, articulating in dignitary terms, like the biblical hermeneutics, the essential components of legitimate politics (Throup, 1995). Elsewhere, the old schisms splitting the ethno-regional churches (the AIPCA and the *Dini ya Msambwa*) and the mainstream churches no longer existed in the same robust manner that had given them energy in the 1930s and 1940s. But the ill will that they once generated is still visible in the background, best seen in the way local politics is still played in places like Kiambu. Here the old quarrels between the Gikuyu Independent Churches (the faith of choice of the underclass) and the mainstream churches, principally the Pentecostal Church of East Africa (PCEA) and the religion of the landed Kikuyu elite, still colour the language of campaigners at each election year.

To be sure, the Church is itself divided by the cleavages of class and tribe. As we shall see later on, churches in Kenya can be described with reference to the ethnic groups that constitute their membership. Surprisingly, this ethnic character does not appear to have impaired their capacity to work for democracy, contrary to popular beliefs about the divisive nature of ethnicity and ethnic consciousness.

One important point is to be noted, however. Because, as in colonial Kenya, the Church remains somewhat unregulated, it has become an important civic umbrella for associational life, sheltering and giving sanctuary to groups that the State may otherwise criminalize. In so doing, the Church often incubates dissident groups and nurtures nascent democratic forces until they are strong enough to confront the State. This role means that those who study the Church in Africa need to assess its strength carefully, and not only by the size of its membership, but also by the strength and size of secular groups that it houses and gives sanctuary.

A second aspect of Kenyan civic life relates to the State itself. As a conquest State, the colonial State never developed roots in society. Experienced as an alien imposition, it evolved as a low-trust institution, distrustful as well as distrusted. Deracialized but not democratized at independence, it straddles all political and civic life (Mamdani, 1996), colouring the way that civil society interacts and relates to it. Because it is distrustful, the State is generally supervisory and administrative, run by a prefectural system of despotic provincial commissioners, district commissioners, divisional officers, chiefs and sub-chiefs. Their key function is surveillance and control of restless local populations. Once seen as serviceable to the demands of the colonial system, this structure now serves an equally unaccountable African administration

The institutional persistence of the colonial State has given longevity to another associational form that emerged in colonial times: the informal group. Much politicking in Kenya still takes place outside of formal institutions and structures: funerals, especially among the Luo and Luhya of Western Kenya, weddings and family and clan get-togethers are all important associational fora. Indeed, given the mythical and symbolic significance of some of these functions, especially funerals, the State would hesitate to rush into ill-advised regulation. These fora thus provide the one opportunity for local leaders to meet their constituents without the blessings of the administration.

The importance of these informal fora will vary according to the attitude of the State towards more formal institutions. In Kenya at present, most formal groups must meet stringent registration requirements laid down in the NGO Coordination Act and the Societies Act. Until September 1997 (when the law was changed), their activities had to be licensed under the Public Order Act or their membership risked being dispersed by the riot police. Given this institutional context, it is no wonder that people prefer to associate only with those that they trust. The consequence is that many people's most important associational activities take place within the family, the clan and the tribe.

Third, some of the institutions established by the settlers (such as agricultural and professional associations) have evolved and become Africanized. The KFA has had a highly chequered political career, its fortunes ebbing and flowing depending on the political forces on the ascendancy. During the reign of the first post-independence president, Jomo Kenyatta, the association flourished, a seed-bed of Kikuyu agrarian capital. On the ascendancy of today's president, Daniel arap Moi, it tumbled (Moi's goal had been to undercut the power of the Kikuyu landowners who had tried to obstruct his constitutional entitlement as vice-president to succeed Kenyatta automatically if he should die in office). Other farmers' groups such as the Kenya Co-operative Creameries (KCC) have had similarly mixed fortunes.

In professional categories, the LSK has survived and grown. For two decades after independence it was dominated by white lawyers and their firms, concerning itself mainly with the welfare of its members. The society was patronized by the President and rarely spoke out on political issues. As more African lawyers took the bar, the society could no longer remain aloof from politics. From the mid 1980s, it became a key player in civil society, teaming up with the Church to emerge as an important pro-democracy actor.

CIVIL SOCIETY AND THE STATE IN KENYA TODAY

Thus far, we have outlined the theoretical and historical perspectives that are the bedrock of today's State–civil society relationships. Those remarks hold together well when tested against evidence gathered in recent empirical work, described in this part of the chapter. Although some of the more controversial propositions in part one obviously need more thorough proof, the key components of the theoretical perspective are supported by new and interesting data.

Much of the evidence and the analysis that follow draw from raw data gathered in the course of three different studies and a series of personal interviews conducted over the last two years on different aspects of civil society in Kenya. All the figures in table form are compiled from raw data gathered in a Civic Education Evaluation Study done for the United States Agency for International Development (USAID), Kenya, from January to March 1997. In this study, a total of 173 people were interviewed; 140 were interviewed individually and 33 took part in focus group discussions. The interviewees were drawn from all but one of Kenya's eight provinces, and most might be considered members of the grassroots elite. Their

Table 5.1: *Participation in Key Organizations*

Type of Organization	Participation (%)
Church or other religious groups	74
Welfare groups (family/clan associations)	72
School committees	70
Other community groups (mostly informal)	67
Student or youth groups	64
Environmental protection groups	62
Political parties	58
Farmer's associations	57
Private business groups	54
Human rights organizations	51
Labour/trade unions	41

Source: Compiled from survey data (Thalman et al., 1997)

education levels were higher than the national average and many were either artisans, small-scale business people or lay leaders within the local parishes. Women and men were equally represented, with a very slight bias towards women, and a majority were between the ages of 25 and 45. A control group of 38 people was set up. Although there were certain differences between the control group and the respondents in terms of their political knowledge and information, on the issue of associational life, the two groups were largely the same.

One of our questions was whether Kenyans' associational identity corresponds to the arguments set out earlier: that people undertake civic activity under the umbrella of Church and ethnic associations. Table 5.1 presents the beginnings of an answer, tabulating the types of organizations to which respondents said they belonged.

The most important groups for the interviewees were the Church, school committees, welfare associations, community groups and youth and student groups. Although the Church ranked highly, there was a marked difference between respondents who told us that they were members of a particular church and those who said that they had participated in associational activities within the Church. There were, in other words, more people participating in church activities than the proclaimed members of those churches.

To make sense of these data, one has to put them in the context of Kenyan politics. The high participation level in the churches is consistent with the low level of regulation suffered by the Church community and its function as an umbrella for a range of other activities. Many who say that they have participated in Church activities are often involved in associational activities that are more secular than spiritual. Welfarist rural groups like Mothers-in-Action, Mothers' Unions, Fathers' Unions, Church Action Groups and Youth Groups and camps form an integral part of Church activity. Many social networks and political activities are conducted under the cover of these groups. Similarly, wives of prominent politicians are active members of Mothers' Unions and Mothers-in-Action Groups, using these to consolidate political support for their spouses. Indeed, the Church is the entry point into the local community for an aspiring politician. In our survey, even NGOs in civic education admitted that they used the church as an entry point into the community. They told us, and we subsequently confirmed (see Table 5.2), that the Church was the most trusted grassroots organization. All this suggests that participation levels in the Church can easily lend cover to a range of civic activities that are hardly religious.

Another question was whether unions and farmers' associations provided an important alternative forum for civic action. These organizations performed much more dismally than expected, however; farmers' associations recorded low participation and unions recorded the lowest level.* As most respondents were rural, one might have expected a higher connection here to groups linked to land and farming. But our analysis of the role of the Church in Kenya's associational life might offer a clue. Trade unions, unlike the Church, have invariably been treated with suspicion by government in independent Kenya. In the early days, they were seen as hot-beds of radicalism and even communism. As a result, unions never took root; those that survived have been patronized by the State, directly indebted to it for cash handouts and survival. Against this political background, it is likely that few believe unions can successfully further their interests.

Much the same can be said of farmers' associations. Co-operatives are squarely under the administration, throttled by the Co-operative Societies Act, which gives the Minister for Co-operative Development draconian powers over their management and supervision. Although in theory co-ops are meant to be self-organizing and democratic, in practice their management has been highly centralized within the ministerial bureaucracy. The general rule is that the more economic power the co-operatives wield, the greater the extent of ministerial intervention. This intervention has had a deleterious impact on their performance and mortality, however. As one writer has noted, although the survival rate of co-operatives has been steadily increasing since the 1960s (40 per cent) to the early and late 1980s (72 per cent), in some ways their productivity and performance has shrunk considerably (Gyllstrom, 1991: 98–148). A key reason is the constraining institutional environment.

Welfare associations showed a high level of participation all round. As already noted, these are likely to be high trust organizations for historical and cultural reasons. They record participation levels as high as the Church.

Looking at this mapping from a European perspective, the picture is a little surprising. Kenyans appear to place little value on *instrumental* or

---

* As Dr Mark Robinson correctly alerts me, this level of participation may be explained by the fact that most of the respondents in the survey were from the rural areas, whereas union activity in Kenya tends to be a wage earner's activity and is, therefore, more prominent in urban centres.

Table 5.2: *Confidence in Key National Institutions*

Institution	High confidence (%)		Low confidence (%)	
	A lot of confidence	Quite a bit of confidence	Some confidence	No confidence
The Church and religious organizations	53	31	15	1
The media	10	31	53	5
Trade unions	3	24	61	12
The electoral commission	3	13	49	35
The judiciary	2	16	64	19
Political parties	2	5	69	15
Kenyan police	1	4	44	51
Members of parliament	1	9	75	15
The president	0	14	60	26
The provincial administration	0	7	55	38
The county councils	0	5	55	63

Source: Compiled from survey data (Thalman et al., 1997). Totals do not all add to 100 due to rounding and double voting.

outward looking associations. In other words, many of our respondents are not members of lobby groups or other associations designed to change policy and effect social and political changes (aside from those who are members of political parties). They are members instead of inward-looking, self-improvement and self-expression groups. This characteristic might be read as a sign of civic apathy, but we suggest that it reflects a widespread lack of trust in existing political and State institutions.

To assess just how deep this distrust runs, we also asked respondents to tell us how they perceived key national institutions. In particular, we asked them to tell us how much confidence they had that national institutions were generally working for the people's welfare. The responses are set out in Table 5.2.

From the responses, only the Church and other religious organizations scored an aggregate high confidence rating of 84 per cent. The media was second with an aggregate score of 41 per cent. All other national institutions were in the low confidence range.

When respondents were asked whether they thought they could influence the government, a majority were certain that the government did not care what people like themselves thought. Others felt that some ethnic groups had more influence than others on government decision-making. Both responses may give us a clue as to why so many people are members of *segmental* groups (based on kinship) as opposed to *functional* groups (based on occupational or class ties).

These data show some relationship between participation and confidence levels. High participation is consistent with high confidence levels for the Church, somewhat consistent for trade unions, but wildly inconsistent for political parties. A large percentage, 57 per cent, said that they had participated in a political party over the last year; only 7 per cent, however, had high confidence that parties were working for the welfare of the people. This unexpected result is not inconsistent if we assume a background of political cleavages, ethnic polarities and low political trust. People may have little faith in political parties generally but have considerable confidence and trust in the parties to which they or their kin belong.

The data on participation and confidence also raise two important questions for theory. One regards the role of community welfare groups, especially those with ethnic affiliation, and the other regards the emergence of the Church as a crucial mediator of grassroots politics. Welfare and community organizations, which include clan and family groups, account for as much associational life as the Church. The analytical question is whether it is prudent to discount these groups from African civil society studies merely because they are rooted in ethnic identities and kinship reciprocities. In African politics, much of what matters profoundly to people takes place not outside but within the groups in which they feel safest.

Concerning the role of the Church as civic umbrella, these data raise some complications for analysts. If civic action can only be safely carried out under the umbrella of the Church, can groups that genuinely disagree with the Church but, nevertheless, need sanctuary from political intervention, boldly express their views? In other words, do the institutional constraints imposed by the predatory State in the civic sphere give undue ideological veto power to the churches, which the government is wary to punish? Does the Church itself then become a 'totalizing' agent, like the State, as it arm-twists civic organizations that it shelters to Christianize their programmes and agenda?

The point here is that the institutional context is all important. It is crucial to explore the ways in which the Church, for example, interacts with the civic institutions, Christianizes their agenda and unleashes its own hegemony on them. Most of the civic organizations in the survey were urban based, professional and secular and, because they lack contact with the grassroots, they are easily hostages of the Church. They do not have the same geographical or temporal proximity that nurtures trust and mutual exchange between the Church and the people. To succeed, they must use the Church for entry into the community. That entry way acts as a constraint to them in two ways.

First, there is some evidence that these institutions cannot use the forum provided by the church to teach things it obviously objects to. A human rights' organization is unlikely to use a forum provided by the Catholic Church, for example, to affirm the right of a woman to have an abortion in the first trimester.*

---

* If that action were undertaken, it could well be the end of the relationship and so of the programme. In one instance, this issue threatened to split the constitutional reform movement in Kenya. When human rights NGOs drafted a model constitution, they asked the Church to front the campaign for reform to give it a national appeal and grassroots support. This civic bargain almost came apart on account of a provision in the model constitution affirming the right of every Kenyan to make crucial life choices, including the right to choose a homosexual lifestyle.

Second, because NGOs and other civic groups typically do not have the local networks needed to select participants to their programmes they often use the Church to select these participants. The Church then becomes not just a shelter but also a crucial mediator of the conduct of associational life in the village. A large number of the first contacts that NGOs have are parish priests and members of the Church that they have used as the entry point into the community.

Our data gave a strong indication that such a process of ecclesiastical self-selection may be at work. Although only one of our 40-odd survey organizations claimed strong institutional affiliation to the Church, a large majority of the beneficiaries of these programmes were strongly connected to the Church (most interviewees were from the three big mainstream churches: the Catholic Church had 55; the Church of the Province of Kenya, 38; and PCEA, 13).

The data also suggest that other elements of associational life at the grassroots – particularly the unions, farmers' associations and parties – are as likely to be patronized by the State as by the Church. The ideal of pluralistic and autonomous *functional* (versus kin-based) civic institutions flourishing in the face of a hostile State is unsupported by evidence.

Of course, there is some measure of pluralism evident through the Church umbrella, which itself reflects the ethnic and class cleavages throughout Kenyan society. The Anglican Church has held together only because its leadership is able to manage ethnic differences astutely and to accommodate ethnic tensions when they arise. All the other leading mainstream churches have a coalitional character, forming alliances with different ethnic groups. The Anglican Church is mainly made up of the Luo and the Kikuyus. The PCEA is dominated by the Kikuyu elite, especially Kikuyu landed capital. The African Inland Church (AIC), the closest Kenya has come to an established church, is predominantly Kalenjin and Kamba. The Methodist Church is strongly based in the Eastern Province and dominated by the Meru. The Seventh Day Adventists (SDA) is to be found in lower Nyanza and draws heavily from the Kisii. The Quakers are in Western Kenya and the bulk of their membership is Luhya. The Legio Maria is almost exclusively Luo, (formed and registered in the 1960s with the help of the late Jaramogi Oginga Odinga, then Vice-President, the Legio Maria expended much prophetic energy foretelling a bright political future for Odinga). Indeed, the only church that can claim to be truly national is the Catholic Church.[*]

Notwithstanding this ethnic profile, the churches are rarely tribalist when speaking out on democracy. This ethnic neutrality might have arisen

---

[*] Why the Catholic Church has managed to avoid this ethnic profile is a tantalizing question. Much more historical and empirical work is needed. Possible lines of inquiry include assessing its strongly ideological character and the way this attribute may submerge segmental differentiation, its non-elective leadership style, which probably takes away the need for political bargaining and payoffs so characteristic of the Anglican and Presbyterian churches, and its rather centralized decision-making, which minimizes conflicts over issues of management and politics between the centre and the branches.

because the Church has been able to elaborate a theology of power that holds rather well across ethnic lines (Benson, 1995: 177–99). To be sure, the increasingly important role of the Church in the channeling and control of the civic sphere and energy in Africa is part of the explanation for its success as a pro-democracy force in South Africa, Malawi and Kenya. This growing strength has reshaped the nature of the political sphere itself. In places where the church is as important as in Kenya, the reformist churches are the effective counterweight to State predation.

An additional contribution to theory are our findings on the nature, extent and strength of the State in shaping Kenyans' lives. Indeed, the insidiousness of the State seems to be a favourite blind spot of much civil society literature. The responses from the survey suggest that trust levels may actually be *lower* than we intuitively may be led to think. This lack of confidence in the State is an increasingly familiar African tale. Whereas some researchers have been writing off the African State as soft, juridical, decayed or weak, the African people have known differently. The State is 'alive and well' (Sangmpam, 1993) and capable of harming its opponents. Nowhere has this been demonstrated more clearly than in those African countries where incumbent regimes have been re-elected after the first democratic elections. In most of these (Kenya, Zambia and Togo, for example), the State has emerged stronger than predicted and, in all cases, has continued its nasty ways, frequently preying upon civil society.

Moreover, the suggestion that a vigorous civil society necessarily ruptures State hegemony misses an important insight: the State is not an indifferent or idle bystander to civic activity. Frequently, as in Kenya and as convincingly demonstrated by Ngunyi (1996), democratic activism forces the State to move into the civic space, to restrict this space legally (as with the NGO Coordination Act in Kenya), or to prop up statist NGOs and civic organizations.* Beginning in the late 1980s and throughout the early 1990s, the government of Kenya has grown increasingly intrusive in the civic sphere. Professional and clerical organizations at the forefront of the democratic campaign (such as the LSK, the International Commission of Jurists, the National Council of Churches of Kenya (NCCK), the Catholic Church and the Presbyterian Church of East Africa) have been targets of official reprisals. In the 1990s, the State begun to beat them back by propping up rival organizations or engineering Trojan factions within the more vocal of these organizations. To check the NCCK, there is the Redeemed Fellowship Churches of Kenya, dominated by the African Inland Church, to which President Moi belongs. There is a faction of the LSK closely allied to the Attorney General to oppose those within the Society seen to be supportive of reform. To counter the radical Islamic Party of

---

* There is ample evidence from Kenya as to just how insidious this State relocation can be. The former Chief Executive of the NGO Council, the umbrella body for Kenyan NGOs, estimates that in the last two years government officials, including a number of cabinet ministers, have registered close to 200 NGOs, a strategy perhaps to ensure that the government has a large enough majority to take over the NGO Council itself. (The Council is the umbrella body for Kenyan NGOs.)

Kenya, there is the United Muslims of Africa, founded by Omar Masumbuko, an open supporter of President Moi and of the ruling party.

Third, even when the State does not directly prey on civil society and civic space, its relationships with political society and the business community shapes the way in which civil society evolves, affects its performance and mediates the way civil society institutions are perceived and, more critically, funded.

When the State shrinks political space for the opposition, rendering the political parties both ineffective and institutionally weak, the organized parts of civil society often take up some of the national political issues as part of their agenda. If parties are negatively perceived as no more than the electoral vehicles of political entrepreneurs, civic organizations can be both a source of principled leadership and a sobering influence on political parties. But this political role for civil society tends to drive civic organizations into direct competition with political parties, thereby sundering the capacity of both to deepen democracy. Since the 1992 general elections in Kenya, to give one example, civil society organizations have been more focused and vocal on constitutional reform and other broad issues of governance than political parties. In some ways, these institutions have become effective vehicles for interest aggregation and articulation, a traditional party function. The result has been a rather frosty relationship between political parties and the more organized sections of civil society.

In concluding this section we note the following important research themes, suggesting that these are part of what policymakers and African scholars need to examine if we are to deepen our understanding of the capacities of African civil society to contribute to democracy.

First, there is no institution in Kenya that is free of ethnicity. This observation implies that rather than focus on ethnic differences as the key analytic tool in studies of African democracy and civil society, we need to recast the question. We must ask instead how some organizations (particularly the Church) have managed these differences in a manner that has not led to rupture and acrimony. Why has ethnicity not undermined the capacity of the Church to be a force for democracy?

Second, having recognized the low trust that characterizes political exchange between State and society, is there perhaps an argument that analysts should accept in their definition the family, the clan and the tribe as the starting point for the reconstruction of a more realistic theory of the African civil society and of democratization in the continent?

Third, given the continuing predatory nature of the State in Africa, should studies of African civil society not focus as decisively on the State as a continuing variable in the increasing de-institutionalization and weakening of civil society?

Fourth, and finally, how can high-trust organizations such as the Church be used in further efforts to strengthen African civil society without undermining the emergence of a genuinely pluralist society? Although some answers to these questions may emerge later on, we will now look at the role the donors are playing in Kenyan civil society.

DONOR SUPPORT FOR CIVIL SOCIETY

Capture, Release, Capture

The story of donor support for Africa is one of high drama. It needs to be told, because it shapes all else that we have seen in the 1990s.

By the early 1980s, the State in Africa was in crisis. First, incipient ethnic sub-nationalism had undermined the case for the nation-State, signaling that the social contract that underpinned the African State's post-colonial models of development was increasingly being questioned (Ngunyi and Wachira, 1997). Nationalist, anti-liberal and hostile to ethnic pluralism, that contract required African people, in the halcyon days of independence, to trade in their liberty for official guarantees of prosperity. Second, to support the role it had planned for itself, it became a key player in the economy and took on large social provisioning programmes – the State had grown large and unwieldy. This over extension had in turn led to substantial attrition of its managerial capacity as 'characterized by ramshackle regimes of highly personal rule' that were 'severely deficient in institutional authority and capability'. To survive the predation of the State, citizens had taken flight into 'groups and survival mechanisms that compete with the State, including suffer-manage' (Sangmpam, 1993).

In the main, the State was seen as patrimonial and clientelist, bottling up creativity and undermining the growth of a rule-based entrepreneurial culture. Lacking in bureaucratic probity, this State spawned ineptitude, corruption, inefficiency and, eventually, crowded out the private sector.

To reverse the continent's fortunes, African economies had to adopt a variety of measures to 'improve governance'. According to the World Bank, the way to undercut prebendal politics was to install a new policy regime rooted in a sharp dichotomization of the public and the free market spheres. The problem with Africa, so the consensus ran, was that interest groups allied to the State routinely used their power to vote themselves 'increases in public expenditure while diffusing the resultant costs through rises in general taxation' (Olukoshi and Mkandawire, 1995), or else engaged in directly unproductive profit-making through manipulation of civil service bureaucracies, parastatals and the complex regulatory environments that created opportunities for punitive illegal taxation.

Shrinking this type of State, therefore, became the conceptual hook on which neo-liberal reformers hung their programmes throughout the early and mid 1980s. Governments were to supply supportive policies, meaning that they were to abandon protectionist policies, pare down their civil service bureaucracies, privatize State-owned enterprises (SOEs), remove tariff barriers and open up to trade.* In addition, they were required to

---

* The intellectual case for international trade and global integration, which is part of the World Bank orthodoxy, is deftly argued by Sachs and Warner (1995) in *Economic Reform and Global Integration*. They argue that the key failure of most developing countries is that few have been continuously open from the start of the post-war period. On the whole, Sachs argues, these have recorded better economic performance than the closed ones.

remove market distortions such as food subsidies, price controls and commodity movement restrictions. Trimmed of its bureaucratic baggage, the State would become essentially protective: defining and securing property rights; providing effective legal, judicial and regulatory systems; improving the efficiency of the civil service and protecting the environment (World Bank, 1997).

The authoritarian withdrawals in Eastern and Central Europe justified and amplified the donors' brief. Seen in Western diplomatic circles as the triumph of Western liberalism, these withdrawals added moral fervour to Western reformers. Not only was economic reform necessary, but also its long-term survival was now seen as dependent on democratic change. The pursuit of democracy and economic reform became, for many Northern donors, the overall goals of their aid programmes.

How would economic reform feed into broader democratic transformation? In the view of some theorists (Diamond et al., 1988), shrinking the State would encourage the emergence of a genuinely productive African middle class able to play by the discipline of anonymous market forces. Structural adjustment was thus not only economically rational, it also made long-term political sense for would be supporters of democracy. It was a force that can liberate the one class capable of leading the continent to democratic governance.

Thus far, we have the theory. In practice, donors did not agree on how to put into practice what they now agreed were the key ingredients of successful economic and political reform. In the case of Kenya, most donors worried about corruption and the government's intransigence to calls for democracy.

In mid 1990, the government violently cracked down on pro-democracy protesters in Nairobi. That October, the United States became the first Western country to tie its aid to Kenya explicitly on political and legal reform, suspending further disbursements until the government restored the independence of the judges of the high court and the court of appeal. This independence had been stripped away in a precipitous amendment to the Kenya Constitution in 1988 to check judicial scrutiny into the treatment of dissidents by the police.

In 1991, Denmark followed the US, suspending its aid to the Rural Development Fund on grounds of corruption and mismanagement. Then, in the autumn of 1991, the hammer fell. The Consultative Group for Kenya suspended balance-of-payment support to Kenya, awaiting further progress on a select number of governance issues. Almost on cue, the government released political prisoners and repealed one-party law to allow political competition.

Soon after these reforms, however, the donor coalition that had forced the Kenyan government to back down soon collapsed. Official donor thinking, seemingly coinciding with the fragmentation of the domestic opposition to the government, also splintered into three. There were those donors who were no longer interested in political reforms. These, the

French, the Italians, Swiss and the Japanese would leave well enough alone, totally delinking their aid from political reform, itself clearly a political vote for the status quo. There were those who styled themselves the positive conditionality donors. They did not suspend aid but rather used it as a carrot, supporting projects that they felt would advance positive reforms. These soft conditionality donors were mainly the British and the Germans. Finally, there were those donors who did not balk at using direct political sanction, if needs be, suspending aid in an effort to push political changes. These, the negative conditionality ones, sometimes termed hard conditionality donors, include the United States, Denmark, Sweden, Canada and the Nordic countries.

With the rupture of the 1991 donor coalition came a change in the nature and overall aid commitment by donor category. On the whole, aid from the soft and no conditionality donors either remained at the pre-1991 level or climbed substantially. In the case of Japan and Germany, the aid went up to a point where they are now the largest donors to Kenya. Support from the hard conditionality donors went into precipitous decline. The case of the United States is instructive: at the turn of the decade it was the third largest donor to Kenya – it is now seventh. Its total aid has fallen from about US$77 million in the mid 1980s to around US$20 million, a 74 per cent decline.

But this donor realignment also became the occasion for donor interest in civil society. Although the hard conditionality donors' overall support fell rather precipitously, it also became increasingly important for emerging CSOs. All hard conditionality donors have become a significant presence in Kenya's civil society, especially crucial to the survival and growth of urban-based advocacy groups led by professionals. The soft and no conditionality donors have remained insignificant to civil society programmes.

Multilateral agencies appeared to continue working on the principle of the minimum consensus. Thus the European Union, the World Bank and the International Monetary Fund (IMF) have had no significant interest in civil society. Such interest as they have had has been limited to activities that donors would rarely disagree about; such as providing support for the electoral process. Other than bilaterals and multilaterals, foundations have also been important to civil society support in Kenya. Other than the German political foundations, which are really bilateral donors in disguise because all their funds come from the Ministry of International Cooperation, and the Ford Foundation, most other foundations are not significant donors, making only occasional grants. In this regard, this chapter does not focus on them. In the next section, we assess the overall support to civil society by the United States, the Swedish International Development Cooperation Agency (SIDA) and the Danish International Development Assistance (DANIDA), the key bilateral donors in civil society support.

A Tale of Three Donors

The foregoing brief historical sketch reminds us of an important truth. Donors did not come to support civic organizations out of a belief and faith in their potential. Rather, donor support for civil society was meant to confront the state. Having failed to persuade the State of the folly of its ways, they alighted on the remarkable option of supporting the State's own citizens against it: giving them money and resources so that they could lobby for positive change and check its more egregious excesses.

We should assess donor support for civil society in the context of this back-handed compliment. The data that follow are culled from three different studies that I have been involved in over the last two and a half years. The first was an assessment of the impact of political conditionality on constitutional reform in Kenya (1996), the second was a strategy paper for NORAD (the Norwegian Agency for Development Co-operation), conducted under the auspices of the Norwegian Institute for Human Rights (1996), and the final study was a civic education evaluation done for USAID (January 1997). The figures in Table 5.3 are aggregates.

Table 5.3 shows overall support to CSOs by the three key bilateral donors over a three-year period (1993–96). (I have deliberately left out donor support for election monitoring covering financial years 1992 and 1997; there is usually massive donor interest in the elections and a substantial part of that funding goes to local NGOs for election monitoring. Counting this episodic support would skew the picture because very little election monitoring money goes to support long-term programme work or institution building.) USAID is by far the largest donor to civil society, contributing more than three times what SIDA and DANIDA respectively give in a year.*

It is clear that donors to civil society have so far taken a sectoral concentration approach. The largest category is gender advocacy, which takes one out of every five dollars of all donor support to civil society. Donor policy

---

* This figure may mask the rather precipitous decline of official US assistance to Kenya. From a high of US$77.5 million, US aid had fallen to US$53.3 million. Yet aggregate figures can mislead. US funds are disbursed under different headings and spending authorities. Considered under these different headings, the impact of the decline is more evident. Funds under the Economic Support Fund stood at US$30 million in 1983. By 1988, they had fallen by 52 per cent to US$14.4 million. They climbed marginally the next year, fell by another 20 per cent the year after and were altogether suspended in 1990 after the US conditioned aid to Kenya on political and economic reform. Support under this heading has not been resumed. Civil society support, however, is disbursed from the Development Fund for Africa. The amount spent under this heading stood at roughly the same level as that for the Economic Support Fund at the beginning of the 1980s, but has declined steadily since then to an average of US$18 million per year today. This figure is also somewhat misleading, however; the actual amounts disbursed may actually be less. Over the 1993/1994 financial year, for instance, much of the money intended for Democracy and Governance activities was not actually spent. They were held up by negotiations between USAID and the Kenyan government over what eventually came to be termed the DG project. After much dithering, the government refused to sign the framework agreement and everything collapsed. In the meantime, many project proposals had been deferred, awaiting the conclusion of the agreement.

Table 5.3: *Donor support to civic activities (in US dollars)*

Programme Area	USAID	DANIDA	SIDA	Totals	Ranking
		Donor and level of support			
Gender	607,970	101,455	409,031	1,118,456	1
Capacity building/ institutional support	576,551	464,275	—	1,040,826	2
Research and publications	898,629	99,039	—	997,668	3
Law and human rights	621,547	103,130	205,448	930,125	4
Civic education	488,900	22,100	208,807	719,807	5
Media	246,532	146,620	41,866	435,018	6
Democracy scholarships	187,200	—	—	187,200	7
Doctors fees	—	93,066	—	93,066	8
Miscellaneous	—	—	61,268	61,268	9
Totals	3,627,329	1,029,685	926,420	5,583,434	

Source: United States Agency for International Development (USAID), Danish International Development Assistance (DANIDA), Swedish International Development Cooperation Agency (SIDA).

differences are stark on this issue in particular. SIDA spends most of its funding on this category, committing about 39 per cent of its total support to civil society to gender issues (it is important to point out, however, that a large proportion of these funds was actually spent on financing attendance at the Beijing conference). Support for capacity building for civil organizations is the next priority, absorbing 18.6 per cent of the total. Law and human rights activism is another important heading, taking up 16.3 per cent of total support. Sectoral concentration is also reflected in organizational concentration. Most donors concentrate their funding to just about 40 civic organizations, an average of US$142,500 each over the last three years.

The aggregate figures should not mask the power relations between donors and NGOs, however. A common grouse from NGOs was the unreasonableness of donor requirements. Some charged that donors were too focused on reports and financial accounting and less on programme quality and impact. Two organizations worried about the intellectual role played by donors in setting the civil society agenda. They said that there were situations in which the process of proposal revision eventually led to a situation where the final programme belonged to the donor, not the NGO. A key problem seems to be a perception that there is no real commitment to donor/recipient partnerships, no matter what the policy papers say.

On their part, donors complained about a lack of financial probity and discipline on the part of NGOs. Some NGOs gave fraudulent accounts and shirked on performance. Many, all the donors we interviewed agreed, were poorly managed. Lack of organizational depth led to numerous opportunities for slippage. One donor, however, excoriated his colleagues on the grounds that some of the requirements they imposed on NGOs were unrealistic. A key variable in the success of any funded programme was the political environment. This donor, Oxfam, wondered how many donors were 'ready to live with the political consequences of their funding decisions'. This suggests that performance targets needed to take consideration of political factors.

In addition, these aggregates may also mask the fraternization and coalition formation between donor organizations and NGOs and the way in which this skews actual funding. For instance, although we have worked out the averages, in the actual fieldwork it was obvious that some organizations were donor favourites, receiving significant funds from each of the key civil society donors. Although the interviews with donors suggested that funds were disbursed according to the absorptive capacities of the organization, some donors readily admitted that the reputation of the leaders of these organizations was an important factor in the funding decision. There was certainly evidence of favouritism. In one case, it was clear that one donor was partial to one organization, describing the executive director of a favourite organization as almost his 'son'. In another case, one organization was clearly favoured, receiving more than a quarter of a donor's total funding to civil society over a two-year period. In yet another, more than 50 per cent of the donor's support for capacity building in civil society went to one organization alone.

The institutional profiles of the funded organizations raise further questions. For one, for example, there is a clear predominance of lawyers in the field: 10 out of 40 surveyed were involved in law-related activities and 13 were headed by lawyers, not including the number of lawyers actually employed by these organizations. This suggest that the funding focus is rather narrow. A second issue was the age of many of these organizations; a majority are less than six years old and only four in our sample are more than 15 years old. We learned that in 1992 and 1993, donors surfeited with funds for civil society went around shopping for good organizations. The result was donor 'over-funding and civil society under-consumption' (Ngunyi, 1996).

This power-struggle cocktail, political footlooseness and the newness of 'civil society' as a concept and the fragile partnerships formed within it, spawned both practical and theoretical problems. Donors are still putting money into civil society and yet many are unclear what impacts they are having. Performance indicators are now the subject of intense discussion among donors. Within USAID, draft indicators have been prepared but are yet to be operational. Other donors indicate that they have planned to follow suit. One Kenyan NGO suggested that indicators might mislead, especially because these are likely to measure quantitative as opposed to qualitative impacts. Another suggested that donors should approach civil society funding much like venture capitalism; out of every ten investments donors make, eight might go bust. The two that work, however, more than compensate for the funding experimentation. Donors counter that funding does not belong to them, hence the need to have indicators to convince headquarters that taxpayers' money is being used well.

Shadowing these relationships and attendant battles is the political and social environment in Kenya. We found that formal civic organizations are divided sharply by both vertical (territory, ethnicity) and horizontal (urban/rural divide and class) cleavages. Frequently, civic groups are further divided by policy and programmatic differences, patterning themselves on the larger cleavages between opposition and government. In the civic education evaluation, for instance, we found out that civic education NGOs in Kenya are dominated by a few ethnic groups, typically those that also dominate opposition politics. This may account for the perception, captured by some of the field reports, that supporters of the ruling party felt that civic education is a weapon against government and that CSOs are out-riders of the opposition, or else they are 'proto-parties' and political action committees.

Donors skew the picture even further, typically limiting their support to English-speaking, urban-based middle-class groups, thereby playing a part in the marginalization of the popular sectors of civil society, especially rural economic groups and community-based organizations. Some donors seem aware of the potential of their funding to feed into existing social cleavages and to privileged conservative, pro-status groups and elitist NGOs. They point out, however, that they do not have the administrative capacity to run a nationwide grants programme. They provide a corrective by insisting that a certain proportion of the funds for a particular programme does have a rural component. This condition may ameliorate the more perverse 'five-star hotel seminar and workshop' programmes so evident of donor-funded civic programmes in the early 1990s, but they do not address the deeper ethnic and social cleavages that pervade funded civil society programmes. Although this rural conditionality has forced a number of Nairobi-based organizations to establish links with rural groups, many of these relationships are forged through the Church (suffering all the difficulties alluded to earlier) and some may even suffer Briefcase Empowerment Syndrome, a caricature of a Nairobi-based NGO representative grabbing his empowerment kit and rushing off to inject some rural folk with donor-funded prophylactics.

This research suggests that some of the assumptions that underlie current theorizing of African civil society are inadequate to the realities. The literature tends to dichotomize civil society. Good civil society is populated by professional groups, the Church and human rights lobbies, and bad civil society is made up of ethnically inspired groups. In the main, civic bonds founded on segmental loyalties, such as those of clan and tribe, are currently off limits for theory, seen negatively as part of the problem that modernizing, functional and instrumental civil society should overcome if democracy is to take root in Africa. Thus the most virtuous of civic organizations is one that has learned to leave tribal loyalty behind, one that is animated by the forces of class and ideology. Positive social change is seen to entail a community's 'growing consciousness of (class) at the expense of (tribe)'. Based on this assumption, tribe is seen as a residual category, inhabited by only those few who have not, through urban wage labour or Western education, suffered the creative pangs of detribal-ization (Lonsdale and Berman, 1992: 212–13).

But our data, analysed more fully in Thalman et al. (1997), seem to suggest that tribe and class are often contiguous categories, both in time and in space, intersecting and intertwining. For there is no contradiction that the urban elite that leads the donor-funded segment of civil society should both select its kin and the local elite in its civic education target-ting. This practice confirms Lonsdale and Berman's perceptive insight that 'people can enter into class struggle as much to prevent themselves from being treated as members of a separate moral and social category as to defend their economic interests in common with those who appear (...) to be their class colleagues' (Lonsdale and Berman, 1992). Many among the African elite are keen not to let their class positions and new beliefs separate them from their social surroundings.

Given this understanding, there is no idealized civil society out there waiting to be discovered. Civil society is contextual, and the forces both of class and of kinship can animate its capacity to fight for and help root democracy. There can be no *a priori* assumption that only civil society based on non-kin ties can serve democracy.

Overview of Donor Funded Civil Society

Donor Capture

As emphasized in the preceding pages, a key feature of donor support for civil society is an intense concentration on a limited number of organiza-tions and issues. Surveying the five largest democracy and governance donors in Kenya (SIDA, USAID, DANIDA, the Ford Foundation, and NORAD), we found a clear bias towards particular organizations. The Kenya Human Rights Commission (KHRC), the Centre for Governance and Development (CGD), Research and Civic Awareness Program (RECAP) and the International Federation of Women Lawyers (FIDA) were the runaway favourites. There are several explanations for this concentration.

One explanation is that it is significant that the NGOs with heavy donor support are also the human rights and law-based organizations. These two issues are central to the mandates of the Ford Foundation, USAID and SIDA. Given that these donors fund unsolicited proposals, it is likely that there is an unconscious process of donor self-selection at work here. If so, there is a danger that donors may end up funding projects that resemble what they see in their own countries as opposed to what might be more urgent for the recipient country. In itself, this emphasis would undermine the impact of the programme.

A second explanation is that most donors readily admit that reputation, both of the organization and of the key individuals, is also a determinant of the decision to fund. In practice, this means that newer NGOs with relatively unknown managers have a more difficult time accessing certain donors.

The undue advantage that accrues to older NGOs with recognized managers may lead to a form of donor–civil society mutual capture.*

One of our earlier studies indicated that rent-seeking activities (including over-invoicing and fictitious attendance at seminars) take place primarily in the institutions whose leaders have either captured the donor or have been captured by the donor (Ngunyi, 1996). In the absence of performance indicators, and in the context of the goodwill generated by the mutual capture, some organizations are subject to too-friendly oversight by the donor. Shirking on performance is relatively easy.

All the donors in the civic education evaluation, except one grassroots development organization, admitted that they had no relationship with the final beneficiaries of their funding. There were, therefore, no countervailing reports on what the NGOs did. Evaluations undertaken were often coordinated by the NGOs who set up appointments and designated who the evaluator from the donor would talk to. Beyond the reports and these stage-managed evaluation interviews, donors may not really have independent criteria for assessing the impact of the civic institutions that they have funded.

Equally problematic, donors work with unsolicited proposals. Proposal writing can become a process of second-guessing the donors. If it is generally known that a certain donor, say SIDA, is keen on gender issues, a proposal with a good deal of gender content will be sent out. Given the professional sophistication of urban CSOs in Kenya, it is clear that urban groups have an easier time capturing the donor imagination than rural civil society organizations, many of which are managed by less well-educated leaders.

Hence, there is an ensemble of civic organizations battling for space near the donor pork barrel. Given the clubby nature of donors in a small country like Kenya, and the fact that the word spreads, this crowding often leads to the recycling of similar activities by the same group but for different donors. In one instance, one of the programmes we surveyed included a conference on 'Building Democracy in a Multi-Ethnic Society' for which USAID gave US$20,000 and SIDA US$10,000. The total of US$30,000 is an unjustifiably high amount to spend on a two-day, non-residential workshop in a country like Kenya.

The Donor as an Alternative State

Grant-making in the democracy and governance sector has seen the donor gradually evolve into an 'alternative State'. The shrinking of the indepen-

---

* In two cases we found a situation where the executive directors of two different human rights NGOs were regularly consulted by a donor on proposals submitted by other human rights organizations. Such individuals can use their privileged positions to shut out possible competitors for donor funding. In one case, one called up the executive director of a competing but friendly NGO that had submitted a proposal to a donor and assured him that he had put in a good word for his proposal and that chances were that the funding would come through. The funding did finally come through. Clearly, when this kind of intervention occurs, it vests enormous clout in an individual if others come to believe that he or she is key to receiving funding from a particular donor.

dent State has resulted in the emergence of other State-like actors with resources and authority similar to those of the State.

The mechanisms of this evolution are complex but they cover a whole range of agenda items. First, for a start, African civil society has no political language of its own. The language of political reform in Africa is a language generated by donors. Terms like 'empowerment' and 'aid re-engineering' are part of the lexicon of the aid business, this language figures prominently in the proposals of local NGOs and in their presentations at seminars. One wonders whether this language can be used among civil society groups in rural Kenya. Even more worrying are suspicions that this dependency on donor language is perhaps part of a larger intellectual dependency.

Second, the extent to which local politics is often mediated by donors is remarkable. The donors are often the first organized group that the opposition in Kenya speaks to when it has an idea to sell. When the Democratic Party of Kenya was formed in 1992, a professor of law and a leading commentator wrote, without any hint of irony that the democratic party was 'a party the World Bank should like'. When the government refused to register the Safina party fronted by palaeontologist Richard Leakey and opposition leader Paul Muite, Leakey and his friends expended considerable efforts trying to lobby the donors to pressure the government into registering the party. They did not spend as much time trying to win Kenyan public opinion.

Third, the acquisition by the donors of the accretions of the State has led to donor/State polarities within civil society. The State expends considerable energy trying to capture segments of civil society, partly to check the expansion of its more critical segments but also to counteract the impact of donors. As the State creates patronage networks in civil society, the donor appears to do the same. It is instructive that in the parliamentary debates on the NGO Coordination Act in Kenya, one of the key complaints voiced by Members of Parliament was the receipt of donor funds by local NGOs and the use of these funds to fight the State. It was clear that many saw the law as giving the government the statutory framework to check the growing power of those NGOs funded by donors.

As Ngunyi has noted, this emergence of the donor with a statist profile 'has led to the trifurcation of civil society into the State-driven sector on the one hand, the popular sector in the middle, and the donor-driven sector on the other hand. As the State encroaches and captures civil society actors on one end and the donor on the other, the independent sector inevitably shrinks' or is pushed to the margins of mainstream political dialogue (Ngunyi, 1996). In this regard, it is revealing that key actors in civil society in Kenya, such as co-operatives, farmers and informal groups, hardly ever figure in the reform debate in spite of their obvious power and influence. More remarkably, even when they demonstrate their power to extract concessions from the State in a manner that the more donor-friendly organizations are unable to accomplish, they remain outside the mainstream.

Rent-Seeking in Civil Society

Civil society, as noted, often reproduces the cleavages in society. In addition, key CSOs often adopt the profiles of existing political institutions and structures. This often includes bad political practices. The Leeds Study revealed that civil society can become an arena of accumulation: rent-seeking activities such as over-invoicing, fraudulent billing for seminars and faking of seminar participants' names are common. As a result of personal and institutional competition to corner funding, territorial behaviour can become very pronounced in the funded corner of civil society.

Many civic organizations in Kenya are small and dominated by either their founders or executive directors. In fact, MONGOs (My Own NGO) and NGIs (Non Governmental Individuals) are rife in Kenyan civil society. These are performances by the blue-eyed boys and girls of an unsuspecting busy donor. This is how Ngunyi (1996) reports on one of our early encounters with lack of transparency and accountability in civil society:

> *During our research work, we (made) two visits to one of the heavily funded institutions. We were told that its Chairman was on leave for one year on a visiting fellowship overseas. The acting Chairman unwittingly told us that he had specific instructions not to 'talk to anyone regarding the operations of the institution for one year ... only the Chairman can answer questions about our institution'. The treasurer was more dramatic. In a bid to keep us out, he threatened to expose us (as) a KANU (government sponsored) 'audit' group masquerading as scholars. He refused to talk to us until 'Chairman comes back', six months down the road.* (Ngunyi, 1996)

This was clear evidence of the total dominance of the chair. Where such chairs are unaccountable, patronage can run deep. Consulting contracts for training, civic education and other small research services are not competitively given out. The organization nurtures what has been called exclusive systems of patronage wherein patronage is reserved for a small group of friends of the executive director.

RECONSTRUCTING THE STATE, DONOR AND CIVIL SOCIETY RELATIONSHIPS

The State and Civil Society: Coming to Grips with the Relationship

The agnostic tone struck in this chapter regarding current theoretical and funding approaches to African civil society are rooted in a general optimism about the potential of African civil society and of the hopes for democratic renewal in Africa. The chapter has the overall objective of pointing out the gaps in current approaches, however, showing where those approaches may offer solutions worse than the ailment. This task is especially urgent because much of the theory on African civil society has programmatic objectives intended to furnish a philosophical justification for current interventions in the continent. Having argued that much of the theory is inadequate, this last section highlights the neighbourhoods we must ply if we are to find theories more faithful to the realities we seek to change.

First, there is need for much more attention to the African State. A good deal of its supposed weaknesses are not empirically established; they are drawn from the parlous condition of the State in Europe in the last century. A key limitation in the empirical investigation of the African State has been the lack of settled operational variables – what makes a State? The difficulty of a task is, however, a bad argument for its scholarly neglect.

Moreover, by comparing the evolution of civil society in Africa to that of European civil society, the literature ignores the ways in which the foisting of colonialism on Africa changed the trajectory of the evolution of the State and, hence, the civil society that developed within the institutional framework established by that State. In particular, the evolution of the colonial State as a low-trust institution should give pause to those who devalue segmental loyalty and kinship identity as a basis for civic action. The French declaration of the rights of Man celebrated not only rights of individuals but also 'fraternity', a fact obscured by Anglo-American rights discourse. Fraternal bonds are the refuge that the African middle class takes when faced by a predatory State. Political and economic reprisals against members of an ethnic elite are always interpreted as attempts to finish that ethnic group.

Second, studies of African democratization need to resist the unwarranted theoretical jump from 'the State is not viable' to 'civil society is the key to Africa's success'. Civil society in Africa, as elsewhere, has arisen historically and relationally. The importance of informal groups, spontaneous protests, suffer-manage (or, making do), lack of discipline and laxity as foils of civic action has everything to do with the predation of the African State. African society's relation with the State ought, therefore, to be placed in its historical continuum, seen as the natural, although not inevitable, consequence of the evolution of that State.

What has been lacking so far in much of the literature is a more sensitive analysis, one that carefully explores the complexities of State/society interaction. In particular, an analysis is needed that explores the interpenetrations between political and civic institutions, the political and social forces unleashed by that interaction, the changing patterns of elite behaviour implied and the larger question of how all these undermine or support democracy.

Third, because the State in Africa has evolved as a low-trust institution, it is neither neutral nor disinterested in civil society's political choices. Much of its institutional logic focuses on fragmenting opposition. In discussing the pluralizing potential of African civil society, therefore, there is a need to deal with the double jeopardy confronting African civic groups – the task of survival in a hostile institutional environment coupled with the mission to change State behaviour. Complicating the picture is the role of the State as a player in civil society, sometimes directly, sometimes through proxies. This participation sustains the distrust between groups in civil society, sometimes nurturing the polarities that Ngunyi has observed.

Fourth, and finally, scholars should not set too much store by economic reform or its potential to democratize the African State. Efforts to shrink the State via adjustment rest on an obvious paradox: shrinking the State is an act of auto-limitation. It is the State that must pare itself down (Hutchful, 1995). Because regimes are not self annihilating, we can expect that they will manipulate and selectively implement adjustment programmes in ways that do not threaten core regime interests. Rather than strengthen civil society, economic reform may serve to shift the sites of repression.

Moreover, exogenously driven reforms often give governments the feeling that they are being bullied. This interpretation may considerably undermine genuine commitment to reform and deepen State antipathy to both domestic reform constituents and donors. Local pro-reform groups are then perceived as fifth columnists for the donors, making them accept-able targets of State reprisals. Donors, on their part, are often seen as allies of the domestic opposition. In Kenya, reform efforts from donors have fed into a siege mentality that is pervasive in key State actors. Feeling buffeted from all sides, principally by the opposition and donors, the State often implements reforms in a manner that will not substantially erode its hold on the economy or undercut the State elite's economic power.

Sometimes the reforms are sequenced and paced in a way that maximizes benefit to the State elite, both instrumentally and politically. The Kenya government began its privatization programme by off-loading the smallish, often profit-making enterprises in which some of its key officials and cronies were investors. The shares in some of these enter-prises, such as those in Firestone (Kenya) Ltd (15 per cent government share-holding) and Eveready (Kenya) Ltd, were sold grossly undervalued. The parliamentary oversight body, the Public Investment Committee, also queried the sale of Kensalt, a State-owned enterprise believed to have been sold to politically connected businesses for a paltry sum. On the key para-statals, often the arenas of the State's redistributionist and patronage politics, much remains to be done. Where bills for large privatizations have been drafted, as in the case of Kenya Posts and Telecommunications, the government has structured the proposed privatization in a manner that raises the suspicion that it intends to retain substantial managerial control. The point is that economic reforms that the State patronises in this way are likely to strengthen the State elite, enrich their cronies and undermine the actual reform measures and constrain the emergence of significant democratic forces within civil society.

In turn, this suggests that we must also reject the assumption that civil society groups have equal access to political as well as other resources.

Class cleavages, differentiated access and favouritism define the way different groups relate to the State and to political society and the market.

Donors and Civil Society: Pre-Empting Civic Death

Much of what donors have done in Kenya in support of civil society has had a significant impact on political change. No doubt the repeal of one party law in Kenya was spurred by donor pressure. Critically, the constitutional reform debate now underway has been led by donor-funded NGOs. This and more can be done.

But aid is an addiction, fostering financial and, more perniciously, intellectual dependency. A word of caution then: the road to perdition may be strewn with good intentions. The key question for donors is the possibility of giving principled and sustainable support to civil society. This suggests broadening as well as deepening knowledge of African civil society; in particular understanding what might sap or energize it.

First, there is surely a case for a good-faith effort to find rural groups worth supporting. Many urban-based groups are no doubt well meaning and will probably make valiant efforts to link with rural groups and to impart lobby skills to them. But their good intentions is about all they can offer. Many are ill-prepared for the difficulties of communication entailed in working at the grassroots, they may be blind to pressing local needs, the cost of conducting surveys on needs can be prohibitive and they may be distrusted and lack a continuing presence in the community. They can become only itinerant problem solvers.

Long-term support to African civil society may profit from building partnerships and twinning arrangements between local and urban groups,* thus providing an important corrective to the current preoccupation with civil and political rights. Groups at the grassroots are likely, as we saw in our survey, to have an economic and social mandate as opposed to a legal one. Many of the organizations that are invisible to donors are in the economic sphere, yet have often been able to cause shifts in government behaviour through civic action. For instance, although the government in Kenya has been intransigent to demands for constitutional reform, a campaign fronted by the urban middle class, it has moved swiftly to negotiate peaceful outcomes with farmers' groups whenever they have taken to the streets. It backed down when the tea farmers threatened to shut down the industry if the government persisted in its efforts to foist Mr. Eric Kotut on them, the disgraced former governor of the Central Bank. It relented when milk farmers demanded autonomy from the government patronage in Kenya Co-operative Creameries. It has recently opened dialogue with coffee farmers and millers who are challenging the right of the Coffee Board of Kenya, a State monopoly, to be the only legally authorized auctioneer.

---

* This is one of the recommendations made in Thalman, et al. (1997).

Twinning arrangements linking these economic groups with human rights and legal advocacy groups could be beneficial to both: rooting the legal groups in society and giving the economic groups advocacy skills. These links would also help urban middle-class groups to capture and channel the political energy that comes from spontaneous civic action in the rural areas.

Second, donors and civil society ought to be ever alert to the *raison d'être* of their relationship. The intransigence of the State was the occasion for the consummation of the donor–civil society relationship. The donors' first love was always the State. After all, aid has traditionally been a government-to-government business. Civic groups in South Africa are learning this lesson rather painfully. In the context of an open and transparent Mandela government, support for civil society has declined precipitously. Most organizations never anticipated this change; forced to live with less, they have learned lessons from the anorexic American corporation – how to become ever leaner.

But the donors were also guilty of failing to plan. Surely, if aid will inevitably remain a government-to-government business, it is logical for those who give it and the NGOs that receive it to anticipate that one day it must all cease. This means planning for exit and investing in sustainability. Donors' most frequent complaint about their civil society support is that civic institutions are not sufficiently accountable and that most are not sustainable. No donor in the studies mentioned in the foregoing distinguished between *institutional sustainability*, that is, the sustainability of the NGO as an organization and *programmatic sustainability*, that is, the sustainability of the programmes initiated by the NGOs they funded. Most are also unclear about what investing in sustainability meant. One donor, OXFAM, said that it always invested in sustainability and had over the years evolved mechanisms for handing over projects to the beneficiaries.

One gets the impression that NGOs and donors worry more about institutional sustainability, hence the frequent question of 'what are you doing to raise funds locally'. Although this is a legitimate concern, programmatic sustainability is probably of more immediate importance to democratization. It is on this that the sustainability question should focus.

6 PERU: CIVIL SOCIETY AND THE AUTOCRATIC CHALLENGE

Pepi Patrón[*]

As argued in the book's introductory chapters, it is important to remember that civil society, at least in its form as organized community life, existed throughout the world long before Western audiences became interested in the topic. It has been an empirical reality for centuries in Peru. As in pre-colonial times, such social groups continue to be the focus around which life and work are organized for an important sector of the rural population, and the space where solidarities and collective ends are achieved.

Nevertheless, the discourse on civil society is something new (Cohen and Arato, 1992: 2), as is the existence of aid for the explicit purpose of strengthening CSOs. Although the concept was originally introduced into academic circles in Latin America from a Gramscian perspective, its use now extends beyond the limits of academics. As early as the beginning of the 1980s, the concept appeared in political discussions, in the media and even in public discourse. Today, that language reaches donors and those CSOs favoured with foreign support. Those donors are the subject of this paper.

The use (and eventual abuse) of the civil society concept, however, cannot be examined apart from the wider context of Peruvian history during the last few decades. One of the hypotheses developed here is that the actual concept of civil society is directly linked to the weakening of the popular movements that ruled the Peruvian socio-political scene in the late 1960s and the 1970s. Such movements were closely linked to left-wing organizations and parties concerned with the notion of class and the idea that the State represented the economic interests of the dominant classes, the 'civil society' of the bourgeoisie. The solution was to capture the State

* The author wishes to acknowledges the help of Juan José Ccoyllo in the preparation of this chapter.

with a working-class perspective. The failure of the State to change was in turn seen as responsible for the decades-long presence of military regimes, the rise of populism, as well as subsequent reform attempts to insert control by political (as opposed to civil) society over the State apparatus. The Cuban Revolution, the socialist regime in Chile and the reforms of Velasco Alvarado in Peru were particularly important elements in this history. The heroes of the 1970s were popular movements. Yet, by the end of the 1970s, many popular organizations had disintegrated.

A second hypothesis suggests that 'civil society' is now linked to a broad range of *other* political and social objectives. The popularity of the term came about partly as a result of new social actors (for instance, representatives of entrepreneurial or women's organizations) and the need to account for this growing pluralism in the 1990s. Much had changed in Peru, including the need to make sense of ten years of internal war, since civil society was conceived as the face of popular movements during the 1970s. Our review of donor documentation and interviews reflect some of those changes, but they also illustrate how the concept is used by different agencies, foundations or Northern NGOs to express a plethora of perspectives. Some of our interviewees, indeed, refer to the civil society concept as a muddle with room for almost everything (see Roncagliolo, 1997: 38).

In this chapter we will examine the ways in which this pluralistic civil society relates to Northern donors and to the State, as well as to market forces. We will try to show, as the second chapter has argued, that the language of civil society is language about, and language that shapes, power relationships. In the Peruvian case, the nature of the State shaped by the current regime is of primary importance in defining these power relationships. Based on interviews with people in government and in academic, grassroots and donor communities, the first section maps Peruvian civil society and various relationships among civil society groups, the State and the market; the second section is devoted to describing donor activities within civil society and their power relationships with regard to the State and other actors. Some general impressions on how ideas about civil society improve the prospects for development and democracy are displayed in the last section, pointing the way forward for policy-makers.

MAPPING CIVIL SOCIETY IN PERU

A Brief History of Later Evolution

Efforts to achieve democracy in Peru face ancient and deeply rooted problems. The traumatic European conquest of the Inca empire, which laid the foundation for modern Peru, opened an enduring social chasm between the conquerors and the conquered. Through three centuries of colonial life, Peru was ruled by a social, economic and institutional order born of that original rupture. In the following 170 years as a republic,

Table 6.1: *Important dates in Peruvian history*

1821	Peru becomes an independent republic after war with Spain.
1821–50	The republic is governed by 'Caudillos' of all sorts.
1879	War with Chile.
1890–30	Called the Aristocratic Republic. From 1919 to 1929, a dictatorship under Leguía.
1930–68	Seesawing of democracy and dictatorship.
1968–75	*Coup d'état* and dictatorship of General Velasco Alvarado over elected President Belaunde
1975–79	*Coup d'etat* from General Morales Bermudez, who called for a Constitutional Assembly in 1979. New Constitution in 1979.
1980	Back to democracy with the re-election of Fernando Belaunde. Beginning of Shining Path violence.
1985	Democratic election of President Alan García.
1990	Democratic election of President Alberto Fujimori, within a context of hyper-inflation and terrorism.
1992	Self-coup (*auto-gulpe*) of Fujimori, closing of Congress and the installation of a Constitutional Congress. Shining Path national leader Abimael Guzmán captured. New Constitution in 1993 that allows presidential re-election.
1995	Fujimori's re-election.
2000	New elections planned.

Peru's enormous difficulties in building a nation integrated in all its social, economic, political and cultural aspects have become all too clear (see Table 6.1). Peruvians' difficulties in acting in a united fashion have their roots in multiple divisions, both historical and recent.

The most persistent of these ruptures is ethno-social. The idea of a collective 'us' has racial connotations, and these connotations affect how Peruvians process conflicts related to social origin: the conflicts of status, class, gender, culture and regional background. Democracy requires processes that allow citizens to relate as equals with the same opportunities and the same rights and that guarantee the integration and participation of sectors historically marginalized from the country's civic, social, economic and political life. Reducing extreme inequalities is a key prerequisite for democracy. But inequality in Peru is extreme, a far cry from the 'reasonable level' associated with modern democracies. If we call 'democratization' the process by which extreme inequalities are eliminated, then it is important to say that a crucial turning point in Peru's democratization occurred through the reduction of inequality that resulted from the integration of Andean people into urban society. Paradoxically, this integration sped up during the military government led by General Juan Velasco, which launched what could be called the 'greatest process of democratization without democracy' ever seen in Peru (Foro Nacional/Internacional, 1995: 23). Nevertheless, the process of reducing inequality runs up against the obstacles of racism, extreme poverty, gender discrimination and centralization, all heightened by unequal access to education and other social services.

During the last four decades, social change has shaken the foundations of the State in Peru. The population has exploded, massive rural-to-urban migration has occurred (70 per cent of the inhabitants of Lima are rural migrants) and regional movements for political and administrative autonomy have appeared. All of these factors have contributed to overturning social and political structures, such as the oligarchical State, which had prevailed for centuries. As a result, new actors arose to take their place on the national stage. They are demanding a place in the market (jobs, income and consumption) and a share of social benefits, education and political power. These demands present a potent challenge to centralist practices and, with that challenge, a new awareness that the problems of Peru's many different regions cannot be solved with a Lima-centred approach.

These 'territorial strips' of the Peruvian civil society, as one of our interviewees (Sinesio López, a social scientist who was one of the first Peruvian intellectuals to use the term civil society) called them, are the regional associations and local 'defence fronts,' which played a very important role in the decades preceding the 1990s. The terrorist violence of the Shining Path and MRTA (*Movimiento Revolucionario Túpac Amaru*) is the most violent manifestation of that social unrest; their campaigns indelibly marked the whole of the 1980s and continue today. The 1997 hostage drama in Lima was the most recent example; more than one hundred people were held hostage by the MRTA for more than four months before the military intervened. This near disaster exposed the fragility that continues to exist in a country where terrorist movements have the capacity to challenge the State's very authority.

The beginnings of this period of change can be traced to the reform programme carried out in the late 1960s by the military government led by General Juan Velasco. Velasco's agrarian, industrial and educational reforms sped up the process of social transformation that had begun in the 1950s with the crisis of the oligarchic State. The leaders of the military regime further challenged the old order's exclusive character and its concentration of power and wealth. The practical results of the Velasco reforms were far-reaching: peasants were given access to land ownership, fundamental social rights were recognized, the Quechua language and Andean culture gained renewed respect, grassroots urban organizations appeared (with new names like 'inhabitant' and 'young town' replacing the former derogatory names 'squatter' and 'slum'), self-managed local communities such as Villa El Salvador developed and workers participated in the management and ownership of State-owned and private companies.

The outcome for social mobilization was extraordinary. The popular voluntary associations and social movements that grew out of the Velasco reforms had begun to reshape society from the bottom up: labour unions, professional guilds, student movements, neighbourhood organizations, agricultural guilds and even an Intersectoral Committee of State Workers (CITE) were the prime social and political actors at the time. Their demands for democracy, however, were focused on utilitarian bread-and-butter issues rather than demands for broader political participation. They sought democratic freedom to have better conditions under which to demand their rights. The 'popular' stamp marking international development co-operation programmes during the 1970s must, therefore, be placed within this context. The importance of popular education, the strengthening of social movements and unions and the autonomy of grassroots organizations were among the priorities of international co-operation.

Nevertheless, the authoritarian military nature of the Velasco regime prevented the autonomous institutionalization of these reforms. It hindered their full acceptance by society as a whole and, at the same time, blocked the expansion of political rights. In a certain way, the regime followed the participatory pattern (and the language) of the Cuban Revolution, but the only political party in Peru was the military already in power. The unwieldy growth of the State was another result of the military government's policies, and it had negative effects on public finances. Starting in the 1970s, the State rapidly increased its functions, and the number of government agencies and State employees skyrocketed. Foreign companies were nationalized, new State enterprises were created and the State took over a number of bankrupt private companies. With no Peruvian tradition of civil service or specialized and independent public employees, this rapid growth of the State brought disorder in the application of legal norms and arbitrary behaviour in the exercise of public functions. Yet the State's growth also had a positive effect, bringing government services and public works, often for the first time, to the farthest corners of Peru.

Since the Velasco regime, Peruvian society has continued to experience deep, radical and rapid transformation. Taken together, these currents form what could be called, in the words of Gustavo Gutiérrez (one of the most important representatives of Liberation Theology in Latin America) 'the new presence of the poor' in Peru. As they demand places to live, the new urban migrants are changing the face of the coastal cities, especially Lima, where a third of the nation's population now lives. To a certain extent since the 1970s, their presence has democratized the cities, significantly increasing the number of citizens conscious of their economic, social, political and cultural rights.

The return to representative democracy in 1980 coincided with the appearance of The Shining Path, whose first violent act was to destroy ballot boxes, the instrument and symbol of democratic elections. Since then (including 22 April 1997 when the residence of the Japanese Ambassador was liberated), daily violence has touched and shaken nearly every Peruvian, undermining their sense of personal security and emotional stability. Drug trafficking networks have also grown rapidly, bringing with them corruption, violence and economic distortion.

The democratic governments of the 1980s led by Fernando Belaúnde and Alan García had serious difficulty confronting the decade's most important issues: economic crisis and political violence. Belaúnde is the leader of a once very important right-wing political party called Popular Action (AP) and was the elected president when deported by the Velasco Revolution. He was then re-elected in 1980. Alan García, now hidden somewhere between Paris and Colombia and with several trials waiting for him, was the charismatic, young leader of the APRA (Popular Revolutionary American Alliance), a social democratic party that governed Peru from 1985 to 1990. García's populist policies and corruption led the country to the inflationary calamity of 1989–90 and opposition political forces found it difficult to propose constructive alternatives. As a result, the government's impotence and the opposition's weakness became clear. The State's short-comings and the extensive corruption of the spheres of power led to a *de facto* privatization of essential services like security and justice (which explains, for instance, the support granted nowadays by Northern co-operation agencies to the reform of judicial and other State institutions, discussed in the following section).

Alberto Fujimori, an independent leader with neither a known politi-cal past nor a stable political organization behind him, began his government in 1990 with a series of radical economic reforms grounded in a rationale that emphasized impersonal market forces. The new free-market system requires of individuals an enormous capacity to meet the demands of an increasingly competitive society. Freeing the market, opening foreign trade, reducing public spending, privatizing State enter-prises and implementing other measures have increased inequalities in income distribution. Fujmori's economic policies successfully controlled the hyperinflation inherited from the Garcia administration, but at the cost of the profound recession and increased poverty, which became the trade-marks of the 1990s. At the same time, the Fujimori government launched a counter-insurgency strategy that significantly reduced terrorist activity and led to the capture of Shining Path's leader, Abimael Guzman.

Although Guzman's capture and Fujimori's successful control of infla-tion won him broad support, he faced criticism for the harsh outcomes of his economic policy. His authoritarian behaviour and political inexperi-ence led him to resolve those difficulties with the parliamentary opposition through a military-backed 'self-coup' in April 1992. Congress was closed and a new one elected to settle a new Constitution (which, for example, allows presidential re-election for the first time). This break in the consti-tutional order marked a return to seesawing between authoritarian and democratic governments, which so clearly embodies the crisis of gover-nance that has plagued Peru throughout most of its republican life. Democratic institutions and procedures became mere tools to be set aside whenever the leader so desires. Nevertheless, Peruvians saw the govern-ment's successes against terrorism and hyperinflation as signs of efficiency and rewarded Fujimori and his government with re-election in 1995.

His authoritarian exertion of power remains, marked by an increase in the concentration of power and further alienation of other political sectors. During the first half of 1997, Peruvians saw signs that Fujimori was challenging the very institution of democracy itself. Three members of the Constitutional Court, for example, were dismissed because they opposed an interpretation of the Constitution that would permit the President to run for a third election. A battle by the powerful National Intelligence

Service backed by the President against a Jewish owner of a television channel who criticized the military forces resulted in the revocation of his Peruvian nationality. Indeed, except for the Ombudsman Office, which has great support both within and outside the country, Peruvian democratic institutions are extremely fragile and are vested with a low degree of autonomy from such abuses of power. These democratic institutions are key to strengthening civil society – an element that has shaped Northern donor policy and will be discussed in the following pages.

Today, Peru is facing an autocratic challenge. Because the legislature is subordinate to the executive, the latter passes the most important laws by decree, using legislative faculties ceded to it by Congress. Moreover, Congress's limited power as a democratic institution, particularly in relation to the executive arm, upsets the balance of power and weakens the process of democratic legitimization through which citizens identify with State institutions and with democracy. This process, fundamental to building a democratic political community, has yet to occur in Peru. Mechanisms for controlling the exercise of power and public authority are virtually non-existent. The few institutions devoted to this task are inefficient or, worse still, manipulated by government and the opposition to protect allies or destroy political enemies. By stating that it is enough to communicate directly with the people through polls alone, the autocratic leader and his retinue may eliminate public spaces for communication and consensus building, spaces that are key to the process of developing democracy and democratic institutions.

This political and institutional framework, shaped by the context of the new free market economic model, has meant that social and political participation have become bad words from the government perspective. Indeed, the early 1990s were marked by a constant feeling of insecurity that partially manifested itself in the difficulty people faced in establishing common goals and in acting together as a group. Although that feeling of insecurity has greatly diminished, most people continue to live in the short term and act almost exclusively on their own to benefit themselves and their closest relatives.

Stabilization and structural adjustment programmes have introduced new economic policies destined to foster a market-oriented model that emphasizes individual success. People find it difficult to participate in different forms of collective action and to identify with the social movements and institutions that such action might eventually build. The immediate goal is to survive. The big social movements that arose in the national sphere during the 1970s – regional movements, peasants' movements and union and students' movements – have since given way to organizations responding to a country shaped by years of internal war and to the urgencies of life. The individual acting alone in the informal world, at least 36 per cent of the working population (Foro Nacional/ Internacional, 1995: 17), does not usually act collectively as a member of an organization. Popular movements and social mobilization, as mentioned in our first hypothesis, are not the trends of the 1990s. The 'popular' character of civil society is lost. Talking about civil society now means talking about a plurality of organizations that in one way shows the very *weakening* of those movements. We will talk in the next section about this new feature of Peruvian civil society.

Some Features of Peruvian Civil Society in the 1990s

Civil society in Peru today is, perhaps for the first time in its history, a *plural* civil society, or a 'universal' civil society according to authors such as Lynch (1992), in which the existence of different interests, representing different classes, groups and sectors within the society is acknowledged. The participants of this plural civil society include new umbrella groups and voluntary associations at either end of the spectrum (business associations and survival organizations led by women), as well as traditional actors such as professional guilds, labour unions (playing a very marginal role now), regional associations and student movements.

By the end of the 1980s and the beginning of the 1990s, several business associations appeared in Peru (mainly based in Lima), and took their place as actors in civil society. The organizations representing business in public debate (the National Confederation of Private Entrepreneurs' Institutions (CONFIEP), the Exporters' Association (ADEX), the Peruvian Association of Banks (ASBANC) and the Peruvian Institute of Business Administration (IPAE), among others) now play a key role in Peruvian civil society and its relationship with the State, particularly by organizing events like IPAE's Annual Executives' Conference (CADE).

Although it is evident that such organizations do not respond to the urgency for survival and are not strictly necessary for the existence of private enterprise, they do provide an important function for the broader civil society. Their deliberative and voluntary nature gives them the possibility of autonomy. Indeed, these professional bodies have been able to underline key failings in the market and political system that affect not only business (for example, that without rule of law there cannot exist a well-functioning market) but, more important, social and political organizations as well. These organizations thus inadvertently become advocates for sectors that they more or less ignored before. Among them, micro entrepreneurs from poor communities have become an important sector of the emerging society and are in the process of identifying needs and common interests and trying out forms of organization and institutions. The existence of COPEME (an association of NGOs supporting the small and micro entrepreneurs) constitutes a sign of its associative intentions. Nevertheless, the clear identification of civil society with the market itself needs to be avoided; one must be careful of equating civil society simply with the sum of contractual relationships.

Other key actors in the new Peruvian civil society are women fighting for the subsistence of their families. Among the nation's impoverished majority, women are usually in charge of family subsistence, either alone or through organizations such as People's Kitchens, Mother's Clubs and the Glass of Milk Program. This situation generates a clear and important social contradiction: each family's private reality revolves around the woman, but the public model of power and authority is masculine. Peruvian society may be basically matriarchal but it is also profoundly macho. The contradiction between the private need to feed one's family and the imperative of public action to guarantee survival is thus a very important social issue, demanding that we open our concept of civil society to include the family. Our concept of civil society must also deal with the notion of 'voluntariness'; it is hard to call participation in emergency or survival organizations strictly voluntary, because vital needs, the very conditions for subsistence, are at stake. Moreover, these survival organizations are spaces where democratic participation and consensual practices are being fostered.

These efforts for survival include a growing network of primary health care programmes run largely by women. In emergencies, such as the 1991 cholera epidemic or the annual summer onslaught of intestinal infection and infant dehydration, grassroots organizations have managed to provide minimal preventive health services efficiently, generally with little help from the State. Along with proving the importance of grassroots organizations, this success has underscored the need to involve the community, especially women, in designing and implementing basic strategies and programmes to improve family and children's health and nourishment. Both the proliferation of such organizations and the stable role they play in community life means they are now facing the most serious consequences of the economic crisis.

By 1994, there were around 20,000 grassroots women's organizations. If each included about 20 members, the total would come to 400,000 organized women. In Lima alone, People's Kitchens distributed roughly 570,000 portions in 1993, reaching 10 per cent of all families in the capital (IEP, 1995: 18). Moreover, the kitchens are now centralizing their activities; there is a Federation of Committees of Self-Managed People's Kitchens of Lima and Callao as well as zonal and district committees and a Metropolitan Coordination of the Glass of Milk Program. These organizations are becoming more democratic themselves, serving as examples of effective mechanisms of solidarity among the poorest.

For these reasons, women's organizations are becoming favoured interlocutors for channelling emergency and social welfare programmes, enjoying public recognition throughout the country. Since the 1980s, they have operated with the support of domestic and international development agencies in efforts to tackle the consequences of structural adjustment.

We will see in the next section that when some donors talk about interventions oriented towards poverty alleviation, they refer to just these grassroots organizations led by women. Understanding women's movements in their different forms, including the contradictions between their growth and the amount of State and international support ladled upon them, is thus important for understanding Peruvian civil society.

In the development of civil society during the 1990s, another important change is the appearance of neighbourhood organizations. The new dynamism of the local governments is clear both in the provinces and in Lima. The creation of district development committees, inter-institutional committees, working committees and dialogue committees, often at the initiative of local authorities, shows a new and more dynamic way for civil society to relate to local powers, a fundamental condition of democratic life. In November 1997, we witnessed in Peru a very interesting (and new) procedure called 'recall of local authorities'. All around the country, there were almost 70 cases of local authorities who were questioned (because of problems of corruption, for instance) by local organizations. This democratic proceeding allowed these organizations to change those authorities through democratic election. The level of participation was very high and the results show a renewed interest of CSOs in local power.

In urban areas throughout the country, it is also important to underscore the active role played by chambers of commerce, Lions' and Rotary clubs and other community service groups, both in concrete initiatives and in organizing people around issues of shared interest. Among these are parents' associations and classroom committees in schools, which take on promotion, management and leadership roles that were once left to the State or the schools' private owners.

Still another change in the profile of civil society has come about through economic reform. The current government's economic liberalization programme means that the State will no longer intervene directly to promote co-operatives, market agricultural products, set prices or provide agricultural credits. Some of these functions have to be assumed by the producers themselves, organized in private, community or multi-community companies.

As a result, the rural guilds, created during the 1970s to confront the State or receive concessions from it, are changing to relate to the State in a less contentious way. In rural areas, the biggest agricultural guilds (the National Agrarian Confederation, the Peasant Confederation of Peru and the National Agrarian Organization) that arose during the 1970s and 1980s are increasingly substituted by local, district and sub-regional organizations, such as village central committees, village development committees, district federations and producer's committees. The State's withdrawal from rural areas is reorganizing and re-articulating rural civil society, forcing it to find new ways to relate to the State and other organizations of Peruvian society.

Last in our map of new actors in Peruvian civil society is the non-governmental organization (NGO). These intermediary bodies between funders and grassroots organizations (and between funders and other organizations) are no longer commonly equated with civil society itself (a perception still found in certain literature and in some Northern co-operation agencies), although they do constitute an important part of it. During the second half of the 1990s, according to the Directory of NGOs for Development, there may be a minimum of around 2,000 organizations of this kind in the country. According to a number of our interviewees, however, this information is probably inaccurate because the definition used is too vague and too encompassing (including, for instance, one-person NGOs or those created by government itself). A safer estimate would number NGOs in the region of 800 indigenous and foreign organizations.

The history of NGOs in Peru before the 1990s is long and complex. We found different versions among those we interviewed and in the literature consulted. One of the people interviewed, Federico Velarde, a Peruvian sociologist whose links with national and foreign NGOs are maybe among the oldest and strongest, explained it best by saying: 'The NGOs have passed from revolution to democracy'. This means that during the 1970s, the beneficiaries of the revolution were to be those popular organizations active during the decade; the beneficiaries of democracy, however, are to be all the people. Because NGOs belong to the third sector (that is, neither the State nor the market), those that encouraged development during the 1970s and the first half of the 1980s were linked to the so-called popular movement and hence to a 'restricted – though implicit – conception of civil society' (Ballón, 1996: 38–9). Northern NGOs, particularly European organizations linked to the churches played a very important role in the development of these popular movements, seen as creators of the space in which social change took place according to the interests and needs of the majority (Ballón, 1996: 39). The NGOs' early link with left-wing parties was evident, as was their confrontation with the State.

About the middle of the 1980s, within a context of violence, the transition to democracy created a sense that institutions mattered and that there was a need to develop citizenship. NGOs went from the privilege of denunciation to an emphasis on the proposal and an interest in influencing the country policies. As we have argued, during the 1970s, voluntary associations and social movements acted in a demand-based and defensive fashion, without pushing to democratize society as a whole or develop political democracy. The insistence on the purely *popular* nature of civil society denied it the plurality of a *democratic* civil society that would include all citizens with their different perspectives and interests.

In the 1980s, NGOs assumed the responsibility for 'strengthening civil society' as a whole and were assigned a substantive role as a guarantor in the process of transition into democracy (Ballón, 1996: 41). The opening of new spaces like city halls, parliament and regional governments resulted in an important change in the activities of the NGOs. The organization of life itself, citizens' as well as women's activities (the so called functional or survival organizations), are now also to be considered an important part of civil society. This notion of plurality within civil society implies important changes in NGOs' programmes and activities. The issue is no longer revolution of one privileged class or subject. The goal is society with its rich and complex diversity.

Today, Peruvian NGOs are redefining, evaluating and establishing goals. Many of those interviewed, long linked to NGO activities, mentioned the consequences of budget reductions, restrictive fiscal policies by development agencies and their demands for project sustainability. They face the challenge of supporting different forms of CSOs, of getting connected to other economic actors and agents (private enterprises, micro enterprises), of negotiating with the State and of influencing public policies (Ballpro 1996: 58–60). Although important in certain areas, like human rights or women's training, some people argue that 'it's surprising… how irrelevant NGOs' joint work is considered in global terms' (Beaumont, 1996: 95).

Among the actual issues, however, one of the most important concerns NGOs' very presence in civil society. Can Northern NGOs operate in a developing nation such as Peru without imposing their own Northern systems on Peruvian organizations, thus creating a greater dependence without necessarily providing the capacity to be independent? To what extent are they assuming functions that are in the sphere of the State? Are they taking over responsibility in areas like food, health or rural development? We will talk about these items in the next section of the chapter.

Why Does Civil Society Matter Politically? What is at Stake?

Civil society appears as a sphere of voluntary organizations and, therefore, as a space where democratic life and pluralism can be fostered. Making democracy function effectively is a task for society as a whole and not simply for the country's formal political structure. In this section, the power relationships between civil society, State and market will be examined in more detail.

In the Peru of the 1990s, governance seems to be rebuilding itself from below as the population generates its own spaces and structures to resolve the problems of government. As we have seen, these alternative spaces include participation in local government, social service organizations, neighbourhood organizations, survival agencies and business organizations. This new social dynamic becomes especially clear during emergency situations when hunger, violence and unemployment threaten. For example, women's organizations successfully fought Shining Path terrorists when they tried to take over the women's People's Kitchens and other food networks, even though the terrorists brutally killed some womens' leaders.

People's organizations are also generating roles to replace shrinking State services. For example, the promoters of the Glass of Milk Program committees also treat cases of diarrhoea and dehydration, sometimes at the request of the Ministry of Health. Clearly, it is possible to supplement the State with grassroots organizations to provide basic social services. Nevertheless, there are almost no specific programmes designed to provide people with greater knowledge and technical skills or to institutionalize community participation in providing social services. Furthermore, Fujimori's recent decision to decentralize the Glass of Milk Program by giving the resources to district governments was resisted by women's organizations because it ignored their own autonomous organization.

Currently, little is expected of the State (even though broad sectors of the population oppose the State's withdrawal from areas considered priorities, such as the provision of basic services) so that there is a bottom-up regeneration of civil society that, neglected by State institutions, has begun to formulate demands and find solutions. The creative, if fragile, responses to Peru's overwhelming social and economic problems show that the initiative exhibited by grassroots organizations and informal entrepreneurs, among others, might, if nurtured in a climate of broad democratic freedoms, provide a way out of a multi-dimensional crisis. One of our main problems now is the State's lack of interest in strengthening those organizations not under its control. Another problem is the concentration of power in the executive branch, particularly in the person of the President. This is the autocratic challenge that civil society (and, in their own ways, Northern donors) must answer.

Another serious obstacle to democratization lies in widespread notions that reduce equality and citizen participation and, thus, democracy itself to a question of market competition. The assumption that equality is an affair of the market and the laws of supply and demand implies the existence of equal opportunity and equal access to markets with national dimensions and the capacity to integrate. These conditions do not exist in Peru. Overcoming Peru's extreme inequalities is the responsibility of both society and the State, problems that cannot be left exclusively to market forces, especially as the market neither includes the majority of Peruvians nor covers the entire national territory. Defining citizenship exclusively in terms of individual competition in the market and identifying the market with civil society, which is part of the 'common sense' of neo-liberal ideology, restricts the progress of democratization in Peruvian society. Democratization implies that these citizens have active participation in organizations and in other collective ways of fulfilling a collective purpose.

Peruvian civil society has not evolved the autonomy that would make it a realm of participation and citizen development. Given the newness of organizations and their struggle to survive, fragmentation and disintegration continually threaten. These tendencies breed behaviour foreign to the basic norms of social life, turning shared spaces into areas in which 'anything goes' and where the 'law of the jungle' reigns (Foro Nacional/Internacional, 1995: 18). Individuals find it difficult to identify themselves as part of a world of social actors whose behaviour is defined and stable.

Nevertheless, new forms and processes of social integration, based on relationships of need and solidarity, are arising in the shape of associations of small and medium-sized producers and merchants seeking to enter the market, and organizations are developing for security or food distribution that seek to meet the most immediate challenges of survival. But in a context of extreme poverty these new forms of integration, dynamic as they are, still confront serious barriers to building a solid base on which to grow, institutionalize and reproduce throughout society as a whole. The decline and frailty of many organizations of civil society hamper the appearance of interlocutors who could define, in fairly precise terms, their relations among themselves, with the State and with the donor community.

In this setting, mechanisms providing CSOs and actors with access to political power are unclear. The political parties, which should be a fundamental part of the democratic system and are crucial mediators between civil society and the State, have lost their ability to respond to citizens' problems and social demands. The parties' problems and vicissitudes may make the transition from civil to political society appear too difficult within a democratic framework or, conversely, too dangerously 'simple' in an authoritarian one. The latter may conjure up illusions of 'direct democracy', based on communication via television and 'legitimized' by opinion polls, which erases the intermediary representative bodies of civil society. Political leadership arises in different ways from the most important realms of Peru's variegated civil society of the 1990s. The presence of a large number of independent political leaders with neither a known political past nor stable political organizations behind them shows clearly how hard it is to link civil and political society in an organic fashion.

The necessity of leadership in the country is an urgent issue. Leadership demands the participation of intellectuals, of new people's leaders, of people with credibility and of people of high moral principles and with summoning skills. This need is perceived almost unanimously by all social sectors in Peru, as the crisis within the political parties seems to go on and on (Foro Nacional/Internacional, 1995: 42). Organizations such as the German Friedrich Ebert Foundation, the American National Endowment for Democracy or the International Republican Institute are working, in different ways, on party political issues, but crisis seems to be a long-term problem.

The mediation among civil society, political society and the State is possible thanks to the existence of public spaces. These are real and metaphorical places where citizens shape consensus and express their dissatisfaction in an attempt to influence the public agenda. Nevertheless, such spaces are not 'topographical' places: they are anywhere and in any form where issues of general interest can be discussed, differences noted and consensus reached in a rational manner (Arendt, 1958: 50–1). This is what is meant, after all, by deliberative democracy: a truly participatory democracy (Habermas, 1992: 446–7). The presence of such public spaces is, according to Charles Taylor (1995: 260), the central element of civil society in democratic regimes; however, the almost absolute lack of such spaces is a fundamental feature of contemporary Peru.

Obviously, at the level of the State political apparatus, parliament institutionalizes a kind of debate, but it has poorly mediated conflict between opposing interests. Other public spaces, such as the political parties, have not taken up the slack and have not functioned as places where meaningful agreement can be reached on shared goals. What is needed are spaces outside of the institutions of political society that come from civil society itself.

Some efforts, supported by international development co-operation funds, have tried to generate such spaces: the Democratic Forum, whose very name shows its nature as an open arena; the *Cabildos Abiertos* (open council meeting) in some local municipalities; the *Concertatión* meetings in some inland towns; workshops and seminars organized for leading women of the People's Kitchens and of the Glass of Milk Program; and *Foro Educativo*, centred on educational problems. The case of women is particularly illustrative. The difficulties women face in having their voices heard in the political system can be understood as a lack of truly public space where the problems faced by women become issues of shared, not marginalized, interest. In other words, there is a bottleneck between civil society and public agenda caused by the absence of public space. (The Democratic Forum may be an interesting exception. In 1998, it is successfully organizing a petition to call for a referendum preventing the re-election of Fujimori for a third period.)

MAPPING NORTHERN DONOR INTERVENTION

A Brief History of Donor Intervention

To prosper, civil society needs not only space but a sense of common identity. This section explores why that common identity has been so difficult to forge and what international cooperation has been able to do to foster it. Key is the systematic persistence of abject poverty, Peru's greatest problem. Poverty has excluded the vast majority from genuine citizenship and civic participation, and it is poverty that first brought the donors. They have stayed, however, for other reasons.

Peru's relatively old nation-State status has not generated a country of citizens who identify themselves with the nation (López, 1991: 7–8). In place of, class and race have become the primary characteristics of an individual's identity and geography. In Lima, administratively and emotionally distant from the provinces, the wealthy and powerful organize the economy and politics, while indigenous people live in abject poverty in the countryside and inland areas, largely ignored (Sagasti and Alcalde, 1997: 78). Although the reform-oriented government of Velasco Alvarado attempted decentralization of power outside of Lima, reform was unsuccessful. Today, the country's centralized character has led residents of Lima to abandon what they call simply the 'rest of the country' and allow rural impoverishment. These divisions not only reinforce poverty but they also exclude most of the population from real citizenship, particularly if we consider the full civil, political and social aspects of citizen's rights (Lynch 1992: 83–5; Sagasti et al., 1995: 93). Common in today's literature and among our interviewees is the belief that Peru is, therefore, not a country of citizens and that *poverty* is the main limitation for developing citizen status.

That impoverishment, combined with extreme violence and drug trafficking, meant that Peru became an aid-receiving country at a very early stage of international cooperation. Today, it remains near the top of the list of countries receiving aid from the US (although Haiti receives more), Japan (in addition to Pacific Basin concerns), Germany and the Netherlands. Historically, however, international co-operation has undergone important changes. The recent changes are fundamental and we will try to outline them briefly.

Since the 1960s, development co-operation between North and South operated under the paradigm of modernization and development (Valderrama, 1993: 17). Although the criteria varied among donors (geopolitical interests in the case of the US, commercial interests in the case of Italy and solidarity in the case of Scandinavian and other European countries), many we interviewed assert that the direction of support for development depended largely on the activism of Third World movements in the 1970s. Notions of 'national liberation', 'revolution' and 'popular movements' were consequently key phrases in many aid agencies, even though at the same time they focused on the State as the principal agent of development.

During the 1970s, much aid came as charity but, none the less, it had an important impact on today's civil society. In coordination with the Peruvian State, philanthropic agencies such as OFASA (an Adventist organization) and Caritas (a Catholic organization) provided material support such as food, pots and sewing machines for poor people in urban shanty towns. To receive these donations, women were asked to organize themselves in groups of at least eight to ten people (perhaps the origins of the People's Kitchens). Caritas continued this type of project into the 1980s and 1990s, working with People's Kitchens and Glass of Milk Programs (Córdova, 1996: 34). These initial efforts gave impetus to social organizing, one of the key characteristics of Peru's contemporary civil society.

The 1980s, considered Latin America's lost decade, presented the foreign debt crisis. The 1985 decision of President Alan Garcia not to pay the debt resulted in serious financial flow restrictions. The debt crisis and the growth stagnation to which it gave rise was in turn exacerbated by the rise of terrorism. Violence and economic recession seriously discouraged private investors and even technical assistance decreased dramatically. COEECI (the Coordinating Body of the International Foreign Cooperation Institutions) was founded during the most violent years of that decade to offer protection and coordinate activity among the many agencies based on the outskirts of Lima that had been attacked or threatened by terrorist groups.

Foreign NGOs started to channel aid to promote the 'social conditions for democracy', a goal that became paramount during the worsening quality of life of wide sectors of the population (Ballón, 1996: 43). This kind of NGO intervention raised political suspicions, however. The governments of Belaunde and García accused international agencies, and Northern and local NGOs working to protect human rights of financing Shining Path and MRTA activities. Some human rights NGOs were accused of being more concerned with terrorists' rights than civilians' or soldiers' rights, generating a continuing uneasy relationship between the Peruvian government and official aid agencies and NGOs alike.

By the 1990s, many other things changed within development co-operation. The logic of foreign aid in the country has been directly affected by the events in Eastern Europe; the fall of the Berlin Wall caused changes both in the organizations' priorities as well in the issues and programmes considered eligible for technical assistance. Programmes to strengthen the market economy and support democracy in particular were suddenly more popular. The post cold war world involves new priorities organized around peace, governability, the struggle for survival and recent formulations relating to 'global human security' (Jaworski, 1994: 17).

For one, Fujimori's goal of reinserting Peru into the international financial system meant that from 1993 credit started to flow once again from the private sector and from multilateral organizations (the World Bank, the Inter-American Development Bank (IDB) and the European Union, among others). The emphasis of the multilaterals was threefold: the struggle against extreme poverty aggravated by structural adjustment; the promotion of democracy; and the encouragement of economic reform through privatization, tax reform, public administration reform and the development of a free market economy. According to our interviews, some Northern agencies approached these tasks through an 'institutional strengthening' approach, whether focused on State institutions (in the case of the United States Agency for International Development (USAID) and the Canadian International Development Agency (CIDA)) and CSOs and institutions or both (particularly important for CIDA, the World Bank, the IDB and Northern NGOs).

To take up the goals of poverty reduction and democracy promotion in particular, local participation is considered crucial. Participation has, in turn, been approached through donors' relations with both NGOs and government agencies. One strategy has been to use local and foreign development NGOs, sometimes despite government reluctance, because these intermediary organizations are seen to work closely with the poor through grassroots organizations and local membership organizations. As some of our interviewees (from different types of agencies) said, it is not easy for donors (whether CIDA, Oxfam or the Friedrich/Stiftung (FES)) to fund CSOs directly. Helmut Kurth, Director of FES in Peru, indicated that FES and USAID are planning to work together as a way to reach appropriate organizations – a difficult task.

Similarly, another strategy has been to tie participation conditionality into bilateral and multilateral agreements with government agencies. Local needs assessments are required for much of the assistance distributed through the government (up to 52 per cent of official aid is channelled through the Ministry of the Presidency and FONCODES (the National Fund for Compensation and Social Development)). Sanchez-Leon states it very clearly: 'In accordance with the World Bank, the local participation grants project relevance and sustainability, facilitating its acquisition by the population, thus becoming an incentive for community organizations' (Sanchez-Leon, 1996: 24). The demands placed on communities to form 'local executing agencies' to use those delegated funds has, therefore, become a mechanism, encouraged by FONCODES, for civil society mobilization through schools, churches, municipal authorities and women's organizations. The Director for Peru in the World Bank, Isabel Guerrero, is very clear in stating the importance this institution gives to local participation.

According to authors such as Beaumont, however, this State-encouraged mobilization may mean that autonomous CSOs will become 'operators of the State's social policies' (Beaumont, 1996: 96), thus losing their independence and their ability to criticize. Valderrama states also that there would be a risk 'of turning the NGOs into plain instruments of economic and social stabilization policies' (Valderrama, 1993: 111). A specific argument could be made about women's organizations that have assumed the role of agents organizing and executing programmes developed by the State. Sometimes they are engaged by the State itself, sometimes by agencies that have bilateral contracts with the government (Tamayo, 1997: 9). Another example is the Freedom and Democracy Institute of Hernando de Soto, which was supported by USAID and the US government and which collaborated with Peruvian government programmes giving official property inscriptions and bonds to informal workers and owners and assisting in the struggle against drug trafficking.

The current situation in Peru is then peculiar, as the State summons civil society because of pressure exercised by the co-operation agencies. At the same time, some NGOs are very distrustful of this relationship with the State. They point to evidence of the State creating its own NGOs to avoid existing ones considered too critical of State policy. Others expect that a strong relationship with State institutions may allow them to influence public policy, thus giving permanence and sustainability to their programmes and projects. According to people we interviewed, including Rafael Roncagliolo, this approach characterizes some health care, nutrition and population programmes that were implemented with the aid of international co-operation through the State, base communities and NGOs.

These historical experiences have had an influence on the new agenda of donor intervention. The following section shows how these trends are shaping today's civil society.

Some Features of Donors' Interests in Civil Society

Because Peru was an early aid recipient, the population of donors today is diverse: there are Northern government bilateral aid agencies, like CIDA, USAID or Italian Co-operation; multilateral bodies, such as the United Nations Development Programme (UNDP), the World Bank, Organization of American States or the IDB; foundations such as Ford, the FES or the National Endowment for Democracy; and private NGOs such as Oxfam, Caritas or Bilance.

The largest amount of aid comes from the first two kinds of Northern agencies. The total donor contribution to aid programming in Peru, including NGO grants, may be in the neighbourhood of US$600 million, with the US and Canada easily at the forefront. As of 1996, USAID was working with a volume of US$150 million, CIDA dispensed roughly US$80 million and the Germans some US$40 million – together, over half of total foreign aid. Overall, aid represents less than 5 per cent of GDP (compared to the much more heavily indebted countries of Kenya and Sri Lanka), and 90 per cent flows directly to the State for programming within the country. This concentration of resources and information with the Peruvian government has meant that it is difficult to make accurate estimates of flows from outside. We will come back to this problem of concentration.

Furthermore, within that larger aid pool, it is difficult to know which organizations are working on a civil society agenda because a clear definition of the term is lacking. The donor representatives we surveyed used the term in a very general way: excluding the State but sometimes including the market. It is interesting to note that in the 'Directory of Co-operation Agencies' published by COEECI in 1996, the concept of civil society is not mentioned as such. Nevertheless, the repeated references to 'power sectors', 'basis organizations', 'communities' and 'poor urban and rural population' can be seen as a way of talking about civil society, both in the organizational and in the political aspects we emphasize in this volume. The answer to the question about the existence of a common or shared notion of civil society in our interviews was clearly negative: such a concept depends on each agency or NGO, on its history, its tradition and, in a very important way, on its sources of financing.

Yet it is clear that the discourse has entered development conversations, offering many reasons for Northern co-operation agencies to turn to civil society. Some agencies argue that this emphasis has arisen because of the (apparently debatable) results of co-operation: 'after 30 years of co-operation for development, poor people continue to be as poor as before or even poorer', stated the President of COEECI and Peruvian Director of Oxfam, whereas others attribute the change to the winds of transition (from socialism to capitalism, from solidarity to pragmatism) blowing through the world. There appears to be a consensus that the concept of development needs to be rethought. Jaworski describes this situation very clearly: 'the term (development) got so many senses that it couldn't keep any of them, turning itself into an inseparable suffix: economic, social, cultural, educational, nutritional, global, local, popular, human, women's, childhood, environment, agricultural, industrial development... but also military and nuclear' (Jaworski, 1994: 25). The shift to an emphasis on civil society is one part of an effort to recast the debate on development.

In the Peruvian context, this rethinking on development affected how different aid agencies relate to civil society, both in its definition as organizations and in political projects. In the first instance, there is a clear distribution of labour among the donors. The foundations 'continue to focus on the overarching goal of promoting democratic development' (Ford Foundation,

Annual Report, 1995: 111) and, for Ford, this focus has meant a concentration on research centres, universities and human rights groups shaping reform of the courts and the police; also, in the case of the Ombudsman Office, Ford is supporting research on gender issues. An interesting example is the 1995 Ford Foundation Program of Education and Culture that provided Peruvian private universities with grants and projects worth about US$600,000 out of a total budget of US$1.5 million. Other foundations (such as the FES, Konrad Adenauer, Stiftung or Kellogg), also support academic research, although this kind of work is undervalued by many bilateral agencies. Few bilateral agencies are interested in supporting research about the country in general or about civil society in particular because they are interested in projects that have 'impact' on society and media.

The multilateral and bilateral approach to the civil society debate comes from their struggle with the poverty implications of structural adjustment at the same time they continue to promote democracy, human rights and institutional strength. The concentration of multilateral assistance programmes in the poorest sectors of the country is constant, despite the presence of new actors (such as entrepreneurs' associations) as recipients of multilateral aid.

One of the most interesting innovations in bilateral development co-operation is the creation of counterpart funds, which began to operate in Peru the late 1980s. According to Federico Velarde, an officer linked to the *Fondo Contravalor Peru–Canada* since its foundation, the mechanism shows how international support can be particularly productive. These funds, collected from the local sale of donated food, machinery or debt swaps are used to finance local development projects. The first, the Peru–Canada Fund, is managed by a board of representatives of the Canadian and Peruvian governments as well as NGOs. Funds have since been created by agencies from Japan, France, Spain and, more recently, in Switzerland. This innovation could be developed and strengthened in the near future, reinforcing social organizations and local development projects carried out directly by local agents, and minimizing the displacement effects on local agriculture.

Northern NGOs have approached the civil society debate in terms of empowerment; an effort to redress the relative capacity of grassroots organizations to influence the lives of their communities. In practical terms, empowerment has largely meant training, an element considered fundamental by both Northern and Southern NGOs. The need for people to develop their own skills to negotiate with different interlocutors, whether from the State or from other aid institutions, has become a fundamental issue.

Over and above negotiation skills, however, resource mobilization has become paramount; any training not linked to sustainability may be pointless. In a country like Peru, where extreme poverty characterizes many grassroots organizations, external efforts to 'train' CSOs may be rejected as irrelevant in the face of survival. As one of our interviewees from a European agency explained, 'you cannot ask people to take part (in any kind of project) if they are not going to get any profit'. Organizations from the Netherlands, Sweden and Great Britain have, therefore, emphasized the necessity of strengthening their local counterparts so they can in turn mobilize more resources.

Many official Northern agencies have adopted this focus on reinforcing local capabilities as a precondition for democratization. In some cases, the emphasis has been on strengthening democratic institutions through mechanisms for increased participation by CSOs. The strengthening of the independent operation of some State institutions (such as the judiciary or the Ombudsman Office) is a key factor in the consolidation of democracy in Peru fostered by some agencies (including USAID and CIDA) despite their unpopularity with the State. Capacity building has also become a focus of the World Bank (for example, its focus on the Peruvian congress and a very important reform of the judicial power), UNDP (Ombudsman Office) and IDB (Ministry of Economy). USAID, for example, states:

> *USAID will focus on influencing strategies and supporting leadership that maximizes sustainable economic growth. USAID will help to build the economic and political foundations for increased opportunity. We seek to help to empower the women, men and children of Peru by strengthening their individual capacities, promoting their economic opportunities and expanding their political freedoms. As development is sustainable only if it is participatory and people-oriented, USAID will emphasize grassroots participation in its development program.* (USAID/Peru Vision Statement: Partnership in Development, 1996: 2)

CIDA, an institution that insists on the defence of human rights, States in its article about participatory development: 'this approach stresses the need to strengthen community organizations and popular participation in the development process, in concert with decentralization of decision-making to local levels of government' (CIDA, 1995). The accent CIDA puts on civil society as a condition for the democratization of Peru is very clear in its activity programmes (including its local initiatives, gender equity and base community projects).

Another significant example of civil society development is the work carried out in support of Peruvian organizations defending human rights. Almost all are grouped under the auspices of the Human Rights National Coordinator, who has become an accepted interlocutor among different sectors of civil society, and, significantly, despite its evident reluctance, with the State itself. The grave human rights violations committed in Peru in the past 17 years by both subversive groups and the State have made the building of democracy and development especially difficult. For example, the torture and assassination of two members of the National Intelligence Service (NIS) by their own colleagues has raised enormous public protest.

In view of the pressure exerted by public opinion, the President (known for his almost unconditional support of the NIS) demanded prosecution for those responsible. What is remarkable about the case, however, is how exceptional it is; various Peruvian governments, including the current one, have been unwilling to treat human rights as a key characteristic of good governance or to launch systematic campaigns to publicize the importance of human rights as the basis of civilized coexistence. Defending everyone's right to life, freedom of speech, freedom of organization and the freedom from arbitrary arrest without distinction and without partisanship (not the case of some NGOs during the 1980s), is a crucial starting point.

In this aspect, co-operation agencies have played a very important role. Human rights constitute a fundamental issue of democracy with regard to the administration of justice, civil–military relations, the exercise of State power and, because of universal concern about human rights, Peru's relations with international organizations (the United Nations (UN), the Organization of American States (OAS)) and other countries. Canada and some European countries lend great importance to work on human rights issues. An important case is the return of displaced people to the regions most affected by the internal war during the 1980s. The UN in particular has been working directly (although also through the mediation of some NGOs) with the local population. The most interesting example of this kind of work is the return of people to Ayacucho, the province where the Shining Path was founded and one of the places most affected by internal war. The UN is co-operating with local women's organizations (the Shining Path killed most of the men and the women who remained took control in their communities) in helping families to return from Lima where they escaped to in search of security and work.

The importance given today to the development of the private sector is another important element in the aid portfolio. Certainly, the unanimity of the new ideology is striking. Everyone praises the advantages of the market, people talk about the necessity of formalizing wide informal economic sectors and supporting micro enterprises as the engine of the national economy. There is general acceptance of the need to generate jobs and to struggle against the causes of poverty, not only its consequences.

Focused on what Jaworski calls 'organizations of the people's economy' (Jaworski, 1994: 218), one change in donor strategies has, therefore, been the growing support to alternative financing, allowing wide, informal sectors to join the market. Micro-credit programmes or *Fondos Contravalor* are good examples of this kind of activity. Although this type of financing does not mean a major change within classic financial instruments, it radically alters the nature and conditions of possible borrowers: people and groups not eligible for financing from traditional banks, women, the needy, the illiterate, people without identification documents, the displaced, community groups and others are now being accepted and encouraged to participate (Jaworski, 1994: 218). Backed by international support from agencies like CIDA or USAID, the work of institutions like

IDESI (Institute for the Development of the Informal Sector) or COPEME (associations for NGOs for small and micro enterprises) are good examples.

Others point in the same direction. In an interesting article titled, 'A little bit of State, a little bit of enterprise... the NGO in the Peru of the 90s', Martin Beaumont describes this phenomenon: 'some NGOs which used to grant direct credit to little and micro entrepreneurs (thus potentially competing with the banks) now sign agreements with the banks that manage the funds and the NGOs offer a series of *different* services for low-range manufacturers: training in technology or management' (Beaumont, 1996: 102). This entrepreneurial emphasis could be an effort to develop additional skills with a stronger effect. According to Jaworski, some European governments (especially Germany and to a lesser extent, France, Switzerland and Belgium), as well as some European NGOs, are willing to support schemes and mechanisms (rather than projects) aiming to strengthen the financial standards of the people's productive units (micro enterprises, self-managed workshops, informal manufacturers) as well as their alternative financing structures (Jaworski, 1994: 223).

One of the problems with this emphasis on the private versus public sector, however, is the danger of State retreat. The radical withdrawal of the Peruvian State from various economic activities, including provision of social services, has been justified on the grounds that the market is not only an efficient resource-assigning organ but also capable of magically solving social problems. This justification has special relevance for CSOs. Structural adjustment programmes have reduced the capacity of the State to respond to social demands, creating a void where CSOs have begun to work in providing services (as we saw in the case of primary health care).

Some of the people we interviewed, including Peruvian government representatives, hold a neo-liberal concept of civil society, identifying it with the market saying things like 'private entrepreneurs are the real civil society'. It is noteworthy that this domestic approach is more conservative and anti-government than that espoused by most outside agencies. The Chief Economist of the World Bank 'sees government and market as complements rather than substitutes' (Stiglitz, 1997: 8). The neo-liberal understanding of civil society's relevance to democracy is also limited to its most formalistic incarnation whereby strengthening civil society represents 'a well-formed vote' restricted to participation in election processes and other formal aspects of democracy. The relationship of society with the State is, therefore, reduced to changing authorities in each democratic election, limiting the role of the State to collecting taxes and paying foreign debt. One former Minister of the Economy went so far as to say that the State has nothing to do with social justice, justice is a market problem.

Another important characteristic of aid programming is the goal of poverty alleviation, mentioned in almost all interviews. The dilemma posed by the negative impact of structural adjustment policies that have significantly reduced the quality of life in poor neighbourhoods is specifically underlined by aid agencies. The European Community, for instance, outlined in its special report of February 1996 that the triennial programme 1995–97 (reaching US$90 million in 1995) has as its first priority the struggle against poverty (according to the priorities established by the Peruvian government) and, in second place, food security. They aim to reach the poorest and work in a decentralized way, 'having as an objective to formally recognize the fundamental role played by civil society in the development process' (European Community, 1997: 5).

Overall, in spite of their differences, there is no doubt that international co-operation agencies did and continue to influence the development of civil society in Peru, whether by accident or by design. In particular, the delegation of health and food programmes to CSOs by local governments has contributed to the size of CSOs and the complexity of their networks. The same may be said about entrepreneurs' associations, although some experts we interviewed think that these remain too dependent on international funding to be able to defend their own interests. The strengthening of women's organizations and the creation of 'local executing agencies' and networks of informal workers can all be seen as important consequences of international co-operation.

IDEAS ABOUT POWER RELATIONSHIPS

The relationship between the Peruvian State and Northern donors is very complex. The decision of the Peruvian State not to pay the foreign debt in 1985 and the 'self-coup' of President Fujimori in 1992 deeply affected the relationship between the Peruvian State and Northern co-operation agencies. Although multilateral, bilateral and private agencies have restored their relationships with particular State institutions since the country's return to the international financial system, their relationship with the current regime itself has not been so easy. Bilateral co-operation depends on political criteria because aid agencies are subject to their own governments' relationship with Peru in promoting their projects.

An interesting example is the work of *Transparencia*, a non-partisan Peruvian organization that focused on civic education to ensure that the 1995 election would be both fair and transparent. Among its activities, *Transparencia* intended to carry out a process of electoral observation and a quick count, summoning over 6,000 youth volunteers throughout the country. Fearing possible conflict with the government, some bilateral agencies pointedly refused to finance their activities, leaving the funding to private foundations. Thus, political ties play an important role in project implementation.

Another complication in the donor–State relationship is the concentration of power in Peru. Formally, the Peruvian State has autonomous and independent powers (executive, judicial, legislative), yet there is domestic and international consensus that power is concentrated within the executive and in the hands of the President. The high degree of centralization of the Peruvian State, the lack of regional government and the weakness (economic and administrative) of local governments have repeatedly led to difficulties between Northern donors and State institutions. One hopeful sign, however, is the recent success in judicial reform after 20 years of piecemeal efforts to change the system of appointments, purge corrupt or politicized members of the judiciary and renew relevant legislation. Today, after a troubled course set largely by changing governments, parliaments and ministers of justice, Peru has new civil, penal and procedural codes and new statues for the judiciary. The World Bank is now very much involved in ensuring this reform is settled in a clear, precise manner (note, however, that the new Council of Magistrates engaged in this reform with the Bank has been frozen through a new law).

In practical terms, this concentration of power has meant a hoarding of information and personalized control of national development plans. According to several testimonies, the key problem is the absence of a clearly defined normative framework or institution outside of the President's office to centralize projects and channel relevant information. No law for co-operation exists and the Executive Department for International Technical Co-operation (SECTI) established in 1992 depends directly upon the Ministry of Presidency. At the end of 1996, SECTI published a five-page document entitled 'International Technical Co-operation Policies 1996–2000', outlining the national goals for development that were provided by the Peruvian government, as well as mid-term international technical co-operation policies. The long-term view seems to have disappeared. With the dissolution in 1992 of the National Planning Institute (INP) that had been responsible for coordination with other relevant bodies (Foreign Office, Ministry of Finance), the notion of integrated social and economic planning has evaporated. Valderrama writes that 'at present, Peru has neither (a) projects portfolio nor a systematic analysis of the resources offered by the co-operation. The co-operation is managed on the basis of dialogues with embassies and international co-operation agencies as well as pushed by government pressure' (Valderrama, 1993: 79).

There is no one other than the President to handle project criteria or the problems or priorities of international co-operation agencies. Institutions such as the Ministry of Transport, the Ministry of Health, the National Program for Food Assistance (PRONAA), FONCODES or the quite new Ministry of Women and Human Development, are directly linked to the Ministry of Presidency. That means these organizations must negotiate external resources at their own risk and manage important co-operation items aside from SECTI (Sagasti and Alcalde, 1997: 41–3). It is important that in the National Budget for 1998, 24 per cent of the total amount goes to the Ministry of Presidency under direct control of the President. There is neither a database for investment projects in Peru nor a yearbook available to record up-to-date information. SECTI even employs Northern NGO support (UN, Spain and Germany) to carry out the task of organizing and publishing information, but with no results to date. SECTI seems to have turned into a 'reception desk of sectoral projects' (Valderrama, 1993: 77).

Both the formal structure of the Peruvian State and its operation seem to be a serious problem for the rational exertion of international co-operation.

Yet another serious issue is the tying of aid to the donor country's commercial interests. Widely discussed in Peru and elsewhere, studies on co-operation insist that 'international co-operation for development is an additional dimension of international relations' (González and Jaworski, 1990: 13) and that aid for Southern countries must follow the foreign and trade policy line of donors. In the history of co-operation with Peru, one of the clearest cases of aid linked to commercial ties resulted in a much debated case of corruption that still has consequences in the highest spheres of both countries. It is the case of Italy's financing of the never-completed metropolitan electronic train. A great deal of money remains missing and ex-President Alan García, now in hiding, is charged with involvement (among other accusations). Italian authorities have also being accused of complicity and investigations are continuing.

Another issue shaping the power dynamic of aid and civil society in Peru is the 'cocktail party' factor. Although it is right to assume that major policy decisions are made at donor headquarters, the selection of the institutions, organizations and mediators of projects has everything to do with personal contacts. The prestige of people and institutions, buttressed through invitations to parties and meetings with embassy staff, is as important as institutional strength. One of the people we interviewed said that agencies like IDB or even USAID had been deeply touched by the speeches of some important NGO directors at these social gatherings. In the case of large agencies, however, competitive tendering for important projects is more and more frequent (as is the case, for instance, of some large-scale USAID health projects).

Also, another issue in the power dynamic centres on the role of the local NGO as intermediary. There is a problem in the very institutional precariousness of many local NGOs and the fact (not frequently mentioned in the literature but often in the interviews) that some NGOs serve simply as employment vehicles for unemployed professional and technical groups. One of the outcomes is the perverse culture that exists within some Peruvian NGOs whereby results matter less than the capacity to 'sell' new projects to international agencies.

Thus a kind of vicious circle has arisen where about 5,000 professional people live within a fictitious job market (Rafael Roncagliolo's term for those working in Peruvian NGOs) encouraged by international financing. The change that came from the current criteria of financial institutions, like sustainability or results-efficiency, was seen by many NGOs as a threat to their power. Most Northern interactions with CSOs are mediated by NGOs, of course, in turn raising issues of permanence, organizational autonomy and project sustainability. Institutions like Oxfam concerned with linking themselves to grassroots organizations admit that only a third of their activities are carried out in a direct relationship; fully two-thirds are funnelled through intermediary NGOs. CIDA reports that its own distribution is half and half. Agencies are now, therefore, facing the problem of

NGOs taking the place of target populations, generating a job market for professional people and guaranteeing no institutional permanence.

Of course, key to the whole power dynamic is money. In the opinion of many we interviewed, the lack of resources is one of the most important explanations for the gap between intended outcomes and final results. In many cases, the NGOs responsible for carrying out bilateral, multilateral and foundation projects have neither the means nor the infrastructure required to implement them. Yet money is not all that is involved. One of the individuals we interviewed, an expert on co-operation issues in Peru, listed the following as further gaps within international co-operation organizations:

- Bilateral support generally demands the development of its own schemes, by its own highly paid consultants, in ways that do not always correspond to local possibilities.
- Northern co-operation agencies are also often guilty of distorting local organizations' aims and agendas, substituting local efforts and forming strong links of dependence on external financing (as in the case of entrepreneurs' associations mentioned earlier).
- One of the most important problems is the lack of control and evaluation of the results obtained. Corruption and abuse in administering resources are no longer exceptional and the political use of the support is often mentioned. Most frequently accused is President Fujimori, who seems to live permanently on political campaigns, especially inland, making use of external resources to bribe communities into voting favourably.

These, then, are some of the tensions within the framework of international co-operation. These power relationships have to do with the way in which power is exercised in Peru today. The autocratic challenge is all too clear.

Final Implications

In Peru, donors' activities in strengthening civil society have not been a case of old wine in new bottles. Changes are significant enough to allow us to talk about something new. As initially hypothesized, the most important conclusion is that international co-operation in Peru has changed because Peruvian society has changed. A civil society that, during the 1970s, was basically a popular civil society with large social movements as its principal actors, has given way to a plural civil society where women, grassroots organizations, business associations and small entrepreneurs are considered the new players. Organizations changed their relationship with the State from one of confrontation and opposition to one based on problem-solving proposals, precise initiatives and concrete steps.

Similarly, the strengthening of democratic institutions has replaced the accent on revolution that was the mark of the 1970s, not only because of international agendas but also because of what we have called the 'autocratic challenge'. The popular stamp marking co-operation criteria in the 1970s has been replaced by ideas of democracy, sustainability and institutional strengthening. The emphasis on civil society building has further, and ironically, been strengthened by structural adjustment as rigidly neo-liberal elites have introduced economic policies destined to foster a market-oriented model that emphasizes individual success and individual organizing.

Aid programmes to strengthen the market economy and to support democracy have also become part of the regular agendas of international co-operation. In a country where governance seems to be rebuilding itself from below as the population generates its own spaces and organizations to solve their problems, fostering civil society has become a developmental priority. Nevertheless, the frailty of many CSOs hampers the appearance of groups that would challenge and define their relationship with the State and with the donor community, and there is a clear lack of State interest in strengthening these organizations.

That reluctance explains why the donor community there has placed more emphasis on people's organizations, even if they have difficulty reaching them effectively. Foundations, multilateral agencies and official co-operation bodies have found it difficult to access the grassroots sectors that now appear as priorities in their programmes and projects. The solution has been to turn increasingly to Northern and Southern NGOs as intermediaries but, as we have seen, even this remedy has created problems.

To take up the goals of poverty reduction and democracy promotion, local participation is crucial. The accent on local needs assessment and the reinforcement of local capabilities is common throughout the Northern donor community, yet the danger of substituting for State services threatens. Within the context of extreme poverty and the withdrawal of the State, questions arise about the possibility that civil society (supported by international co-operation agencies) is substituting for the State in areas like food and health that should fall into its competence, thus favouring what many local actors call the neo-liberal policy of the current regime.

Moreover, as we have seen, those problems are exacerbated by the personalized control of national development plans (if they exist) by President Fujimori. Concentration of power, particularly since the dissolution of the INP, has also meant concentration of information and co-operation criteria and restriction of information publicly available. The need for independent intermediary bodies, mandated with a clear normative framework, is urgent.

If working with civil society really improves the prospects for development and democracy, then what can Northerners possibly do? The chapter has emphasized the following problems and makes a few suggestions for change.

CSOs may be growing, but for the wrong reasons

Although CSOs are expanding to meet the needs of survival, they are inadvertently allowing the State to cede its responsibilities. Perhaps perversely, the proliferation of groups may not, therefore, lead to any strengthening of democracy. Donors need to examine the kinds of groups they are supporting under the rubric of 'strengthening civil society' for fear of undermining the provision of core social services.

NGOs are distrusted

The growth of a fictitious job market in Peru has undermined the credibility of both Peruvian and Northern NGOs. If external programmes designed to 'strengthen civil society' are seen solely as the disbursement of more funds to the professional elite, solidarity between the intermediary organizations and people's groups will continue to break down. Northern and Southern NGOs must develop their accountability *vis-à-vis* Peruvian society and not only *vis-à-vis* co-operation agencies.

Politics are everywhere

In a country split by political violence and distrust, it is especially crucial for foreign agencies to forge political distance. Although all agencies have been painted with the same brush, bilateral agencies in particular need to restrict their dependence on political ties if they mean to reach beyond Fujimori to the people he governs in poverty.

Public engagement is weak

While organizations, although fragile, have proliferated, the space for them to articulate and debate a shared vision has not. Outside the closed circle of international development agencies, there are no local fora, including in the media, where groups can discuss development and the role played by civil society. This democratic bottleneck should become the centre of donors' interventions in Peru. Without public spaces, CSOs will simply wither. These steps *can* help, if made with an understanding of Peru's complex political history and the weight of endemic poverty. Although the challenge of defeating autocracy and poverty belongs to the people of Peru, the challenge of supporting, or hindering, that effort from outside lies elsewhere. This chapter tries to guide that support to where it is most needed and to alert the reader to the power dynamics that shape State–market–civil society relations in Peru. Today, there is good news in the struggles of civil society; tomorrow, we hope for more.

7 THE ART OF STRENGTHENING CIVIL SOCIETY

Alison Van Rooy

The book argues that the idea of 'civil society' has become omnipresent because it rings most of the political, economic and social bells of the late twentieth century. The ideas packed into the two familiar words are rich, overlapping, contradictory and in danger of being all things to all people; at the same time, however, they hold out tremendous inspiration for change. This book has explored that tension between analysis and hope, between language and the world it describes. This is the very stuff of politics.

Donors, like others, have shown different behaviours in response to the debate on civil society. In the name of civil society, some donor activities have made important strides in the promotion of development and democracy. The chapters chronicle roundtables, election supervision, soup kitchen work, think tank interventions, diplomatic *tête-à-têtes* and careful 'expert' advice, all in the name of civil society strengthening. Some of that work (for example, Kenya's moratorium and Soros' copy machines) has brought about important social and political change, but there has been frustration elsewhere.

The irony is that the very little debate there has been on civil society has been valuable precisely because of its vagueness. This vagueness encourages a whole range of agendas to be considered. In policy and practical terms, however, how can one make projects and programmes focused on 'civil society strengthening'? How to deliver funds? Measure progress? It is here that the meeting of political processes sits uncomfortably with the tools that donors have at their disposal: projects, funds and timelines. This conclusion argues that programmes in the name of civil society have been important, and may indeed become more important, but they work best when based on deep knowledge, small funds, and long-term relationships. Enthusiasm drawn from the inspiration of civil society must be measured carefully when meted out in dollars, lest harm be done.

WHAT WE FOUND

The slipperiest part of the debate is the difference between norms (the values inherent in the idea of civil society) and forms (the organizational incarnation of those values). What we *want* to see (the normative) is difficult to distinguish from what we *do* see (the organizations). This book dealt with this difference first by describing the current perspectives on the debate in donor literature and then by illustrating in each country the shape of civil society in its organized form. The message is that the nature and purpose of organizing differs by culture and history in each of the four countries, but all share the act of collective organizing.

If we left the discussion here, however, it would soon lose our interest. We could count and describe those groups by form, membership, structure and shape. We could contrast forms across countries and seek to understand their variation. We could highlight their variety by subject area. In this kind of analysis, it would make equal sense to talk about civil society as to talk about the voluntary sector or the non-profit sector; they are categories of organizations (Anheier and Salamon, 1997).

Yet it is important to go further. The next part of the discussion in this book and in our definition, therefore, delves into the normative field: 'What do civil society organizations (CSOs) do for social justice'? As donors, practitioners and academics ourselves, the authors are primarily interested in the functions of CSOs in promoting social justice. The normative question forces us to look at the 'whys' of civil society, the functions of organizations, the value structures that bring people to build their organizations. We are, after all, interested in the idea of civil society *because* it is a way to describe normative political projects among those organizations, introducing to the debate a discussion of values, conflict, relationships and power.

Once the debate is grounded in the day-to-day challenges of international aid planning, these distinctions become all the more important. The focus on organizations is easy enough, but the normative element is more difficult to describe and evaluate. The danger for analysis is the lure of Kumar's 'emancipatory promise' that civil society is used to mean all good things in all places and at all times. For aid practitioners, the danger is the assumption that one's normative values, even for a goal as irrefutable as democracy, are the same as everyone else's, and that the organizations that bring it about in one country are the same as in others.

This normative danger has shown up particularly in suspicions regarding the State. Western aid agencies have written extensively on the role of CSOs as an opposition or partial alternative to the State (or to a particular regime). Contrary to much popular debate, however, the political projects of influential CSOs may *not* necessarily be designed to diminish the State, although these efforts are always the most visible. Throughout, indeed, we have argued that a responsible, socially active State is part of the preconditions for a healthy and effective civil society. Indeed, the political projects of CSOs may counterbalance other institutions of power, including the trading or hiring practices of international corporations, the global financial system's capital flow practices, the social institutions of sexism or racism and oppression on the basis of caste, among other important social justice goals. If outsiders do not look for these alternate political projects, they may not be seen.

It follows that most CSOs are probably not undertaking the kind of work that is of most interest to donors. As elaborated in each of our case studies, the proportion directly engaged in supporting formal democratization, the promotion of human rights, the legislation of non-profits or other common donor goals is very small. Moreover, as chapter 2 argued, the amount of money allocated to 'strengthening civil society' is very small against the backdrop of aid, and aid itself is of marginal importance even to the most dependent (Kenya) of our four countries. Donor money thus can only be relevant as small, strategic interventions in a bigger picture of social change.

In describing these practical instances of *relevant* intervention, moreover, we found that much of the theoretical discussion does not help to guide policy. When the idea of civil society successfully suits all political tastes, it loses usefulness. We have thus illustrated ways in which theory can be made more useful for addressing the dilemmas of legitimacy, strategy and implementation of foreign intervention.

THEORY

Theories are only interesting if they explain something. The problem with the language of civil society is that it is used to explain almost everything: social disintegration in North America, the democratic surges in China, the transformation of Eastern Europe, the relative wealth of Northern Italy, the efforts to remove Moi from his Kenyan throne and the dominance of the free market, among other ideas. It is used to describe groups with particular motives or is employed as a synonym for 'the people'. It describes not the society we have, but the one to which we aspire. It is deeply populist.

Few of these interpretations help when one is involved in the day-to-day struggle to do something worthwhile with aid dollars. We suggest that a theory on civil society must help us clarify at least the following questions (if not provide answers):

- Who matters in rendering social and political change?
- How is power, political and economic, distributed among the governed and the governors?
- What elements are amenable to outside intervention? What intervention is legitimate? To whom?

These questions force us to look beyond the organizations to the things that they do and the political and economic spheres in which they work. We need theories of civil society that acknowledge the organizational *and* political dynamics. What would be included in such a contribution? Some ideas are elaborated in the following.

Power

The study of civil society is a study of power relations in society. Talk of power, however, makes many people uncomfortable – it generates notions of violence, revolution, social unrest. The compromise position in much donor writing has, therefore, been to focus on democratization, a political idea that is strangely apolitical, apparently harbouring no grounds for legitimate opposition. Leslie Fox, writing for the World Bank, explains it this way:

> *While civil society is a political concept, the tendency among many donors wishing to support it – primarily official bilateral development assistance agencies and their home-country non-governmental organization (NGO) partners – has been to define it narrowly within a strategy of promoting democracy. An alternative conception of 'political', the one used here, takes a more inclusive socio-political view, focusing on the exercise of power to bring about change. In this context, 'political' is used not because civil society engages in partisan politics, but because it confronts powerholders in the State and the market whose interests have often been, and will continue to be, at odds with those of citizens, their communities and the larger society. Challenging power for the purpose of trying to effect change, whether in social, economic or political life, is an inherently political act.* (Fox, 1997: 7)

Fox puts the ball in the right court. The notion that CSOs might be involved in power renegotiation or advocacy *is* contentious among donors. An interesting survey of World Bank staff found just such a reluctance:

> *Respondents were asked to rank the most important sets of attributes of civil society. The largest group (41 per cent) ranked the 'associational' dimension of civil society at the top, followed by the 'human mobilization' dimension (34 per cent), and the 'normative' dimensions such as civility and tolerance (14 per cent). Finally, the dimension of 'advocacy' of deserving causes received the least support (11 per cent). Obviously, the Bank staff do not put great emphasis on the 'normative' and 'advocacy' dimension.* (Ibrahim, 1996: 24)

For two-thirds of the staff, civil society was interesting or useful mostly in terms of getting people together and mobilizing their activity, in this case, to participate in Bank projects. What the survey respondents missed is the message of this book. 'Strengthening civil society' is a deeply political set of activities, not simply a useful thing for getting projects underway.

The implications of this statement are important. For one, the idea of power is itself slippery. Power is a *relational* idea, something between people and organizations, not a commodity poured out in exact measure; it is possible for the powerful to maintain a socially injust system only through a series of relationships. A theory of civil society needs to focus on relationships of power, for it is among these relationships that CSOs must negotiate as they attempt to lever change. To understand the work of CSOs engaged in social change, we must understand how they fit into the larger picture of power players.

This focus on power relationships in turn encourages us to step back from analysis of CSOs' form (membership bases, management structures, degrees of formality of leadership) and to turn to *function*. Theory needs to focus on what organizations *do* more than how they are shaped. This functional analysis is drawn out most clearly in the discussion on clan-based groups, the churches and co-operatives in Kenya. There, the argument is that organizations cannot be discounted simply on account of their form (ascriptive rather than voluntary). Perhaps the degree of ascription *does* matter when coming to a cross-ethnic political solution in Kenya, but we cannot start from the assumption that they cannot matter simply because they take a particular form. We must start with observations about what organizations *do*. Then, we must make choices about the appropriateness of intervention among organizations that are themselves born of that conflict.

The State

Another important element in any theory of civil society must include, as it almost always does, some explanation of CSOs' evolving relationship with the State. The book has emphasized in many places how Western descriptions of civil society's virtues actually have less to do with civil organizing (who is forming into what organizations for what reasons) than it does with the legitimacy accorded to the State or a particular regime by outsiders. In fixating almost generically on the failings of the State, we may have missed other important political projects.

First of all, understanding the State as an abstraction is not very useful, either in theory or in practice. Only once the conversation turns to the relationship between particular CSOs and governments, does it become more interesting. After all, if power is a relational idea, it depends on real institutions and the people who created them. It is hard to talk about power if we cannot refer to particular policies, police forces, legal instruments and cultural beliefs, all of which are nationally specific and irrelevant if generalized to all countries. In a given country, moreover, it is not very helpful to talk about State–civil society relations in tidy opposition. Rather than sitting in analytical circles distinct from the State, CSOs need to be seen on a moving continuum of opposition and collaboration with particular governments and other brokers of power in the debates over poverty and social justice. This, indeed, was what Gramsci proposed.

In this light, a focus on function also helps us to look at our ideals of State–civil society relations, including the central role of a State in providing for its people. As Miszlivetz writes:

> *(A) starting premise needs to be the recognition that the State is potentially, and in the most objective reality, the most important actor in both improving development and building democracy and that civil society can, at best, ensure that such a role is played transparently, with accountability and in a socially enabling manner. Civil society certainly cannot sustainably supplant or substitute the State.* (1997, personal communication)

Theory should, therefore, discuss the myriad of functions identified for the State and other actors in given contexts. If civil society is merely not to supplant the State, what is it to do? In the analysis required by any outsider wishing to intervene, those functions must at least be questioned and explored.

Actors in the Marketplace

Power relationships also exist among civil society actors and market actors, institutions and policies, both local and global. A failure of much of today's theoretical literature has been to ignore the impact that market forces have on the shaping of civil society.

For many organizations, the globalization of trade and international finance is of increasing concern. Severe pressures on national economies by free-flowing capital (as happened in South-east Asia), arm-twisting on national spending priorities made by international lenders, the impact of international labour competition on labour standards, currency speculation and investment in export production over basic consumption needs – all these have dire consequences for the poorest. The combined pressure brought on by poverty and the reduction of State services has had a dramatic impact in the ways people organize. The number of service organizations has sky-rocketed, arguments brought out forcefully in the chapters on Hungary and Peru; and the number of people dropping from organizing altogether (the 'suffer-manage' strategy of Kenyans) are clear effects.

It is at this point that the debate on civil society also joins the broader conversation on market liberalization. Even as just states negotiate their place in the world order, the pressures have been to diminish State services in order to cut spending deficits and to meet loan conditionality require-ments. For donors, whose strategies encourage quicker market liberalization and lower government expenditure on social services, one might argue that the focus on CSOs ends up as support for mops for the fallout. A weakened State, reduced in its ability to respond to demands from its people and their organization, is hardly the only culprit. Theory needs to at least address the intersection of market, government and civil society functions.

Society

We also need a theory of civil society that acknowledges, describes and interrogates values within the broader society. Distinguishing the form from the norm does not mean that norms are irrelevant; it simply means that they are not the same thing.

By our definition, we have argued that CSOs are neither good, nor bad, nor necessarily democratic. There are corrupt and rent-seeking organizations in civil society (the MONGOs (My Own NGOs) of Kenya and the fictitious NGO job market in Peru) as elsewhere in the broader society. A populous and vibrant civil society – the rise of East German skinheads, for example – may easily promote values *inimical* to broader social justice.

It follows that a theory of civil society has to examine what societal factors and preconditions raise the 'quality' of CSOs towards a given set of normative ends. For practitioners, the challenge is in knowing whether any of those preconditions are amenable to intervention. If the prerequi-sites in a particular country are the presence of an informed, active citizenry, how can external agents inculcate those characteristics, particu-larly without gross infringements on national and cultural sovereignty? These characteristics are deeply social, the outcome of a lifetime of social-ization, a difficult and ethically dangerous province for the work of aid donors. Moreover, as the chapter on Peru illustrates, poverty and weak citizenship reinforce each other to undermine the quality of civil society. Levels of poverty determine both the motivation and the capacity of individuals to occupy and remain active inside the space of civil society.

The implication for donors may be that poverty reduction must re-take centre stage as the most import civil society 'strengthening' effort. The theoretical implication is that civil societies may well build themselves.

THE AID INDUSTRY

The discussion leads us to a set of practical concerns: Is there anything that *can* be done? Is there anything that *should* be done? The mistakes highlighted in previous channels are reviewed before an examination of donors' successes. Those best practices have in turn helped us generate the framework for action that follows.

Mistakes

It is no wonder that mistakes have been made, of course, because the field of debate is convoluted, and the day-to-day work of donors and their allies continues to be political, complex and unsure of results. Aid, almost by definition, is always thus. If, however, we were to sift the lessons learned in the research into general piles, they would focus on three mistakes: simplification, instrumentalism and operationalization.

Simplification

Donor activity around 'civil society strengthening' is frequently based on thin justifications for action. There is a range of assumptions made on the universal desirability of certain organizations, political systems and social norms. As a panacea for social ills, both in the North and elsewhere, 'civil society' has evidently come to the rescue of difficult dilemmas, such as:

How to encourage democracy?
Most equate the proliferation of certain kinds of organization with the institution of democracy itself (see Chapter 2). Questions about the function of organizations in promoting or impeding both formal and substantive democracy need to be asked more frequently.

How to reduce the State?
Serious questions need to be raised about the impact of donor intervention on State service provision. This impact can have both negative and positive implications for CSOs.

How to encourage the free market?
Putnam's work on social capital (see Chapter 2) suggests that support to civic organizations can have spin-off effects in the economy. More careful questions need to be asked about links, particularly in countries where associations are made on ethnic or class grounds, and where the economic system is controlled by a select few.

To link CSOs *primarily* with the institution of democracy, a reduced State and a freer market is a misleading simplification. Even if we limit our horizon to civil society organizations expressly engaged in political work, the horizon of goals is much broader. Outsiders will not see those organizations unless they look for them.

Instrumentalism

Part of this sin of simplification is the assumption that one need only *use* CSOs as instruments on the way to bigger political and economic goals:

'Aid donors view civil society in fairly narrow instrumental terms, i.e. support to civil society is designed to further a number of objectives in the spheres of democratization, human rights, and good governance' (Robinson, 1996: 6).

Indeed, in certain countries, the 'installation' of an autonomous civil society has been part of donors' exit strategies, a way to ensure that their programme of work continues after the dollars stop flowing. As Hungary faces the withdrawal of foreign aid in the coming years, for example, the growth of CSOs is being temporarily well supported by USAID and others. The issue here is what happens once the 'instrumental' donor retreats and the relationships among CSOs, market forces and State agencies take on new shapes in the donor's absence.

'Using' CSOs, however willingly they are engaged, also raises a series of other practical issues. In particular, large-scale funding from outside donors to local organizations can lead to co-optation, perversion of outcomes (through the encouragement of fictitious 'civil' organizations, as in Hungary, Peru and Kenya) and the skewing of domestic priorities. How can donors and CSOs ensure that their funding relationship does not swamp the political project? Part of the answer requires deep donor knowledge about the national political landscape.

Another issue is the choice of particular organizations for support and the changes brought about by this resource skewing. The funding of urban rather than rural agencies, or business associations instead of unions, or constitutional groups rather than service provision agencies all involve important choices and may affect in unintended ways the quality of civil society writ large. Again, the only answers lie in deep knowledge of national realities.

All of these issues underscore primary questions of power relationships in instrumental relationships. Both carrots and sticks are at work in the relationships between recipient organizations and foreign donors, meaning that CSOs do not always have the power to set their own priorities or to resist donor offerings. The danger is that those organizations may undermine their own integrity.

Operationalization

Ideas about civil society in the international aid community, however, can have important and progressive impact on social and political change. The attention now paid to actors outside the State and the marketplace is, of itself, a crucial addition. Soros' support for underground copy machines, multi-stakeholder meetings convened in Sri Lanka, inclusion of women's soup kitchens into Peru's national health programme and donor pressure to end the Kenyan one-party system are all important examples of donor *inclusion* of CSOs into their thinking and practice.

What we find, not surprisingly, is that good thinking does not always translate into good practice. The operationalization of donor instruments and measures has not always been successfully adapted to this new type of development goal. Part of the reason is that it is difficult to turn 'civil society strengthening' into 'logical framework analyses', the standard aid agency planning process that turns an idea into a project. Among the authors' complaints about donor practices in their countries are the following illustrations of the failures of operationalization:

Donor emphasis is often on time-fixed projects rather than processes

Organizations complain that funding agencies focus too heavily on supporting specific projects, rather than on processes, even where the intention is explicitly to support a process of change. Overhead costs are cut from budgets, funding is provided on an item-by-item basis and quick, tangible outcomes are requested even for activities not designed to produce immediately visible results.

Donors often fund the most familiar organizations, rather than the most functionally important

Organizations that have structures or names similar to those in donor countries (law societies rather than ethnic clan associations) are more likely to be funded, as are urban professionalized groups that use donor language (including the term 'civil society') over rural ones that describe their world differently. The carrot factor of funding, for which CSOs are equally to blame, creates an added incentive to become more like the donor. 'Donor capture', a topic discussed particularly in the Kenyan case, then becomes its own problem. As the relationship comes to be called a 'partnership', still further problems can be introduced, as happened with some of the Hungarian examples where donors avoided looking into the background of potential recipients. Their misplaced support generated animosity elsewhere.

Donors often fund organizations in their own likeness

The creation of surrogate organizations (or DONGOs, Donor-Organized NGOs) is an understandable outcome of a literal effort to build civil society. This segment of civil society, however, may never develop indigenous linkages, long-term sustainability or social legitimacy. Similar arguments are made in the chapters against the initiation of donor-created coalitions to channel funding on the grounds that unrooted umbrella organizations may marginalize important voices. These practices are further supplemented by the importation of foreign advisors and experts who take on disproportionate influence, for example, the Marriott Brigades in Eastern Europe.

Best Practice

Although all these problems are evident, they are also understandable. What donors (and others) know about the processes of social change comes from their own national experiences and institutions. What values we espouse seem so self-evidently universal that similar mechanisms must bring about similar change. The message conveyed by the best practices of donors, whether bilateral, multilateral or voluntary, is that social change comes about through nationally specific processes and mechanisms and that donors who support pre-existing processes are the most likely to be successful. For this reason, the idea of civil society is tremendously helpful. There are a number of reasons why this may be so:

Civil society forces us to put aid in its place

Interventions by outsiders have been meaningful in ways that do not involve aid at all or only in small doses. Diplomatic sanctions, ambassadorial *tête-à-têtes*, foreign exchanges, the provision of photocopiers or Internet access, policies to include 'civil society participation' at donor meetings, all these are potentially low-budget, high-impact interventions. Aid thus resumes its role as an encouragement to existing movements for change, not the strong arm that sets them rolling.

The idea of civil society forces us to take civil organizing seriously

The chapter on Hungary underlined a dramatic shift in emphasis in international aid. Hungary, which will likely receive foreign aid for only 10 more years or less, was a clean slate for an international community that wanted to contribute to *Hungarian* efforts towards social change. The speed and profundity of the transformation, although it is not yet culturally rooted, was startling for outsiders. What happened in Eastern Europe and the former Soviet Union made the Western world take civil organizing much more seriously. That philosophical change has not only turned up in donors programmes in that region but in other parts of the world as well. The message here is that organizations outside of the State and marketplace matter deeply.

The idea of civil society makes us look at power in society

Because ideas about civil society are inextricably wound up in our ideas about political systems and their legitimacy, we are forced to look at the political and economic environments in which development and democracy occur. Maina argues in his chapter that much of what donors have done in Kenya has had a significant impact, for example, the repeal of the one-party law in Kenya was spurred by donor pressure and today's debate on constitutional reform has been led by donor-funded CSOs. Saravanamuttu argues in his chapter that donors have been forced to confront the deep conflict between separatists and the federal State, a particularly violent State–civil society relationship, as central to their efforts. The outcome of a focus on civil society is to deepen our understanding of the movement of power.

Civil society forces us to look to NGOs and beyond

The notion of civil society helps give a theoretical place to intermediary NGOs, often otherwise simplified as service providers and project implementors. NGOs have a place in this broader picture as brokers, but the real focus of attention has been where many NGOs have always indicated. These other civil society actors also populate the picture: many are informal and have no wish to engage with international aid, the majority may have no interest in policy at all, some are likely strong formal bodies with professional staff and ample local resources and yet others are often struggling with insufficient material or other resources, trying to make a mark on their political world. The discussion on civil society asks us to look at all of these before we make our own mark on those political landscapes.

'STRENGTHENING' CIVIL SOCIETY

Given these debates, what model for planning civil society programmes could be generated? This section walks through a set of recommendations for deepening an analysis of change from a civil society perspective.

Aside from the research in this book, these recommendations draw from a host of other sources of inspiration.

1995

The Development Assistance Committee (DAC) organized a workshop on civil society and democracy to plan its own position, which included a 1997 Organization for Economic Co-operation and Development (OECD) evaluation of successes in programmes to promote democratic development and good governance (OECD, 1993 and OECD, 1995). The same year, the American NGO umbrella organization, InterAction, undertook a series of workshops to help its membership deal with the debate on civil society. The Synergos Institute published a report on getting the private sector more actively involved in cross-subsidizing the work of CSOs (1995).

1996

A thoughtful contribution was made by USAID's Civil Society Unit, which chose to concentrate its programmes on civic *advocacy* organizations rather than on a larger definition of civil society (Hansen, 1996). Also that year, the United Nations Development Programme (UNDP) published its own policy document pledging to involve CSOs more systematically in the agency's programmes and commissioned a series of studies on how it would do that work (Fowler, 1997a; Malena, 1996; Van Rooy, 1996; Line,

1997). And, the UK's development research funding body (ESCOR) commissioned a workshop on the links between CSOs and the strengthening of civil society (Bebbington and Mitlin, 1996).

1997

Canada's South Asia Partnership undertook a series of workshops and is now undertaking a resource book on how NGOs can relate to the debate in their own work (Swift, 1998). Also that year, a conglomeration of international CSOs, including the Institute for Development Research, published on how they might build the capacity of CSOs with whom they worked (Brown, 1997). Leslie Fox also wrote a major volume for the African branch of the World Bank on what the Bank should do to strengthen CSOs (Fox, 1997).

The list could easily be longer, for the topic is of fervent interest to those wanting to join the civil society parade.

Based on our own work and the contributions of others, the following set of guidelines collects criticisms and findings of success into a bundle that may be useful for practitioners. This bundle will be markedly familiar to many practitioners – it suggests what many already do: listen, learn, encourage participation, be thorough, be reactive. Its message is *specificity*. In a field providing hosts of lists for 'strengthening civil society', we suggest a culturally, historically, politically specific strategic planning process, not a blueprint. We propose a series of methodical questions to help outsiders develop the specific understanding needed to make choices in different cultural and political milieux. Although not exhaustive, this set of recommendations and questions covers key criticisms and offers some alternatives for action. We hope that it is a useful step forward.

The Big Picture

Working with CSOs is both practically and politically complex. The first set of guidelines, therefore, asks donors to interrogate, and to seek help in interrogating, their own goals.

Interrogate Goals

Because the debate on civil society is normatively convoluted, it is important that all players are aware of their own motivations. What is the aid agency doing? Why? Who wants the donor to be there? What are the donor's philosophies of change? USAID, in its pointed focus on civic advocacy organizations to promote formal democratic change, is very clear on its own goals (USAID, 1996), even if those are debated. It is important that the philosophical underpinnings of programmes are described and understood; only then can they be debated.

Get the Lay of the Land

It is also important that one's own philosophies of change bear some relevance to the countries in which one works. Each chapter has made a special effort to describe key cultural and political determinants of civil organizing. We have emphasized some of the factors donors need to know, including the dynamics of power among CSOs, NGOs, the market and the State.

Prominent among those factors is the level of political and financial support or resistance put up by home governments. Examples of resistance are certainly easy to find. In 1976, for example, India passed a law requiring voluntary organizations to obtain government approval before accepting foreign donations. In 1996, El Salvador passed a law requiring that the Interior Minister (at one time in charge of that country's death squads) personally allow civil organizations the right of legal existence. Indonesia under Suharto maintained close controls over its country's voluntary organizations and Kenya requires development NGOs to be listed and their incomes registered under a government-controlled board. Malaysia issued new rules in 1997 to control the activity of NGOs and a recent law in Zimbabwe allows the government to take over the assets of any NGO whose behaviour is deemed 'unacceptable,' (Interaction, 1995: 11). These disabling environmental and relational factors are of crucial importance to the success of civil organizing.

How CSOs deal with that resistance or support is also important – democratization and increasing 'civility' are not always the answer. In Peru and Sri Lanka, some organizations turned to violence, others, to a lucrative career in the aid industry; in Hungary, ex-communists quickly changed face to become the new democrats; in Kenya, many organizations undertook a pointed strategy of disengagement while a prominent few were jailed. In looking at democratization throughout Africa, a recent CODESRIA (Council for the Development of Economic and Social Research in Africa) study demonstrated that a relatively few organizations played a disproportionate role and, in some cases, included those like the Sudanese Communist Party that were themselves undemocratic (Mamdani and Wamba-dia-Wamba, 1995).

Similarly, the ways in which the global or local marketplace intertwines with civil society is also important; the Peruvian association of NGOs promoting small enterprise or the Kenyan Co-operative Creameries are important bodies with both market and civil roles. In some cases, however, co-operative efforts have taken on strictly personal motives, accusations levelled in Hungary, which need to be explored.

Getting the big picture also implies an examination of the other forces that are working on civil society. Socially and culturally, one needs to learn about the informal and unregistered 'organizations' of civil society that none the less carry tremendous weight in social change (the clan associations in Kenya, the ex-communist networks in Hungary, the landed white elite in Peru, the clergy in Sri Lanka). One also needs to offer at least a passing consideration of international factors of debt; economic liberalization, protectionism and globalization; trans-border flow of ideas, people and illicit and legal goods; and environmental problems.

Make Political Assessments

If anything, the debate on civil society has shown that political motivations for aid have come out from under the table. The end of the Cold War has seemed to indicate that political change in the direction of Western democracy and economic forms can only promise progress for other countries. This assertion may be overstated in describing the whole scene, of course, but it strikes close to the mark with those donors who have pointedly political interests.

The questions that need to be asked are about legitimacy. Can donor politics be justified in the context of local agendas? Whose agendas are those? What impact might intervention make on shaping political outcomes? The end of one-party State rule in Kenya is a clear example of positive change spurred by donor activity, as were Soros' efforts throughout Central and Eastern Europe. In other cases, however, donor support to CSOs has had clearly negative outcomes, such as counter-Sandinista support in Nicaragua or cold war interventions in Namibia.

Any intervention is, almost by nature, political. Civil society organizations at the centre of much donor attention are usually political bodies that are themselves at the centre of real conflicts, real debates. The question is not whether politics can be avoided, but whether one's particular choice of political stance and partnerships can be justified and, if so, to whom.

Plan Strategically

Given these initial considerations, we recommend a planning process that involves a focus on organizations, their relationships and the environments in which they work. A metaphor of civil society as a building of bricks, mortar and site is used to make the distinctions clearer. While the metaphor suggests construction by outside agents, we intend it to describe the interplay of forces that causes buildings to grow and to take on important functions. It is thus more accurate to think of this building as a living thing, building itself within a complex interplay of forces. The international aid system may have only a small role to play, and so the onus is on learning and watching, not acting. For aid practitioners, the challenge is knowing if and when to intervene.

Bricks

The bricks, the constituent parts of the building, are organized groups. They form for reasons of collective interest, which may or may not have anything to do with the public interest. They may be morally good, bad or neutral in function but they share with other organizations their collective form.

Mortar

Relationships are the mortar that holds the building together. In reality, of course, civil society's relationships rarely form straight or particularly functional walls. One needs to ask how are organizations related: Are they disparate and atomized, or tightly woven into coalitions? (Ndegwa, 1994). What groups exist in opposition to them? How does this opposition shape public policy? In trying to affect civil society, donors must be aware of the relationships among groups, which may in turn be determined by ethnicity, class or race, among other factors. As Roper-Renshaw points out, 'organizations in themselves are just the bricks of civil society... Civil society, above all, is a relational concept' (Roper-Renshaw, 1994: 46).

Building site

But this building is not drawn from thin air; there are preconditions or enabling environments necessary for its existence. The metaphorical equivalents might be the building site and its zoning laws, unions, weather, budget, neighbours, financing and location. In political terms, these include a system of rights, a culture of association, legal protection, the role of the State and market, and the availability of financing among other factors.

Given this metaphor, then, what is it to 'strengthen' civil society from the vantage point of external agents? Strengthening civil society is more than providing equipment and skills (brickmaking) to formal organizations, it is about contributing to organizations' abilities to do their work in conjunction with, or in opposition to, other actors and forces (laying mortar), as well as clearing the ground for work to begin (obtaining the building site). Mortar and site work may not involve funding particular CSOs at all, and may have implications for the entire swath of formal and informal organizations.

Strengthening Bricks and Mortar

The bricks of civil society, its organizations, can be fortified in different ways. The infrastructure of a formal organization (salaries, phones, rent) can be supported by outsiders and the skills of its staff and members can be developed through training; informal organizations can be supported if they wish to take on a formal role. This kind of aid underwrites the material base of civil society, without which organizing in the political realm is difficult. Otherwise, independent access to those material resources requires ample economic surplus (and perhaps a middle class), and a deep tradition of supporting non-profit ventures – attributes that are difficult to find even in rich countries. For many CSOs, poverty is thus not only issue for action, but also an issue of institutional existence.

We must also ask questions about which parts of civil society, which bricks, are being 'strengthened'. This volume has argued that it matters deeply what organizations are supported, and what motivations bring them and the international donor community to the same table. Although 'civil society' writ large has tremendous appeal in today's policy discussions, in its day-to-day incarnations, many players and many motivations are at work.

The following paragraphs touch on some of those players. As a relational idea, the notion of civil society asks that we look at all three sectors.

The 'third' sector

Many equate civil society with the voluntary or third sector; NGOs with public interest goals. In development circles, this starting point has meant a concentration on NGOs as the most effective medium to reach the poor, and strengthening has, for the most part, involved direct and indirect funding. In many cases, however, little differentiation is made between Northern and Southern intermediaries, nor between Southern intermediaries and service providers, membership organizations, co-operatives, etc, which span the civil spectrum. Many of these organizations are not 'NGOs' in the Northern sense but are popular organizations that fill a larger space in their communities. They are journalists advocating for freedom of the press, glass-of-milk organizations run by mothers in ghettos, academic institutions and so on, and may indeed be organizations with transformative capacity that donors might well ignore like the Girl Guides in Kenya or youth clubs in Sri Lanka.

This distinction between NGOs and other organizations in civil society is important because it runs counter to the frequent equation of civil society, in its breadth and complexity, with the term 'NGO'. As Pearce writes, when international agencies recognize the role of NGOs:

> *They are not envisaging peasants organising to defend their land rights or workers organising for better pay and conditions. They have in mind the voluntary organisations who may be able to deliver services more efficiently than the State. They equate NGOs with a regenerated private sector: their importance lies in simply being outside the State, which is held to be responsible for the development failings of the last two decades.* (Pearce, 1993: 223)

It is significant, and startling, therefore, that so little attention has been paid in Northern development circles beyond questions of NGO proliferation to consider the forces that propel a larger civil society (see Hulme and Edwards, 1997). The emphasis is understandable, NGOs based both in the North and the South have long been the intermediaries, the eyes and ears of donor agencies. They are part of civil society themselves, of course, and often take on political and advocacy functions that bring them to outsiders' attentions. Beyond the familiar shape and language of development NGOs, however, the world of other CSOs looms large and unfamiliar. The pressure to deal with these groups has generated the literature we review in this book; but it is a literature that has been poor on helping donors choose which organizations within civil society to support and to what purpose.

The second sector: the market

Another issue is the common inclusion of the private sector in definitions of civil society. For those who share an anti-State perspective on the debate, the inclusion is not surprising. For the donor community, the labelling of private sector organizations as part of 'civil society' has much to do with the link between economic liberalization, civil society and entrepreneurship – bricks that some donors are keen on reinforcing.

Does that then mean that strengthening civil society involves strengthening the private sector? In what ways and at what level? In some countries, removing barriers to micro enterprise may be included under the civil society heading, in others, promotion of international business may be included. Maina's chapter argues that many of the organizations that are invisible to donors are in the economic sphere, yet they have often been able to cause shifts in government behaviour through civic action. Again, the message here is to look for the desired function – repealing a particular regulation, maintaining the rule of law, supervising government behaviour, monitoring environmental problems – and then identify the owner.

The first sector: the State

A further question about the mix of players at the table has to do with the inclusion of some parts of the State within the definition of civil society. By the mid 1990s, devolution of aid to NGOs had reached a plateau and many donors began to look at devolution of power to local authorities as a parallel, or replacement, activity. Decentralization has thus risen, somewhat mantra-like, as a goal for good governance. In some donor policy strategies, local government agencies are included in the ranks of civil society. Not all observers agree, of course; the politics of inclusion has as much to do with conceptual distinctions between the State and the government as it has to do with neat programming categories. Both challenges will have to be met by donors.

It becomes clear that donor intervention in this morass of relationships is a difficult task. In practical terms, intervention may mean organizing networks, holding meetings, providing telephone and electronic communications, supporting travel, sharing information and distributing documentation. For some donors, these non-project, non-capital, non-glamorous activities may not seem worthwhile because they make it difficult to measure results in concrete terms.

Strengthening The Building Site

Another element in strengthening civil society is making it possible for organizations to form and to act; there must be *room* for their existence. The government needs to guarantee the minimal protection of human rights, particularly the right to associate. The guarantee of the rule of law, an advantageous tax system and a fair regulatory environment are strengthening factors as well. In a review of the environment for civil society organizing in several African countries, Mutume writes:

> *The major problem appears to be the lack – or inadequacy – of regulatory frameworks within which NGOs operate in the sub-region. In Zambia for instance, freedom of association is still limited as the police demand 14-days notice of impending public meetings. In addition, NGOs are taxed while only those with close links to government benefit from grants. In Seychelles, the government has set up State-funded NGOs that enjoy large tax exemptions denied other civic organizations. Sometimes, it is the NGOs which unscrupulously manipulate the law as allegedly happens in Malawi, where NGOs are registered under numerous legal instruments as trustees, companies or co-operatives.* (Mutume, 1996)

Further elements are the presence of a free press, universal access to political participation, high levels of education and other basic services, and (as the Peruvian chapter argues) the elimination of poverty. Others would point to the presence of foundations, private philanthropists and a corporate culture that supports third-sector organizations and does not limit their access to the market for non-profit purposes.

Yet there is some concern that Northern disillusionment with the State may mean that donors may dismiss the critical role of the State in its enabling environment. In their critique of the civil society debate, Porter and Kilby write that, 'civil society is not likely to thrive, and for that matter be judged worthy of "strengthening", unless there is an effective strong State which can establish the rules of the game and provide some discriminatory framework for civil society activities' (Porter and Kilby, 1996: 32).

The Real Issues

Even with careful planning, real political and practical issues will arise. Among them, donors will need to deal with political decisions in making choices, using appropriate support mechanisms, taking an appropriate role at the sidelines and planning to leave.

Making Choices

What should donors do about making difficult choices among organizations or issues? How should donors deal with the legitimate role as critic that CSOs can play, even when donors may have set out to support the CSOs' service delivery? Indeed, how should CSOs deal with the legitimacy of donor intervention in their own work? Neither civil society (nor the donor community) is inhabited by a homogeneous mass of organizations promoting shared values. Talking about supporting civil society, both from a 'recipient' and from a donor perspective, involves making choices.

One key dilemma is how to guarantee 'authenticity' of CSOs, and to garner some assurance from the other side of the fence about the legitimacy of the donor's intentions. Certainly, not all CSOs have a genuine base in society, and the practice of donor contracting through unrepresentative organizations can create tension.

Schearer's list of authenticity criteria points donors in the right general direction when he includes: non-profit character, a genuine constituency, probity and a mission that benefits some portion of the public (Schearer, 1995: 17), although these are not easily applied criteria in real life (Carroll's study on NGOs, for instance, showed that membership-based organizations were not any more accountable than non-membership ones; elites still often controlled the process (Carroll, 1992)).

Donors are clearly struggling with authenticity questions as they step into new territory (Van Rooy, 1996). Our message is that this struggle is a necessary step in getting the big picture but that the struggle for earning trust also happens with the organizations affected by donor work. Legitimacy is a two-way relationship.

Use Appropriate Mechanisms

What mechanisms are appropriate for supporting civil society? Throughout our study, repeated mention has been made of the dangers of funding too heavily or too partially, of allowing 'capture', of creating an artificial layer of quasi-CSOs and of administrative overload and competing paper work.

Much of the debate has focused on the pros and cons of direct funding, the practice of giving Northern government aid dollars directly to a Southern organization, by-passing the usual Northern NGO route. There may be problems inherent with direct intervention in the formation and support of indigenous organizations. Priorities may become skewed, programmes tilt towards the 'fundable' rather than the more immediate and direct funding can give rise to opportunistic organizations. There is much concern that funding to middle-class intermediaries, sometimes self-aggrandizing ex-bureaucrats, disempowers popular organizations. Furthermore, over-funding can affect the organization's popular base: 'the concentration of donor support among development NGOs in the South has sometimes led to a weakened civil society and has resulted in or contributed to a disempowering of popular organizations' (Bebbington and Riddell, 1995: 882).

These funding concerns are very real, but other issues have been repeatedly raised. When the authors were asked to generate a should-do list on mechanisms for support, the following leapt to the top of the pile.

Planning

If any project of social and political change is to be enduring it must come from the voices of local people. Any planning process must be guided by the needs and goals of the organizations who will undertake the work. Donors need to create or support mechanisms where their planning mechanisms are subordinated to existing processes in the field.

Scope

A nationally driven plan should be flexible in scope. Bricks, mortar or building sites may have different priorities. The authors recommended that support mechanisms for brick building, therefore, focus on long-term institution building (rather than on projects alone). Institution building would encompass financing for development of the board or management of an organization, backbone core costs for a clearly defined period of time, skills training for the organization's membership (to build local expertise outside of the Marriott Brigade) or equipment. Mortaring activities could include support to existing networks and to local training/support organizations, and support a greater breadth of players (including rural organizations) in decision-making. Mechanisms to strengthen the enabling environment include backup to incentives to banks and businesses interested in supporting local civil societies, and promoting local philanthropy.

Delivery

How financial assistance is delivered also matters. Although it is important that all that money is used responsibly and that auditing is a regular feature, autonomy to capable organizations should be given in the use of funds. Support should require the minimum in paperwork and reflect a long-term commitment; a results-based focus should look beyond tomorrow and depend on ongoing feedback between the donor, the recipient and other players.

Evaluation

Evaluation measures should be designed collaboratively to promote the shared agenda and to check progress. Appropriate forms might include local independent evaluation groups and regular pulse-taking efforts that allow scope for failing and learning on both sides of the relationship. Equally, the donor should also be the subject of regular evaluation.

Coordination

Given the diversity of the debate on civil society, coordination among donors and other actors is important, as is coordination within donor agencies on the impact of their programming on CSOs' efforts. The left hand needs to know what the right is doing.

Remain on the Sidelines

Of course, once all is said and done, the influence of donors in terms of money or political and economic clout is enormously varied but usually small. Social and political change is a long, complex and difficult process, fractured by inconsistencies and conflicts that outsiders cannot hope to affect except in the most strategic of fashions. Where donors are particularly important, as in Mozambique or present day Guatemala, the key is to remain sufficiently peripheral so as not to dislodge indigenous efforts. Donor fads (infrastructure emphasis, trickle-down balance of payments support, structural adjustment policies, results-based management and, now, civil society) may not necessarily help. The Leeds study offers one such example:

> *Undertaking structural adjustment and democratisation simultaneously is an enormous challenge for the governments of many developing countries. The difficulties are intensified by the potential contradiction that developing country governments could be faced by external insistence on the maintenance of SAPs, and by internal demands for greater democratisation and participation in decision-making. Both multilateral and bilateral donors do not appear to have given much reflection to such issues.*
> (Crawford, 1996: xiv)

The message is that responsible donors watch carefully, intervene cautiously and remain on the sidelines.

Plan for Exit

Failing to plan for exit leaves organizations in the lurch. How can agencies avoid undermining CSOs' sustainability by creating dependency on foreign aid? This is a critical issue for donors as well as CSOs (Schearer, 1995: 17), but many organizations that use foreign funding are worried that an over-concern with dependency will undermine their work. In some cases, there is no way to become self-supporting in the absence of a competent host government programme; health and education for the poorest cannot be expected to be self-sustaining.

Furthermore, even when donors have adopted a responsibility to help develop some of the processes that may make service provision less necessary further on, there is little incentive to do so (Bebbington and Riddell,

1995: 42). There needs to be a way within donor bureaucracies to reward good process work, work that involves long-term relationships, particularly in a context that emphasizes short-term results (such as the emphasis on results-based management).

Once donors, and their partners, decide to leave their relationship, then a similarly long-term plan for exit needs to be put into place. Short-term funding horizons may mean that organizations spend more time scrambling for cash than doing the work at hand. Premature or sudden withdrawal may thus cause additional harm. Development is a process of change, not a race to year end. Donors, and their partners, must be as careful in planning their retreat as they are in planning their intervention.

THE IMPACT ON DONORS

When thinking about the impact of the idea of civil society on donor programming, particularly the emphasis on institutions and processes over concrete outcomes, one wonders whether there is a new reality unfolding for aid. Certainly, monies spent have not yet matched the volume of enthusiasm generated by the idea, although dollars, marks and kroner may eventually follow as the implications are explored (particularly now that systems are being put into place in the DAC to track civil society spending). Is the emphasis on civil society a sign of things to come?

It is certainly a sign of an outspoken return to politics. Described in the friendliest and most universal terms, funding to CSOs has most often been explicitly linked to democratization – the installation of formal mechanisms of elections, parliaments and multi-party systems – a deeply political agenda. The end of the cold war has allowed a seeming universalization of other language, as well. Could civil society, after all, be anything but good news? The sweep of social and economic transformation, particularly in Eastern Europe, has sent development watchers scurrying for easy answers. That 'civil society' responds to a range of political motivations, populist, liberal, Marxist, makes it particularly welcome.

The emphasis on civil society is also a sign of an aid industry seeking to regain legitimacy. Making aid effective is hard work; it can only be but a small prod in the direction of change (even in aid-dependent Kenya, only some 9 per cent of gross national product (GNP) comes from aid). How to insert that small contribution to generate positive change abroad and approval at home is a difficult task. Civil organizing, conflict and social change are processes so rooted in local realities that development 'projects' can be only intermittent features on a vast landscape. Even the most responsive and culturally sensitive aid planning can fall prey to corruption, currency slumps, conflict and political whim. Moreover, although public support for aid programmes in most of the North remains very firm (OECD, 1996), there seems to be widespread disillusionment over the effectiveness of aid within official and multilateral aid agencies themselves (Clark and Van Rooy, 1996). Given the difficulty of delivering effective aid, and the disillusionment that follows, is it any wonder that 'civil society' has been grasped with such enthusiasm?

At the same time, we are wary about wholehearted encouragement of donors to delve into a civic area where the preconditions for success are so far beyond an outsiders' reach. Armed only with a menu of projects and tight timelines and accountability rules, what can donors reasonably do? From the stories in this book, the answer is that much has already been accomplished, when undertaken carefully, in consultation, with a long-term vision and in small doses. The danger is that enthusiasm over civil society's theoretical potential will push caution aside. Along with the promise of civil society, and the hope placed in the work towards social justice undertaken by fragile civil society organizations throughout the world, there are real perils.

BIBLIOGRAPHY

'Hemispheric Partnerships Initiative', unpublished draft report to team members, 10 March 1997

Aaron, Henry J, Thomas E Mann and Timothy Taylor (eds.) (1994) *Values and Public Policy*, The Brookings Institution, Washington, DC

Abeyesekera, Sunila (1995) 'Organizing for Peace in the Midst of War: Experiences of Women in Sri Lanka', in Margaret Schiller (ed.) *From Basic Needs to Basic Rights: Women's Claim To Human Rights*, WLD International, Washington, DC

Ake, Claude (1991) 'Rethinking African Democracy,' *Journal of Democracy*, volume 2, number 1, Johns Hopkins University Press, Baltimore

Amalric, Franck (1996) 'In Search of a Political Agenda for Civil Society in the North', *Development*, number 3

Anheier, Helmut K and Lester M Salamon (1996) *The Emerging Nonprofit Sector: An Overview*, Johns Hopkins University Press, Baltimore

Anheier, Helmut K and Lester M Salamon (1997) 'The Civil Society Sector,' special feature in *Social Science and Modern Society*, volume 34, number 2, January/February

Anheier, Helmut K and Lester M Salamon (1998) *The Nonprofit Sector in the Developing World: A Comparative Analysis*, Johns Hopkins Nonprofit Sector Series 5, Manchester University Press, Manchester

Arendt, Hannah (1958) *The Human Condition*, Chicago, University of Chicago Press, Chicago

Bahmueller, Charles F (1997) 'Civil Society is the Buzzword of the hour, but what Exactly does it Mean?' *CIVnet: Journal for a Civil Society*, http://civnet.org/journal/issue/bahmz.htm

Ballón, Eduardo (1996) 'ONGs, Sociedad Civil y Desarrollo', *Los Desafíos de la Cooperación*, DESCO, Lima

Balmueller, Charles F (1997) 'Civil society is the buzzword of the hour, but what exactly does it mean?' Barber, Benjamin (1996) 'An American Civic Forum: Civil Society between Market Individuals and the Political Community', Social Philosophy and Policy, volume 13, number 1, Winter, pp 269–83

Barber, Benjamin (1996) 'An American Civic Forum: Civil Society between Market Individuals and the Political Community', *Social Philosophy and Policy*, volume 13, number 1, Winter, pp 269–83

Beaumont, Martin (1996) 'Algo de Estado, algo de Empresa: Las ONG en el Perú de los noventa', *Los Desafíos de la Cooperación*, DESCO, Lima

Bebbington, Anthony and Diana Mitlin (1997) *Workshop Report: The NGO sector and its Role in Strengthening Civil Society and Securing Good Governance*, International Institute for Environment and Development, London, 27 August

Bebbington, Anthony and Roger Ridell (1995) 'The Direct Funding of Southern NGOs by Donors', *Journal of International Development*, volume 7, number 6

Berman, Bruce (1990) *Control and Crisis in Colonial Kenya – The Dialectic of Domination*, James Currey, London

Bernhard, Michael (1993) 'Civil Society and Democratic Transition in East Central Europe', *Political Science Quarterly*, volume 108, number 2, pp 306–26

Bickford, Louis (1995) 'Civil Society and Its Applicability in the Third World', *Labour, Capital and Society*, volume 28, number 2, November, pp 203–14

Blaney, David L and Mustapha Kamal Pasha (1993) 'Civil Society and Democracy in the Third World: Ambiguities and Historical Possibilities', *Studies in Comparative International Development*, volume 28, number 1, Spring, pp 3–24

Bobbio, Norberto (1988) 'Gramsci and the Concept of Civil Society', in John Keane (ed.) *Civil Society and the State*, Verso, London and New York, NY, pp 73–99

Bratton, Michael (1986) 'Beyond the State: Civil Society and Associational Life in Africa', *World Politics*, volume 41, number 3, April, pp 407–30

Bratton, Michael and Nicholas van de Walle (1997) *Democratic Experiments in Africa: Regime Transitions in Comparative Perspective*, Cambridge University Press, Cambridge

Brodhead, Tim and Brent Herbert-Copley with Anne-Marie Lambert (1988) *Bridges of Hope? Canadian Voluntary Agencies and the Third World*, The North-South Institute, Ottawa

Brown, David (1997) *Report by Southern NGO Capacity Building Issues as Observed by Nine NGO Support Organizations*, Institute for Development Research, Boston

Bryant, Christopher GA (1993) 'Social Self-organization, Civility and Sociology: a Comment on Kumar's Civil Society', *British Journal of Sociology*, volume 44, number 3, September, pp 397–401

Calhoun, Craig (1993) 'Civil Society and the Public Sphere', *Public Culture*, volume 5, number 2, Winter, pp 267–80

Callaghy, Thomas M (1994) 'Civil Society, Democracy, and Economic Change in Africa: A Dissenting Opinion About Resurgent Societies', in John W Harbeson, Donald Rothchild and Naomi Chazan (eds.) *Civil Society and the State in Africa*, Lynne Rienner, Boulder, CO and London

Carothers, Thomas (1991) *In the Name of Democracy: US Policy toward Latin America in the Reagan Years*, University of California Press, Berkeley

Carroll, Thomas F (1992) *Intermediary NGOs: The Supporting Link in Grassroots Development*, Kumarian Press, West Hartford, CT

Castiglione, Dario (1994) 'History and Theories of Civil Society: Outline of a Contested Paradigm', *Australian Journal of Politics and History*, volume 40, special issue, pp 83–103

Cernea, Michael M (1988) *Nongovernmental Organizations and Local Development*, The World Bank, Washington, DC, October

Chamberlain, Heath B (1993) 'On the Search for Civil Society in China', *Modern China*, volume 19, number 2, April, pp 199–215

Chandhoke, Neera (1995) *State and Civil Society: Explorations in Political Theory*, Sage Publications, New Delhi and Thousand Oaks, California and London

CIDA (1995) *CIDA Support for Public Sector Reform: A case study: Peru*, CIDA, Ottawa

CIDA (1996) *Government of Canada Policy for CIDA on Human Rights, Democratization and Good Governance*, CIDA, Ottawa

Clark, Andrew and Alison Van Rooy (1996) *A Dormant Revival?: The Future of Aid to the Sahel*, The North-South Institute and OECD, June

Clayton, Andrew (ed.) (1996) *NGOs, Civil Society and the State: Building Democracy in Transitional Societies*, INTRAC, Oxford

Cohen, Jean L and Andrew Arato (1992) *Civil Society and Political Theory*, MIT Press, Cambridge, MA and London

Córdova, Patricia (1996) *Liderazgo femenino en Lima: Estrategias de supervivencia*, Fundación Friedrich Ebert, Lima

Crawford, Gordon (1996) *Promoting Democracy, Human Rights and Good Governance Through Development Aid: A Comparative Study of the Policies of Four Northern Donors*, Working Paper on Democratization, ISSN 1359–4958, Centre for Democratization Studies, University of Leeds

CRM (1980) 'New Law to Control Voluntary Social Service', Statement issued by the Civil Rights Movement of Sri Lanka, Colombo, 1 February

CRM (1995) 'Proposed Amendment to the Voluntary Social Service Act', Statement issed by the Civil Rights Movement of Sri Lanka, Colombo, 1 November

Diamond, Larry (1991) *The Democratic Revolution: Struggles for Freedom and Pluralism in the Developing World*, Freedom House

Diamond, Larry (ed.) (1993) *Political Culture & Democracy in Developing Countries*, Lynne Reinner, Boulder, CO

Diamond, Larry (1994) 'Rethinking Civil Society: Toward Democratic Consolidation', *Journal of Democracy*, volume 5, number 3, July pp 4–17

Diamond, Larry (1995) *Promoting Democracy in the 1990s – Actors and Instruments, Issues and Imperatives*, report to the Carnegie Commission on Preventing Deadly Conflict, Carnegie Corporation, New York, NY

Diamond, Larry, Juan Linz and Seymour Martin Lipset (eds.) (1988) *Democracy in Developing Countries*, volume 2: Africa, Lynne Reinner, Boulder, CO

Diamond, Larry, Marc Plattner, Yuan-han Chu and Hung Mao Tien (eds.) (1997) *Consolidating Third Wave Democracies: Themes and Perspectives*, Johns Hopkins University Press, Baltimore

Dicklitch, Susan (1997) *The Uncertain Promise of Non-Governmental Organizations and Civil Society in Transitional Societies: The Case of Uganda*, paper presented at the International Studies Association conference, Toronto, 18–22 March

Donini, Antonio (1995) 'The Bureaucracy and the Free Spirits: Stagnation and Innovation in the Relationship between the UN and NGOs', *Third World Quarterly*, volume 16, number 3, pp 21–439

Drabek, Anne Gordon (ed.) (1987) *World Development*, supplement titled 'Development Alternatives: The Challenge for NGOs', volume 15, Autumn

Economist (1996a) 'Gestures Against Reform', 30 November 1996, pp 19–21

Economist (1996b) 'Latin America's Backlash', 30 November 1996, p 15

Ekeh, Peter (1992) 'The Constitution of Civil Society in African History and Politics', in Gboyega Caron and Eghosa E Osaghae (eds.) *Democratic Transition in Africa*, University of Ibadan Press, Ibadan

Elshtain, Jean Bethke (1993) *Democracy on Trial*, House of Anansi Press, Concord, ON

European Community, Economic and Social Committee (1997) *Ruling on Development Aid, Good Governance and Role of Socio-economic Interest Groups*, Brussels

Fernando, Sunimal (1997) *Sri Lanka Country Profile*, INASIA, Colombo

Fierlbeck, Katherine (1996) *Fetishizing Civil Society*, paper presented at the Annual General Meeting of the Canadian Political Science Association, St. Catharines, 2 June

Ford Foundation, *Annual Report*, New York, NY, 1995

Foro Nacional/Internacional (1995) *AGENDA: Perú Project Report: Democracy and Good Government*, Lima

Fowler, Alan (1990) 'Doing it better? Where and How NGOs Have a "Comparative Advantage" in Facilitating Development', *AERDD Bulletin*, University of Reading, Agricultural Extension and Rural Development Department, volume 28, February, pp 11–20

Fowler, Alan (1997a) *UNDP and Organisations of Civil Society: A Programme Framework*, second draft, UNDP, February

Fowler, Alan (1997b) *Striking a Balance: A Guide to Enhancing the Effectiveness of Non-Governmental Organizations in International Development*, Earthscan, London

Fox, Jonathan (1994) 'The Difficult Transition from Clientelism to Citizenship: Lessons from Mexico,' *World Politics*, volume 46, number 2, January

Fox, Leslie (1997) *Legitimate and Effective Partners in Sustainable Development: A Strategy for Strengthening African Civil Society*, draft prepared for the Africa Branch of the World Bank, Washington, DC

Friedrich Ebert Stiftung (1995) *International Development Co-operation: Democracy, Social Justice, International Understanding*, Friedrich Ebert Stiftung, Bonn

Gellner, Ernest (1991) 'Civil Society in Historical Context', *International Social Science Journal*, volume 43, August, pp 495–510

Gellner, Ernest (1995) 'The Importance of Being Modular', in John A Hall (ed.) *Civil Society: Theory, History, Comparison*, Polity Press, Cambridge, UK and Cambridge, MA

Geremek, Bronislaw (1992) 'Problems of Postcommunism, Civil Society in Poland Then and Now', *Journal of Democracy*, volume 3, number 2, April, pp 3–12

Ghai, Yash and JPWB McAuslan (1970) *Public Law and Political Change in Kenya*, Oxford University Press, Nairobi

Ghils, Paul (1995) 'Le concept et les notions de societé civile', *Transnational Associations*, number 3, pp 136–55

Gonzales Norris, Antonio and Helen Jaworski (1990) *Cooperación Internacional para el Desarrollo: Políticas, Gestión y Resultados*, GRADE (Grupo de Análisis para el Desarrollo), Lima

Grandea, Nona (1995) *Choosing the Right Policy Levers: Drawing Lessons from the Government of Canada's Interventions in South Africa*, The North-South Institute, paper prepared for the Good Governance and Human Rights Division, CIDA, Ottawa

Gray, Michael L (1997) *Creating Civil Society?: The Emergence of NGOs in Vietnam*, in press, September

Grootaert, Christiaan (1996) 'Social Capital: The Missing Link?', in *Monitoring Environmental Progress: Expanding the Measure of Wealth*, Conference draft, Indicators and Environmental Valuation Unit, Environment Department, The World Bank, Washington, DC, October

Gyimah-Boadi, E (1997) 'Civil Society in Africa: the Good, the Bad, the Ugly', *CIVnet: Journal for a Civil Society*, volume 1, number 1, May, http://civnet.org/journal/issue1/egboadi.htm

Gyllstrom, Bjorn (1991) *State Administered Rural Change-Agricultural Co-operatives in Kenya*, Routledge, London

Habermas, Jurgen (1992) 'Further Reflections on the Public Sphere', in Craig Calhoun (ed.) *Habermas and the Public Sphere*, MIT Press, Cambridge, MA and London, pp 421–46

Hadenius, Axel and Frederick Uggla (1996) 'Making Civil Society Work, Promoting Democratic Development: What Can States and Donors Do?' *World Development*, volume 24, number 10, pp 1621–39

Hall, John A (1995) 'In Search of Civil Society', in John A Hall (ed.) *Civil Society: Theory, History, Comparison*, Polity Press, Cambridge, UK and Cambridge, MA

Hansen, Gary (1996) *Constituencies for Reform: Strategic Approaches for Donor-Supported Civic Advocacy Programs*, USAID Program and Operations Assessment Report, number 12, USAID, Washington, DC

Harbeson, John W, Donald Rothchild and Naomi Chazan (eds.) (1994) *Civil Society and the State in Africa*, Lynne Rienner, Boulder, CO and London

Healy, Teresa and Laura Macdonald (1997) *Continental Divide? Competing Approaches to Understanding Social Movement Organizing Across North America*, paper presented at the International Studies Association conference, Toronto, 18–22 March

Hegel, GWF (1976) *Grundlinien der Philosophie des Rechts*, Frankfurt am Main

Hernández, Ricardo (1996) 'IDB–Civil society Consultation in Mexico', *The Other Side of Mexico*, number 45, March–April

Holmquist, Frank, Michael Ford, Judith Geist and Gary Hansen (1995) *Civil Society, Political Liberalization, and Donors in Kenya*, draft paper presented to the annual meeting of the American Political Science Association meeting, Chicago, September

Horowitz, David L (1985) *Ethnic Groups in Conflict*, University of California Press, Berkeley

Howell, Jude (1994) 'Refashioning State–Society Relations in China', *The European Journal of Development Research*, volume 6, number 1, June, pp 197–215

Hulme, David and Michael Edwards (eds.) (1997) *NGOs, States and Donors: Too Close for Comfort?*, St Martin's Press, New York, NY

Hulme, David and Richard Montgomery with Debapriya Bhattacharya (1994) *Mutual Finance and the Poor: A Study of the Federation of Thrift and Credit Co-operatives in Sri Lanka (SANASA)*, number 11, Institute for Development and Policy Management, University of Manchester

Hutchful, Eboe (1995–96) 'The Civil Society Debate in Africa', *International Journal*, volume 51, number 1, Winter, pp 54–77

Hutchful, Eboe and Gerald J Schmitz (1992) *Democratization and Popular Participation in Africa*, The North-South Institute, Ottawa

Hydén, Gorán (1997) *Sustaining Civil Society: Strategies for Resource Mobilization*, Civicus Publications, Washington, DC

Hydén, Gorán and Michael Bratton (eds.) (1992) *Governance and Politics in Africa*, Lynne Reinner, Boulder, CO

Ibrahim, Saad Eddin (1996) *Nurturing Civil Society at the World Bank*, paper produced for the Social Policy and Resettlement Division, Environment Department, World Bank, Washington, DC

IEP (Instituto de Estudios Peruanos) (1995) *Once Millones de Mujeres en el Perú*, Lima

Information Monitoring On Human Rights (1995) *Statement on Proposed Amendments to the Voluntary Service Organisations*, Colombo

InterAction (1995) *Zimbabwe Advocacy Workshop Confronts Political Realities*, 12 June, InterAction, Washington, DC

International Centre for Ethnic Studies (1997) *Civil Society in Sri Lanka: A Symposium*, ICES, Colombo, February

Jaworski, Helen (1994) *Hacia Nuevas Formas de Relación con el Sur del Mundo: Economías Populares y Mecanismos Europeos de Financiamiento Alternativo*, Gobierno Vasco, Bilbao

Jørgensen, Lars (1996) 'What are NGOs Doing in Civil Society?' in Andrew Clayton (ed.) *NGOs, Civil Society and the State: Building Democracy in Transitional Societies*, INTRAC, Oxford, pp 36–55

Kaldor, Mary (1997) *Transnational Civil Society*, unpublished manuscript, Sussex European Institute, University of Sussex

Kaldor, Mary and Ivan Vejvoda (1996) *Final Report on the Project Democratisation in CEE countries*, Sussex European Institute, University of Sussex, September

Kamaru, Joseph, *Nyimbo cia MauMau 1 & 2 (Mau Mau Songs)* volumes 1 & 2

Keane, John (ed.) (1988) *Civil Society and the State*, Verso, London and New York, NY

Kennedy, Paul (1994) 'Political Barriers to African Capitalism', *Journal of Modern African Studies*, volume 32, issue 2, pp 191–213

Korten, David (1990) *Getting to the 21st Century: Voluntary Action and the Global Agenda*, Kumarian Press, West Hartford, CT

Kothari, Smitu (1996) 'Rising from the Margins: the Awakening of Civil Society in the Third World', *Development*, number 3

Krasner, Stephen D (1989) 'Sovereignty: An Institutional Perspective', in John A Caporaso, *The Elusive State, International and Comparative Perspectives*, Sage, London

Kumar, Krishan (1993) 'Civil Society: an Inquiry into the Usefulness of an Historical term', *British Journal of Sociology*, volume 44, number 3, September, pp 375–95

Kuti, Éva (1996) *The Nonprofit Sector in Hungary*, Johns Hopkins Nonprofit Series Manchester University Press, Manchester

Line, Milburn (1997) *Reviewing Progress for Building Sustainable Partnerships*, unpublished paper for UNDP, February

Lipshultz, Ronnie D (1992) 'Reconstructing World Politics: The Emergence of Global Civil Society', *Millennium*, volume 21, number 3, pp 389–420

Lonsdale, JM and Bruce Berman (1992) *Unhappy Valley*, volumes 1 and 2, James Currey, London

López, Sinesio (1991) *El Dios Mortal, Estado, Sociedad y Política en el Perú del Siglo XX*, IDS, Lima

Luers, Wendy W (1996) 'Letter From the President', *1995 Annual Report*, The Foundation for a Civil Society, New York, NY, pp 2–3

Lynch, Nicolás (1992) *La Transición Conservadora: Movimiento Social y Democracia en el Perú, 1975–78*, El zorro de abajo ediciones, Lima

Malena, Carmen (1996) *Human Resource Development for Improved Cooperation between the UNDP and Civil Society Organizations: A Proposed Strategy and Action Plan*, paper prepared for the UNDP, New York, NY

Mamdani, Mahmood (1996) *Citizen and Subject – Contemporary Africa and The Legacy of Late Colonialism*, Princeton University Press, Princeton, NJ

Mamdani, Mamhood and Ernest Wamba-dia-Wamba (eds.) (1995) *African Studies in Social Movements and Democracy*, Council for the Development of Economic and Social Research in Africa, Dakar

Matthews, Jessica T (1997) 'Power Shift', *Foreign Affairs*, January/February, pp 50–66

Melucci, Alberto (1988) 'Social Movements and the Democratization of Everyday Life', in John Keane (ed.) *Civil Society and the State*, Verso, London and New York, NY, pp 245–60

Miszlivetz, Ferenc (1997) 'Participation and Transition: Can the Civil Society Project Survive in Hungary?' *Journal of communist Studies and Transition*, volume 13, number 1, March, pp 27–40

Moore, B (1966) *Social Origins of Dictatorship and Democracy*, Beacon Press, Boston

Mutume, Gumisai (1996) 'Africa-Development: NGOs' Battle for Recognition', InterPress Third World News Agency (IPS)

Ndegwa, Stephen N (1994) 'Civil Society and Political Change in Africa: The Case of Non-Governmental Organizations in Kenya', *International Journal of Comparative Sociology*, volume 35, number 1–2, pp 19–36

Nelson, Paul J (1997) *Relating to Civil Society: Structural and Programmatic Innovations at the World Bank and Inter-American Development Bank*, paper presented at the International Studies Association conference, Toronto, 18–22 March

Netherlands Ministry of Foreign Affairs (1996) *Donor Experience in Support of Human Rights: Some Lessons Learned*, Operations Review Unit, The Hague, April

Ngunyi, Mutahi (1996) *Promoting Democracy Through Positive Conditionality*, Working Paper, Leeds University Department of Politics' Project on Aid and Political Conditionality, March

Ngunyi, Mutahi and Wachira Maina (1997) *Emerging Issues in Constitutional Reform in Kenya*, Working Paper, SAREAT's Project on Constitution-making and the Crisis of the Nation-State, Nairobi, November

OECD (1988) *Voluntary Aid for Development: The Role of Non-Governmental Organisations*, OECD Development Centre, Paris

OECD (1993) *DAC Orientations on Participatory Development and Good Governance*, Development Assistance Committee, Paris

OECD (1995) *Report on the Uppsala Workshop on Civil Society and Democracy*, Delegation of Sweden, Development Assistance Committee, Paris

OECD (1998) *Development Co-operation: Efforts and Policies of the Members of the Development Assistance Committee*, 1997 Report, Paris

Olukoshi, Adebayo and Thandika Mkandawire (1995) *Between Liberalisation and Oppression: The Politics of Structural Adjustment in Africa*, Codesria, Dakar

Omveldt, Gail (1990) *Violence Against Women: New Social Movements, New Theories in India*, Kali for Women, New Delhi

Oxhorn, Philip (1995) 'From Controlled Inclusion to Coerced Marginalization: The Struggle for Civil Society in Latin America', in John A Hall (ed.) *Civil Society: Theory, History, Comparison*, Polity Press, Cambridge, UK and Cambridge, MA

Oxhorn, Philip (nd) *The Paradox of Authoritarian Rule: Building Democratic Civil Societies in Latin America*, unpublished paper, McGill University, Montreal

Palmer, Tom G (1997) 'Civil Society No Longer Means What it was Supposed to Mean', *CIVnet: Journal for a Civil Society*, volume 1, number 2, June–July, http://www.civnetorg/journal/issue2/jftpalm.htm

Pearce, Jenny (1993) 'NGOs and Social Change: Agents or Facilitators?', *Development in Practice*, volume 3, number 3, October, p 223

Porter, Doug J and Patrick Kilby (1996) 'Strengthening the Role of Civil Society in Development? A Precariously Balanced Answer', *Australian Journal of International Affairs*, volume 50, number 1, April, pp 31–42

Presidential Commission (1993) *Report of the Commission of Inquiry in Respect of Government Organizations Functioning in Sri Lanka*, Colombo

Putnam, Robert D (1995) 'Bowling Alone: America's Declining Social Capital', *Journal of Democracy*, volume 6, number 1, January, pp 65–78

Putnam, Robert D with Robert Leonardi and Rafaella Y Nanetti (1993) *Making Democracy Work: Civic Traditions in Modern Italy*, Princeton University Press, Princeton, NJ

Quigley, Kevin FF (1996) 'For Democracy's Sake: How Funders Fail – and Succeed', *World Policy Journal*, Spring, pp 109–18

Riddell, Roger, and Mark Robinson (1996a) 'Judging Success: Evaluating NGO Approaches to Alleviating Poverty in Developing Countries', working paper 37, Institute of Development Studies, Sussex

Riddell, Roger, and Mark Robinson (1996b) 'The Impact of NGO Poverty Alleviation Projects: Results of the Case Study Evaluations', working paper 68, Institute of Development Studies, Sussex

Robinson, Mark (1995) 'Strengthening Civil Society in Africa: The Role of Foreign Political Aid', *IDS Bulletin*, volume 26, number 2, April, pp 74–5

Robinson, Mark (1996) *Strengthening Civil Society Through Foreign Political Aid*, ESCOR Research Report R6234, Institute of Development Studies, Sussex

Robinson, Mark and Gordon White (1997) *The Role of Civic Organizations in the Provision of Social Services: Towards Synergy*, Research for Action 37, World Institute for Development Economics Research, Helsinki

Roche, Chris (1995) 'Conference Report', INTRAC Workshop on NGOs, Civil Society and The State: Building Democracy in Transitional Countries, Oxford, 12–15 December

Roncagliolo, Rafael (1997) 'Sociedad civil y radio ciudadana,' *Cuestión de Estado*, number 20, April, Lima

Roniger, Luis (1994) 'Civil Society, Patronage and Democracy', *International Journal of Comparative Sociology*, volume 35, number 3/4, September/December, pp 207–20

Roper-Renshaw, Laura (1994) 'Strengthening Civil Society: The Role of NGOs', *Development*, number 4, pp 46–9

Rosenblum, Nancy L (1994) 'Civil Societies: Liberalism and the Moral Uses of Pluralism', *Social Research*, volume 61, number 3, Fall, pp 539–62

Rudebeck, Lars (ed.) (1992) *When Democracy Makes Sense: Studies in the Democratic Potential of Third World Popular Movements*, AKUT, Working Group for the Study of Development Strategies, Uppsala University

Rueschemeyer, Dietrich, Marylin Rueschemeyer and Bjorn Wittrock (eds.) (1998) *Participation and Democracy East and West: Comparisons and Interpretations*, ME Sharpe, Armonk, NY

Sachs, Jeffery D and Andrew M Warner (1995) *Economic Reform and Global Integration*, Brookings Papers on Economic Activity, Brookings Institute, Washington, DC

Sagasti, Francisco et al. (1995) *AGENDA: Perú: Democracy and Good Government*, Lima: Editorial Apoyo

Sagasti, Francisco and Alcalde (1997) 'Políticas Sociales y lucha contra la pobreza en el Perú. Una aproximación de conjunto', in dos ensayos de AGENDA, *Pobreza, Exclusión y Política Social: Algunas Ideas para el Diseño de Estrategias de Desarrollo*, March, Lima, pp 9–83

Sahn, David E and Alexander Sarris (1994) 'The Evolution of States, Markets and Civil Institutions in Rural Africa', *Journal of Modern African Studies*, volume 32, issue 2, pp 279–303

Sales, Arnaud (1991) 'The Private, the Public and Civil Society: Social Realms and Power Structures', *International Political Science Review*, volume 12, number 4, pp 295–312

Sánchez-León, Abelardo (1996) 'Historia y Evolución de la Cooperación con ONGs', *Los Desafíos de la Cooperación*, DESCO, Lima

Sangmpam, SN (1993) *Pseudocapitalism and the Overpoliticized State: Reconciling Politics and Anthropology in Zaire*, Avebury, Aldershot, UK, and Brookfield, US

Schearer, S Bruce (1995) 'The Emerging Role of Civil Society', *International Development: Challenges to Foreign Aid Programs*, paper prepared for the ODC/Synergos Institute Conference, Strengthening Financing for the Voluntary Sector in Development, The Role of Official Development Assistance, September

Seligman, Adam B (1992) 'Trust and the Meaning of Civil Society', *International Journal of Politics, Culture and Society*, volume 6, number 1, pp 5–21

Sethi, Harsh (1993) 'Action Groups in the New Politics', in Wignaraja, Ponna (ed.) *New Social Movements in the South: Empowering the People*, Zed Books, London and New Jersey

Shils, Edward (1991) 'The Virtue of Civil Society', *Government and Opposition*, volume 26, number 1, pp 3–20

Siegel, Daniel and Jenny Yancey (1992) *The Rebirth of Civil Society*, The Rockefeller Brothers Fund, New York, NY

Silva, Kingsley M de (1981) *A History of Sri Lanka*, Hurst, London

Simone, Abdou Maliqalim and Edgar Pieterse (1993) 'Civil Societies in an Internationalized Africa', *Social Dynamics*, volume 19, number 2, pp 41–69

Smillie, Ian and Henny Helmich (eds.) (1993) *Stakeholders in Development: Issues in Government/NGO Relationships*, OECD, Paris

Sogge, David (ed.) with Kees Biekart and John Saxby (1996) *Compassion and Calculation: The Business of Foreign Aid*, Pluto, London

Stiglitz, Joseph (1997) *An Agenda for Development for the Twenty-First Century*, World Bank, Washington, DC

Stout, Russell (1996) *Legal Systems, Evaluation of Programs Promoting PD/GG: Synthesis Report*, presented by the United States to the DAC Expert Group on AID Evaluation, Room Document number 3, April

Swift, Jamie (1998) [no title, in press], South Asia Partnership, Ottawa

Synergos Institute (1995) *Strengthening Civil Society's Contribution to Development: The Role of Official Development Assistance*, Report on a conference organized by the Overseas Development Council and The Synergos Institute, 1995.

Szelenyi, Ivan (1988) *Socialist Entrepreneurs*, University of Wisconsin Press, Madison, WS

Tamayo, G (1997) 'La Maquinaria Estatal: ¿puede suscitar Cambios a Favor de las Mujeres?' paper presented to *El Conversatorio, Mujer, Espacios Institucionales y Politicas Publicas*, organized by the Programa de Estudios de Género de la Universidad Católica del Perú el CEDEP, Lima, June

Taylor, Charles (1990) 'Modes of Civil Society', *Public Culture*, volume 3, number 1, Fall, pp 95–118

Taylor, Charles (1995) 'Liberal Politics and the Public Sphere', *Philosophical Arguments*, Harvard University Press, Cambridge, MA and London

Thalman, Dart, Heather Sutherland, Wachira Maina and Betty Wamalwa (1997) *A Review of USAID's Civic Education Programmes*, USAID, Kenya Office, April

Thomas, G Dale (1997) *The Meanings of Domestic Civil Society and Global Civil Society*, paper presented at the International Studies Association conference, Toronto, 18–22 March

Throup, David (1995) 'Render unto Caesar those Things that are Caesar's', in Bernt Hansen and Michael Twaddle, *Religion and Politics in East Africa*, James Currey, London, pp 143–76

Tocqueville, Alexis de (1988) *Democracy in America*, Harper Collins, New York, NY

Tomaz, Mastnak (1990) 'Civil Society in Slovenia: From Opposition to Power', *Studies in Comparative Communism*, volume 23, number 3–4, Autumn/Winter, pp 305–17

Tvedt, Terje (1995) *NGOs as a Channel in Development Aid: The Norwegian System*, Centre for Development Studies, University of Bergen, published by the Royal Ministry of Foreign Affairs, Oslo

UNDP (1993) *UNDP and Organizations of Civil Society*, UNDP, New York, NY

UNDP (1996) *Democracy, Governance, Participation: Europe and the CIS*, Second Edition, UNDP, New York, NY

UNDP (1997) *Building Partnerships for Sustainable Human Development: A Government, Civil Society, and Donor Roundtable*, preliminary report, Warsaw, 20–22 February, UNDP, New York, NY

Uphoff, Norman (1993) 'Grassroots Organizations and NGOs in Rural Development: Opportunities with Diminishing States and Expanding Markets', *World Development*, volume 21, number 4, pp 607–22

USAID (1991) *USAID Policy: Democracy and Governance*, Directorate for Policy, USAID, Washington, DC, November

USAID (1995) *Core Report of the New Partnerships Initiative*, draft version, USAID, Washington, DC, 21 July

USAID (1996) *USAID/Peru Vision Statement: Partnership in Development*, USAID, Washington, DC

Valderrama, Mariano (1993) *ALOP, un Perfil Institucional*, ALOP, Lima

Van Rooy, Alison (1996) *Integrating Civil Society Ideas into the Work of the UNDP: Recommendations for Policy and Practice*, paper prepared for the UNDP, New York, NY

Van Zwanenberg, RMA (1975) *Colonial Capitalism and Labour in Kenya 1919–1939*, East African Literature Bureau, Nairobi

Wakeman, Frederic Jr (1993) 'The Civil Society and Public Sphere Debate: Western Reflections on Chinese Political Culture', *Modern China*, volume 19, number 2, April, pp 108–38

Wanigaratne, Ranjith (1997) 'The State–NGO Relationship in Sri Lanka: Rights, Interests and Accountability' in David Hulme and Michael Edwards (eds.) *NGOs, States and Donors: Too Close for Comfort?* St Martin's Press, New York, NY

Wapner, Paul (1995) 'Politics Beyond the State: Environmental Activism and World Civic Politics', *World Politics*, April, pp 311–40

Whaites, Alan (1996) 'Let's Get Civil Society Straight: NGOs and Political Theory', *Development in Practice*, volume 6, number 3, August, pp 240–4

White, Gordon (1993) 'Prospects for Civil Society in China: A Case Study of Xiaoshan City', *Australian Journal of Chinese Affairs*, number 29, January, pp 63–87

White, Gordon (1995) 'Civil Society, Democratization and Development (II): Two Country Cases', *Democratization*, volume 2, number 2, Summer, pp 56–84

Wignaraja, Ponna (ed.) (1993) *New Social Movements in the South*, Zed Books, London

Wood, Ellen Meiksins (1990) 'The Uses and Abuses of Civil Society', in R Milliband, L Panitch, and J Saville (eds.) *The Socialist Register*, Merlin Press, London

World Bank (1997) *World Development Report 1997: The State in a Changing World*, World Bank, Washington, DC

Yankelovich, Daniel (1991) *Coming to Public Judgment: Making Democracy Work in a Complex World*, Syracuse University Press, Syracuse, NY

Yankelovich, Daniel (1994) 'How Changes in the Economy Are Reshaping American Values', in Henry J Aaron, Thomas E Mann and Timothy Taylor (eds.) *Values and Public Policy*, The Brookings Institution, Washington, DC

INDEX